AIRCRAFT CARRIERS

AIRCRAFT CARRIERS

**CUTAWAY ILLUSTRATIONS • PERFORMANCE SPECIFICATIONS
MISSION REPORTS**

DAVID JORDAN

Published in 2002 by Silverdale Books
an imprint of Bookmart Ltd
Registered number 2372865
Trading as Bookmart Ltd
Desford Road
Enderby
Leicester LE9 5AD

A catalogue for this book is available from the British Library.

ISBN 1-8560-5700-3

Editorial and design by
Amber Books Ltd
Bradley's Close
74–77 White Lion Street
London N1 9PF

Project Editor: James Bennett
Designer: Neil Rigby at www.stylus-design.com

Printed in Hong Kong

CONTENTS

CHAPTER ONE

THE DAWN OF THE AIRCRAFT CARRIER

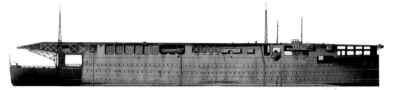

Unlike many historical events, it is not hard to say exactly when the story of naval aviation began. The British Royal Navy showed interest in man-lifting kites in the first years of the 20th century, appreciating that an observer floating above the fleet would enjoy a commanding view – the intrepid sailor aloft could scout for the enemy, or mines and submarines.

BUT THE KITES were simple affairs, and it would be stretching the truth to claim that the ships involved in the trials between 1903 and 1908 were the first aircraft carriers. By the end of the trials, the Royal Navy had already rejected an offer by the Wright Brothers to sell their patents. The Wright brothers were too

LEFT: Squadron Commander Edwin Dunning makes the first successful landing on a carrier on 2 August 1917. Dunning flew extremely slowly, allowing the deck party (here made up of officers) to grab hold of straps attached to the aircraft, and to pull it onto the deck.

confident in the price they could demand for their product, and their proposed fee was high enough to ensure that the Board of Admiralty maintained its view that aircraft were too flimsy for use at sea. The Admiralty instead turned to the airship, viewing its long endurance and altitude capabilities as being perfect for fleet reconnaissance. Partly due to the development of the German Zeppelin, a number of Royal Navy officers came to the view that the German airships presented a serious threat to the United Kingdom. In July 1908, Captain R.H.S. Bacon, the Director of Naval Ordnance, approached the new First Sea Lord, the outstanding and unconventional Admiral 'Jackie' Fisher, with the suggestion that a Naval Air Assistant should be appointed to investigate the procurement of airships. Fisher agreed, and the Royal Navy began construction. The airship, half-ironically christened *Mayfly*, entered naval service on 22 September 1911. Two days later, when the airship was due to fly for the first time, she broke her back when the design team lightened the structure beyond its limits. The whole affair was profoundly embarrassing for the Admiralty, who were rather put off the idea of airships as a result. By this time, events in the United States had overtaken the notion that the airship was the only means of providing effective air support to the fleet.

THE ALBANY FLYER

In 1910, a series of air races and a flight of 241km (150 miles) – a huge achievement at the time – greatly increased public interest in aviation in the United States. The aircraft designer Glenn Curtiss made grand predictions for the future of aircraft, and demonstrated the aerial bombing of a battleship (actually a mock-up moored at Hammondsport, Lake Leuka), prompting Admiral George Dewey to suggest that the US Navy should investigate whether aircraft would be of value to the fleet. Consequently, in September 1910, the US Navy appointed Captain Washington I. Chambers as the head of Naval Aviation. Chambers attended a number of air shows to see what aircraft might do, and in the course of these, he met Curtiss and his contract pilot, Eugene Ely. The enthusiasm of these two pioneers convinced Chambers that operation of aircraft from ships was feasible. The difficulty came in persuading the US Navy. Efforts to get funds were rebuffed, and Chambers' suggestion that every new cruiser should be provided with a two-seater aircraft for scouting duties was ignored. Chambers was undaunted. He had enough money to adapt some existing warships, and persuaded the Navy to authorize the temporary conversion of USS *Birmingham* to permit flying operations. Chambers used the news that the German Hamburg-Amerika steamship company was planning to launch a mailplane from one of their ships to provoke enough patriotism in high places to ensure that permission was granted. A ramp 25.3m (83ft) long, sloping 5° towards the bow, was erected on the *Birmingham*, and Curtiss was commissioned to provide the aircraft.

RIGHT: A Short 184 Seaplane is hoisted from a seaplane carrier in the early part of the First World War (the Union flag seen as an identification marking on the side of the aircraft was soon replaced by a roundel). The 184 saw widespread use, and was used on some spectacular bombing missions against German Zeppelin bases. Although famed for its bombing attacks, the 184 was used mainly for reconnaissance, and could carry a torpedo.

LEFT: A Sopwith Pup is hoisted to the deck from the forward hangar of HMS *Furious*. The Pup was an ideal aircraft for use as the first carrier fighter type. Since it was at first thought difficult – if not impossible – to recover aircraft aboard ships safely, the Pup's good ditching characteristics were useful. Its tractable handling, though, meant that it was possible to land a Pup on the ship, a feat first achieved in 1917.

Curtiss sent an aircraft in which he had set an endurance record, the *Albany Flyer*, along with Ely to fly it. On 14 November 1910, *Birmingham* left her moorings to attempt to launch the aircraft. The weather was appalling, but Ely was anxious to fly, worried that the Germans might succeed in launching their aircraft first (in fact, they had postponed the attempt after their aircraft had been damaged). The short take-off deck meant that it was necessary for the cruiser to steam at 20 knots into the wind to give enough air speed for the aircraft to lift off properly. At 1500 hours, despite the weather, Ely was determined to take off, and started the aircraft's engine. The crew of the *Birmingham* began to weigh anchor, but at 1516 hours, Ely set off, even though the ship was not under way. The lack of wind over the deck was nearly disastrous: the aircraft left the ship before it had enough speed to become airborne. Ely skilfully used the mere 11.3m (37ft) between the end of the flight deck and the sea to pick up speed, and just managed it. The wheels and the propeller struck the water, but Ely kept control. Without any instruments, he flew a few feet above the sea, trying to control his badly vibrating machine while looking for somewhere to land. Ely quickly spotted the beach, and landed there after a 3.2km (2 mile) flight.

PENNSYLVANIA

Thanks to Ely, Chambers was able to continue his work, although the Navy gave him only $500 for the next step. This was to recover an aircraft aboard a ship. The cruiser *Pennsylvania* was given a simple wooden superstructure, some 36.6m (120ft) long, on which the aircraft could land. It was immediately obvious that while landing was going to be an interesting challenge, stopping the aircraft would be even more difficult. Wooden guard rails were built along the deck to stop the aircraft from going over the side, and a large canvas barrier was erected to catch the *Albany Flyer* before it hit the ship's superstructure. Once again, Ely was chosen to pilot the aircraft, but he was a worried man. Although the *Flyer* had been modified so that its landing speed was reduced, Ely was far from certain that he could stop the aircraft before it came into contact with the canvas barrier. Incredible as it may seem today, one of the key reasons for this was that the aircraft did not have any brakes. The solution was elegantly simple: three hooks were fitted beneath the aircraft's undercarriage to engage one (or more) of 22 rope lines, weighted with a sandbag at each end and laid like tripwires across the deck. Ely tested the system on land before he tried it at sea.

Using an outline of the *Pennsylvania's* deck chalked onto the grass, Ely stretched a rope across the landing run and practised until he was satisfied. It soon became clear that the weights at each end of the line needed to be matched, otherwise they would pull the aircraft off-line. Ely also discovered that the arrester hooks had a habit of bouncing over the rope without engaging. But after he replaced the first set of hooks with spring-loaded ones, Ely was able to catch the single rope almost every time: with another 21 on the *Pennsylvania's* deck, he was confident that there would be a sufficient margin for error. Ely and the captain of the *Pennsylvania* (Captain C.F. Pond) had to pay for all this equipment themselves, since the Navy's funding extended only to building the deck. Preparations were completed in early January 1911, Ely taking Captain Pond's advice that landing on the ship while it was at anchor was the most sensible course of action. Frustratingly, the weather intervened, and it was not until the 18th that it was good enough for flying. Ely decided that he would make his attempt at 1100 hours that morning. He took off from Tanforan Field, California, and made his way out to the ship. Thousands of people had turned out to watch, and they were not disappointed. Ely ran into air turbulence caused by the ship's superstructure, but landed safely, catching the eleventh and subsequent arrester ropes. The Curtiss stopped with 15m (50ft) to spare. Ely turned off the engine, and the momentary silence was broken by the sound of cheering spectators and ships' sirens. Ely handled the fuss made by the media with modesty. Having conducted the experimental flights without charging a fee, he went back to display flying, only to be killed nine months later when his aircraft fell apart before horrified crowds at the State Fair at Macon, Georgia.

HMS *Eagle*

Displacement	27,229 tonnes (26,800 tons) (full load)	**Speed**	24 knots
Length	203.45m (667ft 6in) (overall)	**Armament**	9 x 6-inch (152.4mm); 5 x 4-inch (102mm) and 4 x 3-pounder guns
Beam	32.06m (105ft 2in)	**Complement**	834
Draught	6.63m (21.9ft)	**Aircraft**	24
Propulsion	Steam turbines; 32 boilers, 4 shafts		

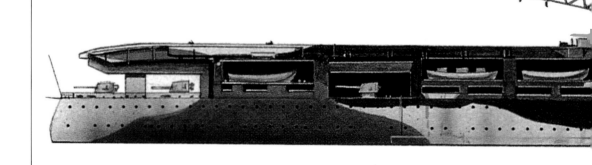

The first naval aviator was only twenty-four when he died. His legacy was to be immense.

BRITISH EFFORTS

After the debacle of the *Mayfly*, the Admiralty accepted an offer from the Royal Aeronautical Club to provide free flying training for four naval officers. The reason for the shift to aeroplanes was not only because of continuing concerns about airships. The Royal Navy's strategy of close blockade of the enemy coast would be diffi-cult in any future war, since by 1910 it was almost certain that the enemy in a war would be Germany. The Germans possessed mines, torpedo boats and submarines in abundance, and these would all present serious obstacles to reconnaissance sorties by surface units. Using an aircraft seemed the obvious solution. The First Sea Lord, Sir Arthur Wilson, rightly took the view that airships would be vulnerable to coastal defences, whereas aircraft would have the agility to evade ground fire.

The four officers selected completed their

HMS *Argus*

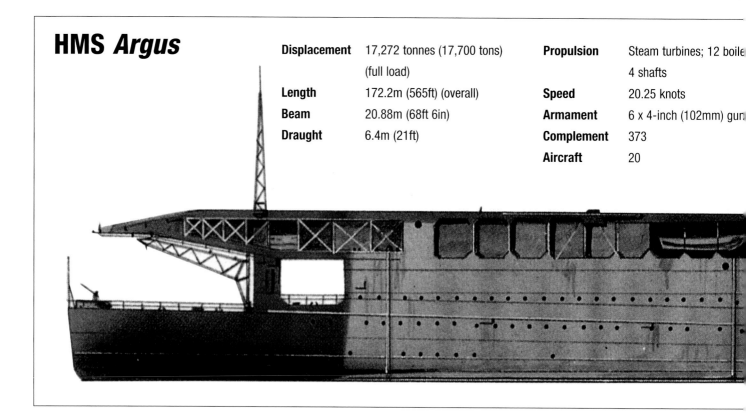

Displacement	17,272 tonnes (17,700 tons) (full load)	**Propulsion**	Steam turbines; 12 boile 4 shafts
Length	172.2m (565ft) (overall)	**Speed**	20.25 knots
Beam	20.88m (68ft 6in)	**Armament**	6 x 4-inch (102mm) gun
Draught	6.4m (21ft)	**Complement**	373
		Aircraft	20

course in September 1911. The most senior of them, Lieutenant Charles Rumney Samson, persuaded Wilson to provide him with a base at Eastchurch from which he could develop the techniques needed for shipboard operations. Samson made the first take-off from a ship by a British aircraft on 10 January 1912. While it is probably fair to say that their Lordships of the Admiralty were never unduly prone to excitement, Samson's achievement certainly interested them. Further experiments were put in hand, under the direction of Murray Sueter. These included trials from cruisers of the Home Fleet, and flights from ships underway at sea.

The trials were successful, but did not encourage Samson to try landing on a ship. He felt that it would be too difficult to land a fast aircraft on a moving ship – and there was an alternative solution: the seaplane. These aircraft were little more than conventional land planes with their wheeled undercarriage replaced with floats. Although the drag from the floats reduced the aircraft's performance, the benefits were felt to outweigh the disadvantages. Because the seaplanes could land on the water, there was no need to build a flying-on platform on the ships operating the aircraft. This was important, since the main armament on the *Pennsylvania* and the *Birmingham* had been covered over by the experimental flight decks. While this was fine for experiments, it meant that the ship would not have been able to use some of its guns in

time of war. In theory the seaplane could also take off without the need for a flight deck, but Samson was concerned that taking off from the open sea would not be easy, particularly in rough conditions. When the Royal Navy went to war, it did so with seaplane carriers with a relatively short flying-off platform and a crane to hoist in the aircraft after it had alighted on the sea.

By this point, however, the Royal Navy was not only considering seaplane carriers.

Murray Sueter had been appointed Director of the Air Department in July 1912, and had issued a specification for an aircraft carrier with a 61m (200ft) deck (intended for flying off rather than landing), but lack of funds prevented its construction. The seaplane carriers, beginning with the conversion of the old cruiser *Hermes*, were the vessels the Royal Naval Air Service used for its aircraft in 1914. Although the naval aviation story began with Eugene Ely, quite when the tale of the aircraft carrier begins is a little more difficult to define. The possibilities had been demonstrated, but none of the world's navies had a proper aircraft carrier in 1914. They had ships that could carry aircraft, certainly, but these were far removed from anything that we would recognize today as a carrier.

WORLD WAR I
When the First World War began on 4 August 1914, the Royal Navy only had the *Hermes* as an aviation vessel, carrying three seaplanes. A German U-boat in the

English Channel sank *Hermes* on 30 October 1914, leaving the Royal Navy without any dedicated ship-borne aviation. This hardly mattered at the time, since the RNAS was busy in France and Belgium, causing confusion and occasional havoc among the Germans in a fleet of armoured cars procured by unusual means and com- manded by the irrepressible Charles Samson. Also, land-based aircraft conduct- ed a number of daring raids against Zeppelin sheds. A Sopwith Tabloid, flown by Flight Lieutenant Reggie Marix, bombed the sheds at Düsseldorf, destroying the Zeppelin Z9 in the process. An even more audacious attack against the main Zeppelin

BELOW: *Eagle* joined the fleet in 1920, and spent much of the inter-war period in the Far East. During World War II she saw service in the Mediterranean and the Indian Ocean, most notably transporting aircraft to Malta.

base at Fredrichshafen followed on 20 November, causing extensive damage. Operations at sea, however, were less impressive, particularly after the loss of the *Hermes*. The Admiralty recognized the need for more aviation vessels, and in 1913 had bought a hull that had originally been intended for a tramp steamer. The ship was given the name *Ark Royal*, beginning a long association between that name and British aircraft carriers. The *Ark* was given a 39.6m (130ft) long flight deck, but construction was slow. By the time she was ready for operations in 1915, the *Ark*'s top speed of 10 knots was too slow to permit the operation of aircraft from the deck, since they needed to be travelling into wind at a greater speed than the ship could achieve. As a result, the *Ark Royal* operated as a simple seaplane tender, hoisting aircraft onto the water with her crane to allow them to take off, and recovering them in the same way after landing. *Ark Royal* was not alone, since three cross-channel ferries, *Engadine*, *Riviera* and *Empress,* were taken on in August 1914 for conversion as seaplane tenders. Their speed of 21 knots meant that they were able to keep up with the rest of the fleet, creating the opportunity for the first air attack by sea-based aircraft.

In November 1914, the Royal Navy decided to launch a raid against the Zeppelin base at Cuxhaven. The operation was planned with two aims in mind. The most important reason for the raid was not to test seaplanes, but to try to draw some of the German fleet out into battle; any success enjoyed by the seaplane raid would be a welcome bonus. The attack involved the three seaplane carriers with an escort of

cruisers, destroyers and submarines, and at 0600 hours on Christmas Day 1914, the seaplane carriers reached the flying-off position. The aircraft were hoisted onto the helpfully flat sea, and at 0700 they were given the signal to start their engines. The biting cold meant that this was more difficult than it sounded, and two of the nine aircraft stubbornly refused to start, despite the best efforts of their mechanics. Two of the mechanics went for an inadvertent – and freezing – swim after losing their footing and had to be rescued before the mission could begin. But within 15 minutes the aircraft were ready, and began their take-off runs. Just after they passed from sight, an inquisitive Zeppelin, the L6, appeared and aimed several bombs at *Empress*. They missed, and affronted at the airship's temerity, the escort HMS *Undaunted* opened fire with her six-inch guns. The L6 decided that this was quite enough and headed off out of range.

While the ships were dealing with this unwelcome visitor, the pilots struggled on through increasing fog. The aircrews realized that they would not even be able to find their target, let alone bomb it, and abandoned this part of the mission. They had been briefed to conduct reconnaissance of the German fleet at Wilhelmshaven as an additional objective, which they did (taking the opportunity to drop their bombs on a cruiser and a seaplane base). The attack was a failure, although the reconnaissance information was useful. Nonetheless, it demonstrated that the aircraft could, given better weather conditions and a little luck, play a major part in naval warfare. The planner of the Cuxhaven raid, Squadron Commander Cecil l'Estrange, made the point that had the

BELOW: The Short Type 184 was built in response to an Admiralty requirement for a torpedo-carrying seaplane and gave sterling service during World War I. After achieving some remarkable early successes the aircraft was most commonly used for reconnaissance. Pictured is one of three aircraft attached to HMS *Vindex.*

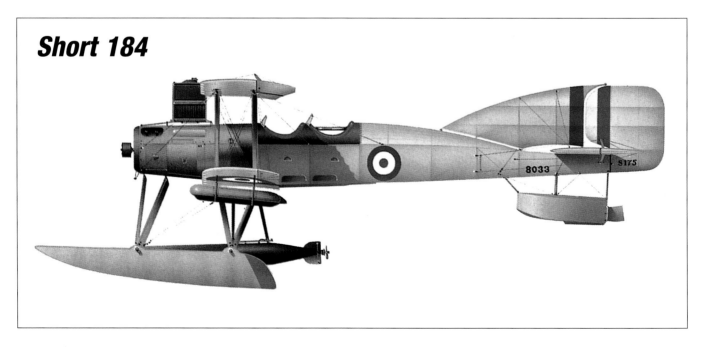

Short 184

8033   S175

Fairey Flycatcher

aircraft been carrying torpedoes, the ships at Wilhelmshaven could have suffered far greater indignities than having some light bombs fall around them. This was not lost on the Admiralty, and despite its understandable concentration upon ships rather than aeroplanes, greater thought was given to the problems associated with operating aircraft at sea.

It soon became clear that the seaplane was not the best platform for conducting offensive operations. As the seaplanes needed to be more robust to survive taking off and alighting on the open sea, they were significantly heavier than land planes. This meant that the seaplanes were slower (not helped by the drag caused by their floats), less manoeuvrable, had a lower service ceiling, and could not carry the same weight of bombs or torpedoes. Events during the unfortunate Dardanelles expedition in 1915 brought these points sharply into focus. Air operations in support of the landings at Gallipoli were hampered by the small number of aircraft available, but some interesting results were obtained on 12 August 1915, when Flight Commander C.H.K. Edmonds took off in his Short 184 seaplane (after an extremely long take-off run), with a 14-inch torpedo slung between the floats. Edmonds spotted a Turkish supply ship and torpedoed it. The supply vessel had already been sunk by a British submarine, but had settled on the bottom in very shallow water. This was not really important, since the incident

showed that a torpedo-armed aircraft could pose a threat to shipping. Five days later, Edmonds demonstrated the point again, when he torpedoed and sank another Turkish supply ship, and Flight Lieutenant G.B. Dacre sank a third the same day. But this did not start a trend, and Dacre's attack was the last successful torpedo attack launched by an aircraft during the war. The reasons for this were straightforward. To take off with a torpedo a seaplane had to carry a dramatically reduced amount of fuel. In addition, the sea needed to be perfectly calm if the seaplane was to take off at all. The limitations of the seaplanes were all too apparent.

THE ZEPPELIN THREAT

At the same time that the seaplanes were achieving their limited successes, the Royal Navy began to give more thought to the problem of intercepting Zeppelins. To intercept an airship, a fast-climbing fighter aircraft was required, and this ruled out seaplanes. The RNAS experimented with the Bristol Scout monoplane, but found that their radius of action was disappointing. The solution, it seemed, was to convey them by ship to a point nearer to the Zeppelin's operating bases. To prove the concept, Flight Lieutenant H.F. Towler flew a Bristol Scout from the deck of the seaplane carrier *Vindex* on 3 November 1915, landing ashore. This neatly demonstrated the problem: the landplane could be launched from a ship's deck, but it would be forced to ditch

ABOVE: The Fairey Flycatcher served with the Fleet Air Arm from 1923 to 1934, and was an extremely popular aircraft with pilots. Wearing the blue and yellow rudder band of a flight leader's aircraft, this Flycatcher I is illustrated as it appeared with No. 405 Flight, Fleet Air Arm, aboard HMS *Glorious*.

ABOVE: The Hawker Nimrod was an elegant naval fighter aircraft, replacing the Fairey Flycatcher from October 1931. The Nimrod was closely related to the RAF's Hawker Fury, although the extra weight of equipment needed for carrier operations reduced the Nimrod's speed.

near a passing ship once its mission was completed. Despite Ely's demonstration that landing on a ship was possible, doing so during fleet operations would be a very different matter. Nonetheless, the awareness that the German Navy's Zeppelin fleet was able to conduct reconnaissance against the Grand Fleet with little risk of interception meant that the Royal Navy was forced to consider using 'one-shot' fighter aircraft to attack the Zeppelins. Despite this appreciation, little had been achieved by the time of the battle of Jutland on 31 May 1916.

JUTLAND AND ITS AFTERMATH

The battle of Jutland was a strategic success for the Royal Navy, but it was not the decisive victory that the Navy and the British people had been expecting. But there were some encouraging points from the battle, notably the benefits to be had from aerial observation for naval gunfire. It was clear that there had not been enough aircraft to do this to full effect, prompting Admiral Sir John Jellicoe to ask for two ships capable of operating aircraft to be provided for the fleet. After Jutland, Jellicoe was convinced

that he required aircraft to give his fleet the ability to destroy Zeppelins and to warn of the presence of German U-boats. In addition to Jellicoe's request, it was becoming clear that the poor material state of the seaplane vessel *Campania* would demand that a replacement be found. Building two brand new ships would take far longer than converting extant vessels – but conversion of any combat ships of appropriate size (cruisers or bigger) would mean a reduction in the gun power of the fleet. A solution was swiftly proposed. At the outbreak of war, construction of a number of ships had been suspended. Two liners being built for Italy, the *Conte Rosso* and the *Guilio Cesare*, had been sitting on the stocks since August 1914, and were likely candidates.

Given the difficulty of operating seaplanes in rough conditions, it was clear that the ships needed to be big enough to permit fighters to fly off the deck. Since it was assumed that these fighters would not land back aboard, the ships also needed to have enough room to carry a large number of aircraft. But this assumption was rapidly challenged and the notion of landing back on

RIGHT: The Shark was the last of a line of biplane torpedo bombers built by the Blackburn company. Ordered by the Royal Navy in 1934, the Shark carried a single torpedo, or up to 680kg (1,500lb) of bombs, as well as two machine guns. A well-liked aircraft, the Shark saw limited service, its replacement by the Fairey Swordfish as a strike aircraft beginning as early as 1936.

CARRIER OPERATIONS 1918

Furious returned from her conversion in March 1918, and landing trials began in May. Although a dozen or so landings were made, many other attempts ended up in the safety net behind the superstructure or over the side of the ship. Tests showed that the problem came from the turbulence generated by the superstructure. The problem of aircraft going over the side was to be tackled by the introduction of longitudinal arrester wires, while a major redesign of the superstructure would be required to solve the problem of turbulence. The latter modification could not be undertaken during the war, but did not prevent *Furious* from taking part on operations, most notably the raid against the Zeppelin sheds at Tondern. Seven Sopwith Camels, each carrying light bombs, were launched early on 19 July 1918, and managed to destroy the Zeppelins L54 and L60 in their sheds, as well as causing damage to the base itself.

But the Admiralty had greater ambitions than this, and spent much of 1918 planning to equip the fleet with aircraft carriers and torpedo bombers. The torpedo aircraft was easily acquired from the Sopwith company, and named the 'Cuckoo' (supposedly since it was meant to lay its 'egg' in someone else's nest). The carriers were not so easily obtained. The Admiralty were confident that a mass torpedo raid against the German Fleet could be mounted, but before this could occur the war ended. By November 1918, the Royal Navy had a clear lead in naval aviation. As well as moving toward flying aircraft off and, more significantly, onto carriers, they had demonstrated that ship-based aircraft could play a major part in operations, and were even toying with the notion of using them independently of surface units. But within less than ten years this lead had been surrendered to the United States.

INTER-WAR CARRIER DEVELOPMENT

There was no single reason for the Royal Navy's decline as the leading exponent of carrier aviation during the inter-war period, but a major factor was the creation of the independent Royal Air Force in April 1918. Virtually all the Royal Navy's aircrew joined the new service, removing the core of the naval aviation force. In addition, the RAF were granted control of all aircraft and other aviation assets, and showed a marked reluctance to invest in naval aviation – indeed, serving in the naval flights was regarded as being detrimental to an officer's career. These two factors did little to encourage the navy to invest in aircraft carriers. The proponents of naval air power were almost all incorporated into the RAF (which was concentrating on strategic bombing), leaving the field clear for those in the Royal Navy who wanted to concentrate on battleships. As a result, the argument goes, the Royal Navy ended up losing interest in air power, since there were few

HMS *Ark Royal*

The third *Ark Royal* gained a legendary reputation in World War II. Seeing action in the Atlantic and the Mediterranean, her aircraft were responsible for the torpedo attack against the *Bismarck* that led to the destruction of the German ship by British surface forces.

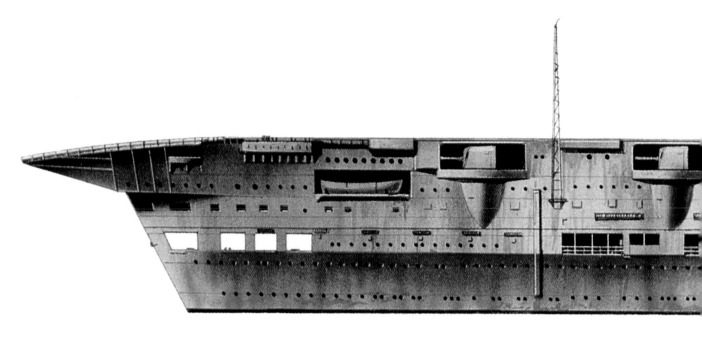

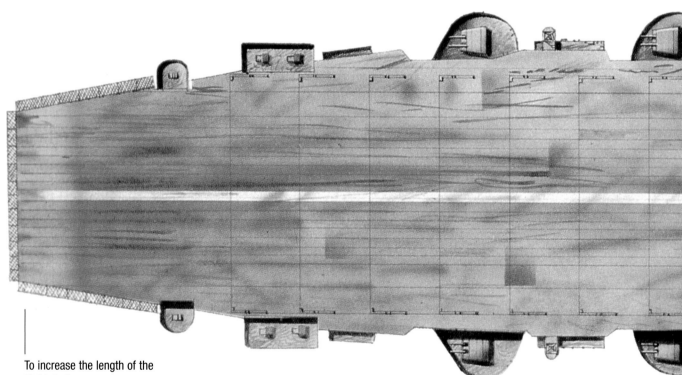

To increase the length of the flight deck, an overhang was provided. The overhang was rounded down, making it impossible to park aircraft upon it: as the need for more aircraft became apparent, later carriers had these flattened out.

Ark Royal mounted a number of larger guns. The 4.5in (114mm) weapons were intended to allow the carrier to bombard shore targets. The notion of using aircraft as the sole offensive weapon had not arisen at this point.

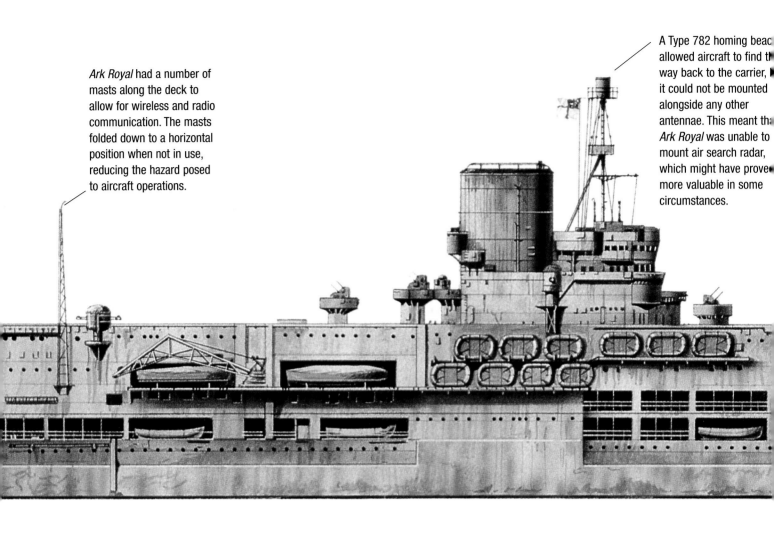

Ark Royal had a number of masts along the deck to allow for wireless and radio communication. The masts folded down to a horizontal position when not in use, reducing the hazard posed to aircraft operations.

A Type 782 homing beac allowed aircraft to find t way back to the carrier, it could not be mounted alongside any other antennae. This meant th *Ark Royal* was unable to mount air search radar, which might have prove more valuable in some circumstances.

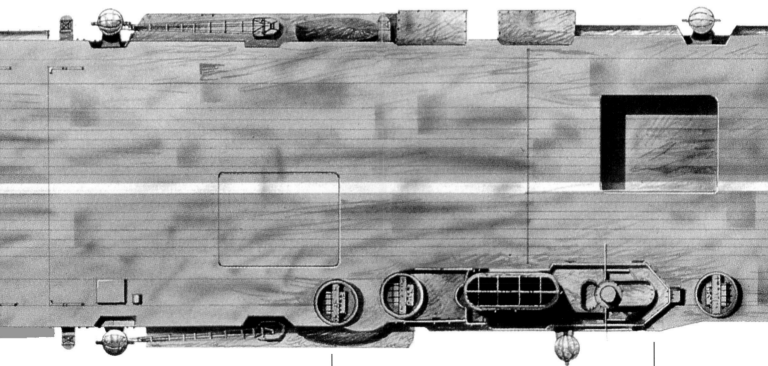

As part of *Ark Royal*'s anti-aircraft armament, 48 2-pounder (0.91kg) 'Pom-Pom' guns were carried by the ship. Experience soon demonstrated that while the Pom-Poms were useful, fast-firing cannon were needed to complement them.

Ark Royal's three lifts were problematic. There were instances where aircraft landed, rolled over the arre wires and ended up in the hangar rather more quickly than the pilot intended.

board gained ever more support (despite persistent doubt as to how this could be achieved). This in turn meant that the ships would need to be long enough to permit the construction of a landing deck, pointing to a ship the size of an ocean-going liner.

In September 1916, authority to convert the *Conte Rosso* to aircraft carrier configuration was granted. At the same time, trials with arrester gear similar to that used by Ely were undertaken at the naval air station at Grain. The trials were encouraging, and from this point onwards, the development of aircraft carriers gained increasing momentum. By the end of 1916, the new Prime Minister, David Lloyd George, ensured that the shipbuilding industry was given the sense of direction that had been lacking when Herbert Asquith had been in power. Aircraft carriers were designated as a special case. The War Cabinet approved the building of two ocean-going carriers, and two more based upon cross-channel ferries – the *Nairana* and the *Pegasus* (formerly *Stockholm*).

These developments met with official approval. In early 1917, an Admiralty committee had concluded that the fleet needed more aviation-capable vessels. The committee appreciated that the swiftest way of meeting this need was by converting existing ships, and proposed that the cruiser *Furious* be converted to a carrier. The proposed conversion was slightly odd, in that the ship was given a flight deck, but retained a huge 18-inch gun turret at the stern.

While *Furious* was undergoing conversion, Squadron Commander Frederick Rutland of the RNAS demonstrated that short wooden platforms mounted on the turrets of light cruisers offered an interim alternative. On 26 June 1917, Rutland flew a Sopwith Pup off a 6.1m (20ft) long platform mounted on HMS *Yarmouth*. The platform did not interfere with the operation of the ship's guns, and meant that aircraft could be flown from a far greater number of ships. This arrangement did not overcome the problem of landing on the carriers, but even this was to be addressed within a month. On 4 July 1917, HMS *Furious* entered service in her new guise as a carrier, with three seaplanes and five Sopwith Pups. Almost immediately, the senior pilot on board the ship, Squadron Commander Edwin Dunning, began trials to see if he could land on the flying-off deck.

This was more difficult than it sounds. Dunning had to fly around the ship's superstructure at a low speed, and land with the engine cut. A deck party would then grab hold of toggles fitted to the aircraft and almost literally pull the aircraft down onto the deck. On 2 August, Dunning managed to achieve the first landing of a combat aircraft on an aircraft carrier. He continued with the trials, with tragic results. On 8 August, he landed on *Furious* once again, but was travelling too quickly. His Sopwith Pup went over the side of the ship, and he was knocked out when the aircraft hit the sea. By the time a rescue boat had reached the ditched aircraft, he had drowned. This tragedy raised a number of questions about the viability of trying to land on *Furious*. It was decided to give the ship a 91.4m (300ft) flight deck aft of the superstructure, and *Furious* went into dock for this work in November 1917.

BELOW: In common with most British fighters of the time, the Nimrod carried two 7.7mm (.303-inch) machine guns, and had the ability to carry light bombs. Some remained in use in second-line roles until 1941, when the type was declared obsolete.

Hawker Nimrod

Kaga

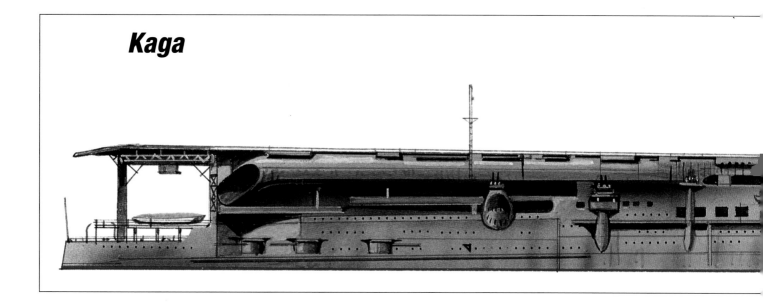

emerged as the USS *Langley*, designated CV1 (CV being the generic designator for an aircraft carrier). *Langley* was followed by two more conversions, the *Saratoga* and *Lexington* (CV2 and CV3). *Saratoga* and *Lexington* had been originally intended as large battlecruisers, but the Washington Treaty meant that they could not be completed as such, without exceeding treaty limits. The ships set a trend for large American carriers, capable of embarking an impressive complement of aircraft, which were able to supply considerable striking power. Their size also proved advantageous to cope with the increasing dimensions of newer aircraft. The USN decreed that only naval aviators could command carriers, which meant that men with direct experience of aviation would oversee the ships and their air groups. This promoted the rapid development of effective carrier operating procedures. Deck parks, crash barriers and the employment of the Landing Signal Officer (LSO) to guide pilots in for their landing all became established practice, swiftly adopted by other carrier operators.

THE ROYAL NAVY

Despite the serious difficulties facing the Royal Navy in the 1920s, the situation began to change for the better in 1931, with the appointment of Rear Admiral R.G.H. Henderson as Rear Admiral Aircraft Carriers. Henderson had commanded *Furious*, and was a firm believer in the use of carriers, but faced a major problem in the general inertia that had afflicted British naval aviation over the previous decade. Although there had been progress, a lack of money and pilots meant that Britain had fallen well behind America and Japan. It

was only as the threat from Nazi Germany increased that major steps were taken to improve the situation. The appointment of Sir Thomas Inskip as the Minister for Defence Co-ordination gave the Navy a new opportunity to press for the return of their own air arm. Despite strenuous opposition from the Air Staff, Inskip sided with the Navy, and instructed that a naval air arm – the Fleet Air Arm – should be created from the range of ship's flights and shore-based units which had been under RAF command since 1918. The change began in 1937, and was just about complete by 1939 – a definite case of 'just in time' planning.

Inskip's instruction came to fruition while the first new British carrier for some time, the *Ark Royal*, was under construction. As the rearmament programme gathered pace, the simplest policy would have been to build more *Ark Royals*, but this option was not pursued. In 1936 Henderson, now the Controller of Naval Construction, took the bold step of commissioning a new design of carrier, which had an armoured deck to protect against enemy air attack. This was not without its disadvantages, since it meant that some space in the ship's hangar had to be sacrificed, reducing the number of aircraft that could be carried. But Henderson knew that the Royal Navy simply did not have the resources to operate large air wings, so this was not an immediate problem (though it was to become one as World War II progressed). Construction of the new Illustrious class began in 1937. With these ships the Royal Navy managed to equip itself with just enough aircraft carriers to meet the immediate demands of war in 1939-1940.

To assist aircraft ranged at the front of the deck, *Ark Royal* employed two accelerators. These could be used to launch the whole air group but this was time-consuming and impractical. Normally, only the aircraft at the very forward end of the deck would use this assistance, the rest conducting free take-offs.

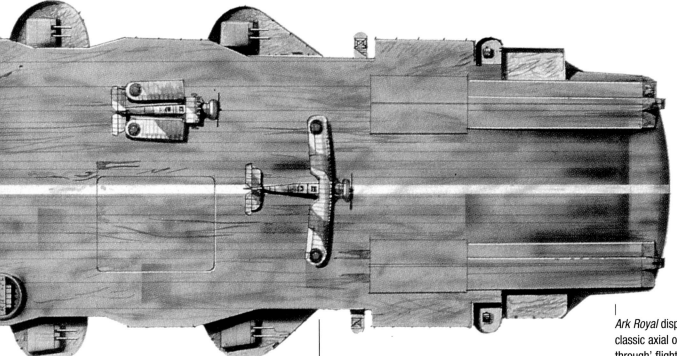

Two Fairey Swordfish can be seen on the deck. *Ark Royal* operated a variety of aircraft types during World War II, including Swordfish, Blackburn Skuas and Fairey Fulmars.

Ark Royal displays the classic axial or 'straight-through' flight deck. When aircraft failed to engage the arrester wires, a safety barrier prevented them from striking those 'spotted' at the bow, but increased the risk to the aircrew. The solution to this ultimately came in the form of the angled deck.

ABOVE: A flight of Fairey Swordfish above HMS *Ark Royal*. Swordfish were involved in numerous notable actions, particularly the crippling of the Italian fleet at Taranto and an operation which crippled the *Bismarck*, allowing the German raider to be caught and sunk by British battleships.

Since the flight deck could not be covered with cleats and wires, British carriers often had openings in the hull to permit the ship to be worked in harbour.

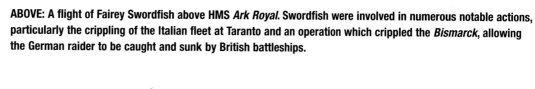

SPECIFICATIONS		Propulsion	Steam turbines;
HMS *Ark Royal*			6 boilers, 3 shafts
		Speed	31 knots
Displacement	28,143 tonnes (27,700 tons) full load	Armament	16 x 4.5-inch (114mm), 48 x 2-pounder
Length	243.8m (800ft) overall		and 32 x 0.5-inch (12.7mm) guns
Beam	28.8m (94ft 9in)	Complement	1600
Draught	6.93m (22ft 9in)	Aircraft	70

to argue its case. This is not entirely fair, since the Admiralty fought for nearly twenty years to regain control of its own air arm. The lack of money and the Washington Naval Treaty of 1922 played a considerable role in limiting what the Royal Navy could do. The Washington Treaty gave the Royal Navy the right to have carriers totalling 135,000 tons, and the Admiralty proceeded under this framework. Three carriers that had been started during World War I (*Argus*, *Hermes* and *Eagle*) would be retained, alongside *Furious* and her two sister ships, *Courageous* and *Glorious* (which underwent similar conversions from cruiser to carrier). This would allow the building of two large or four small carriers under treaty conditions. As a result of financial pressures, the programme was not implemented, and it was not until the 1930s that carrier aviation recovered in Britain. By this time, Japan and the United States had overtaken the Royal Navy.

THE JAPANESE CARRIER FORCE

The Imperial Japanese Navy (IJN) was extremely interested in aircraft carriers. Japan's geographical circumstances and reliance on imports dictated the need for a strong navy. Aircraft carriers would have to play a role in the navy, since there was no other way of guaranteeing the fleet the necessary air support. The Japanese asked for assistance from Britain (then still a close naval ally), and received a semi-official mission led by a former RNAS aviator, the Master of Semphill. The mission resulted in the formulation of Japanese naval doctrine, envisaging the carrier as a key part of a raiding force, supported by fast battleships. Emphasis was placed upon torpedo-bombers, and later, dive-bombers. A naval expansion programme followed, culminating in the construction of the *Akagi* and *Kaga*. The *Akagi* was the largest carrier in the world at the time, carrying 60 aircraft. The developments in Japanese naval aviation meant that the country was potentially well suited to fighting a war in the Pacific. The Japanese progressively saw the United States as their major enemy in the area, particularly since the US Navy had progressed with its own carrier fleet.

THE UNITED STATES CARRIER FORCE

Despite the early potential shown by flights in the US, the USN seemed uncertain about aircraft carriers until 1919. In March that year, exercises with the USS *Texas* demonstrated the importance of aerial observation and the general benefits of having aircraft available to the fleet. No funding was available to build a new carrier, so the redundant fleet collier *Jupiter* was sent to the Norfolk Naval Yard for conversion, to begin in March 1920. The conversion took two years, and the ship

LEFT: The USS *Ranger* (CV4) seen after launching on 25 February 1933. She was the first American carrier to be built as an aircraft carrier from the keel up, but was hampered by the need to compromise the design to meet some of the requirements of the 1922 Washington Naval Treaty. *Ranger* served with the Atlantic fleet during World War II, and did not become as well known as those units that saw service in the Pacific.

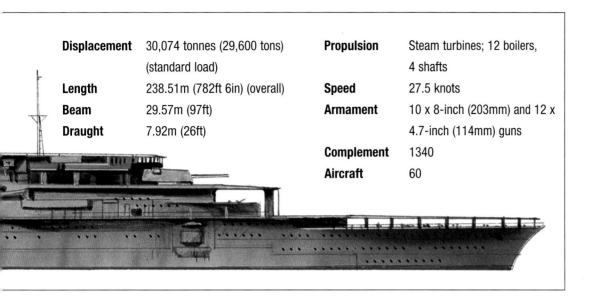

Displacement	30,074 tonnes (29,600 tons) (standard load)	Propulsion	Steam turbines; 12 boilers, 4 shafts
Length	238.51m (782ft 6in) (overall)	Speed	27.5 knots
Beam	29.57m (97ft)	Armament	10 x 8-inch (203mm) and 12 x 4.7-inch (114mm) guns
Draught	7.92m (26ft)		
		Complement	1340
		Aircraft	60

CARRIER DEVELOPMENTS

Although the inter-war years marked a period when all navies suffered from some restrictions, either financial or through treaty obligation, the aircraft carrier as we now know it had begun to emerge. The most obvious development was that of the carrier 'island', replacing the superstructure that had given so much trouble to early pilots attempting to land on board. The alternative was the 'flush deck' carrier, which demanded that the bridge be situated either in the bow or in some form of temporary structure that was folded away during flying operations. The advantages of the island carrier meant that the flush-deckers were discontinued (although the projected USS *United States* of the late 1940s reverted to this configuration). In addition, the longitudinal arrester wire was abandoned as an unnecessary complication. By 1939, the aircraft carrier was an established part of three major navies: but not even the proponents of carrier air power could have fully imagined just how much the aircraft carrier would go on to achieve in six long years of war.

BELOW: A Hawker Osprey flies past HMS *Eagle*. The Osprey was a naval derivative of the RAF's Hawker Hart light bomber. It was designed as a fleet reconnaissance aircraft, and entered service in 1932. The Osprey enjoyed a high performance for the time, and some were built as floatplanes for use from units other than aircraft carriers.

CHAPTER TWO

THE AIRCRAFT CARRIER WAR AGAINST GERMANY

The British carrier-building programme
in the late 1930s meant that the Royal Navy
was in a far healthier position to meet the
threat posed by Germany when war broke
out in September 1939. But it would have
to wait for the newest carriers
to be completed.

EVEN SO, THE NAVY had seven carriers in service, although *Argus* was employed as a training carrier. *Ark Royal* was the newest of the carriers, and could carry the largest complement of aircraft. The others, particularly *Furious*, *Glorious* and *Courageous*, suffered from their age: they had been designed when naval aircraft were smaller and lighter, and carried fewer than the carriers in American service.

LEFT: The deck of HMS *Illustrious*. In the foreground are Fairey Fulmars, while the radial-engined aircraft aft are Grumman Wildcats (named the Martlet by the Royal Navy). The Wildcat was highly regarded by its pilots, and remained in British service until the end of the war, unlike the Fulmar, which was large and relatively slow.

Blackburn Skua

The aircraft themselves were not as advanced as they might have been. The main fighter aircraft was the Gloster Sea Gladiator, essentially a standard RAF Gladiator biplane fighter modified for carrier operations. The Gladiator was almost obsolescent when it entered service, joining the RAF at a time when high-speed monoplane fighters like the Spitfire and Hurricane were only a matter of months away from reaching the front line. This was perhaps not such a disadvantage as far as the Royal Navy was concerned, since many thought operating high-performance fighters from what were relatively small carriers would be difficult. Also, the lack of sophisticated navigational devices meant that the Admiralty judged that longer-range fighter aircraft required two crew members. The other fighter available, the Blackburn Skua (which had begun to enter service in 1938), met this criterion, but was compromised by its dual role as a fighter/dive-bomber. While other fighter aircraft later took on the dive-bombing role, the Skua was possibly the only aeroplane that was ever designed from the outset to perform both tasks. Like the Gladiator, the Skua had only four forward-firing 7.7mm (.303-inch) machine guns, which put it at a disadvantage against modern land-based fighters like the Messerschmitt Bf 109. No 800 Squadron were the first Fleet Air Arm unit to re-equip with the type, and were joined by two other units by September 1939. The key strike and torpedo bomber aircraft aboard the carriers was the Fairey Swordfish, another biplane. An untrained eye could easily have mistaken the Swordfish for an aircraft from the First World War. It was slow and had only two machine guns with which to defend itself. The crew were completely exposed to the elements, and the aircraft's affectionate nickname (the 'Stringbag') gave a good impression of the aircraft's level of sophistication. Appearances are nothing if not deceptive, for the Swordfish was still cheerfully performing a vital front-line role in 1945, adored by its crews and having created a legendary status for itself along the way. To operate these various types of aircraft, the Fleet Air Arm had about 500 trained aircrew, based at eight air stations.

EARLY PROBLEMS

The Admiralty was far from certain how it was going to employ its carriers, since the threat posed by the German navy was far different to that in 1914. Whereas the High Seas Fleet had been built around the battleship, Hitler had created a navy with few major surface units (although they were to cause fearful problems, despite their lack of numbers). The Admiralty decided that the carriers could best be employed against U-boats (a notion that was to be rapidly disabused). The plan was for a carrier, accompanied by destroyers, to head for the position where a U-boat had been sighted. The carrier would employ its aircraft to keep the U-boat underwater, and the destroyers would employ their ASDIC (sonar) equipment to locate the submarine. They would then depth charge the U-boat, and even if they did not destroy it, they would succeed in diverting the U-boats' attention from merchant convoys.

On 14 September, the *Ark Royal* was sent to investigate the report of a U-boat sighting. The carrier certainly diverted the attention of the U-boat commander, who promptly torpedoed the big ship. Fortunately for the *Ark Royal*, German torpedoes were terribly unreliable at this point in the war, and the entire salvo failed to go off. An accompanying destroyer, alerted by the sudden action – which was not quite how the plan was supposed to work – then sank the unlucky U-boat. This might have implied that the tactics were successful, but events just three days later demonstrated just how misplaced they were. On 17 September, *Courageous* was conducting a similar anti-submarine sweep when she was spotted by U29. The U-boat commander fired a salvo of torpedoes, and did not suffer from any reliability problems with them. The *Courageous* sank within a matter of minutes, and the submarine escaped. The Admiralty came to the sober realization that anti-submarine work was not the best role for the fleet carriers, and changed tactics.

Ironically, the first real carrier air action of the war involved a submarine, but it was a British vessel, not a U-boat. The submarine HMS *Spearfish* was damaged off Norway, and the *Ark* was sent to help escort it back to base. On the way, Luftwaffe Dornier 18 flying boats were sighted, and some of *Ark Royal*'s Skuas were launched to intercept them. One was duly shot down by the aircraft flown by Lieutenant B.S. McEwen and his observer, Action Petty Officer B.M. Seymour. This was not enough to prevent a sighting report from reaching German headquarters, and an air attack against the carrier developed in the afternoon. A Heinkel 111 bomber appeared overhead and dropped a 2000kg (4410lb) bomb, which exploded just 30m (98ft) off the *Ark*'s port bow. The ship heeled over to starboard and a huge cloud of soot, loosened from the funnel, shot into the air in protest at the disturbance. The *Ark* then righted herself in stately fashion and carried on. The damage control party found little to do beyond disposing of broken crockery in the wardroom. The pilot of the He 111, Adolfe Francke, returned to base and reported that he had come close to hitting the *Ark Royal*, but had not quite done so. This was good enough for German propaganda to claim that *Ark Royal* had been sunk, and the unfortunate Francke found himself told to write a book explaining how he had done the deed. The infamous William Joyce – Lord 'Haw-Haw' – taunted the British public with the question 'where is the *Ark Royal*?' Initially, the Admiralty

BELOW: A Swordfish is seen from an accompanying aircraft. The paint scheme on the aircraft is one of several worn by Swordfish during their long service: the white fuselage and underwing scheme was proved to be the best for rendering the aircraft less visible to enemy submarines.

ABOVE: Seen in peaceful times, *Ark Royal* sits at anchor. The *Ark Royal* was the first 'modern' carrier for the inter-war Royal Navy, and the first carrier for eight years when she joined the fleet in 1938. She had a short but active war: her aircraft crippled the *Bismarck* and were employed in the Norwegian campaign; the Germans claimed to have sunk her on several occasions. *Ark Royal* finally succumbed to a torpedo from *U81* in November 1941.

HMS *Hermes*

Displacement	13,208 tonnes (13,000 tons) (full load)	**Speed**	25 knots
Length	182.88m (600ft) (overall)	**Armament**	6 x 5.5-inch (140mm) and 3 x 4-inch (102mm) guns
Beam	21.4m (70ft 3in)	**Complement**	664
Draught	5.71m (18ft 9in)	**Aircraft**	20
Propulsion	Steam turbines; 6 boilers, 2 shafts		

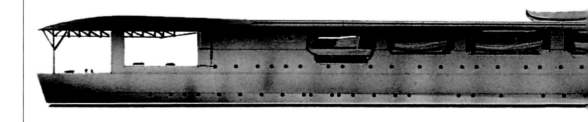

were happy to let this pass, but eventually became so irritated by the question that they felt compelled to show that *Ark Royal* was still in service, even if they did not reveal exactly where she was.

For the remainder of the year, the Royal Navy's carriers were dispersed across the oceans in an attempt to hunt down German surface raiders. *Ark Royal* was sent as part of Force K in pursuit of the *Graf Spee*, and despite many fruitless hours attempting to find the ship, she still played a major part in the *Graf Spee*'s demise. The *Ark Royal* was reported to be part of a major force heading towards Montevideo, and this encouraged the *Graf Spee*'s captain, Captain Langsdorff, in his decision to scuttle the ship. Apart from this, though, the aircraft carrier had not been able to achieve a great deal in the early months of the war.

NORWAY

Although the Royal Navy's carriers were not particularly active in 1939, the following year was far more active. The Norway campaign marked the first true test of the carrier force, but it began inauspiciously. Captain Tom Troubridge, commanding officer of HMS *Furious*, found himself having to signal the Commander-in-Chief Home Fleet to ask for permission to accompany the rest of the fleet to Norwegian waters after it set off without him. *Furious* sailed on 10 April, three days after the other ships, and left her

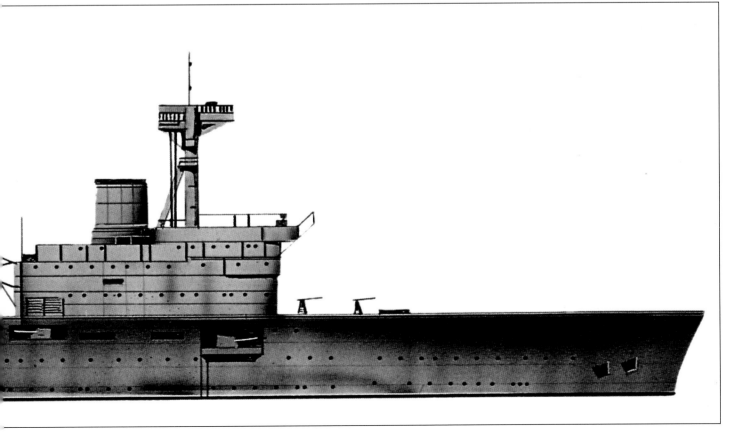

fighters - the Skuas of 801 and 804 Squadrons - ashore at Hatston in the Orkneys. Other Skuas at Hatston had already had a major success before *Furious* set sail, when they sank the German cruiser *Königsberg* in a dive-bombing attack. The Fleet Air Arm was rather disgruntled when the newspapers first chose to ignore the operation and then attributed the success to the RAF. The next day, 11 April 1940, *Furious* launched its 18 Swordfish against German shipping in Trondheim harbour. The cruiser *Hipper* had been reported there, but had in fact left the night before, leaving three destroyers. The shallow water in the harbour meant that the torpedo attack was unsuccessful. Twenty-four hours later, the same units attacked shipping at Narvik, using bombs rather than torpedoes. Conditions were appalling, but the Swordfish managed to find five destroyers and 11 merchant ships, hitting two of them. This encouraged further operations: on 13 April, 10 Swordfish were sent out to coordinate with a sortie by the battleship *Warspite* and nine destroyers against the ships at Narvik. Eight German destroyers were sunk, although none of these fell victim to surface units rather than carrier aircraft.

The lack of fighter cover on board *Furious* meant that the Luftwaffe was able to inflict serious casualties on the Royal Navy. HMS *Eclipse* and HMS *Suffolk* were both seriously damaged by bombing and on 18 April, *Furious* herself was damaged by a near miss. The attacking bomber had been able to circle overhead in a leisurely way, adjusting its aim, before finally dropping the bomb. This demonstrated once and for all the need for fighter cover, and when *Ark Royal* and *Glorious* came to relieve *Furious*, they brought their fighter aircraft

with them. This improved the situation, but operations showed that the Skua was far too slow to compete with modern fighters like the Me 109, despite some successes against bombers. The Skua pilots could boast a number of successful and exciting exploits (one pilot force-landed and fought for three days as an infantryman before finding the part needed to start his aircraft, eventually navigating back to Hatston using a school atlas) – but these could not disguise the fact that they needed better performing aircraft. *Ark Royal* withdrew from the area early in May, and *Glorious* and *Furious* arrived with RAF Gladiator and Hurricane fighters. From 2 June 1940, the British decided to abandon their efforts in Norway, and *Glorious* and *Ark Royal* returned to cover the withdrawal. Despite serious doubts among the ship's officers, the Hurricanes of 46 Squadron RAF landed on board *Glorious*, even though the aircraft had no arrester gear. On 8 June, *Glorious* was given permission to head for home independently of the rest of the fleet (apart from two escorting destroyers). At about 1600 hours, the German battlecruisers *Scharnhorst* and *Gneisenau* sighted the funnel smoke from the small group of ships, and attacked. *Glorious* was not flying any protective patrols, and the attack came as a complete surprise. Desperate efforts to arm and launch Swordfish were thwarted by a hit on the hangar. The destroyers *Ardent* and *Acasta* made valiant efforts to defend *Glorious*, even though their captains must have known the attempt was bound to be fruitless as long as the Germans were in range. At about 1720, *Glorious* was sunk, followed shortly after by *Ardent*. *Acasta* succumbed shortly afterwards, but not before she had managed to damage *Scharnhorst*. The Germans did not stop to

BELOW: The British Wildcat force made a major contribution in the Battle of the Atlantic, with a dozen squadrons aboard the escort carriers from April 1943 until September 1944. This Wildcat Mk V of No 813 Squadron was based on HMS *Campania* and then HMS *Vindex*.

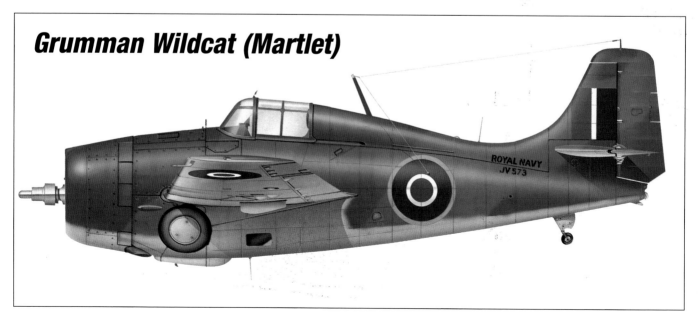

Grumman Wildcat (Martlet)

pick up survivors, and the Admiralty were unable to launch a rescue, because they were quite unaware the battle had taken place until a German news broadcast the next day. Assorted vessels picked up a few survivors, but the loss of *Glorious* marked a disastrous end to a largely disastrous campaign.

The Norway campaign was not without some benefits. It showed that high-performance aircraft could be operated from carrier decks, and the Navy sought a navalized version of the Hurricane as a result. The strategic situation meant that the RAF had first call on Hurricane production well into 1941, but the collapse of France later in June 1940 meant the Royal Navy was able to take over an order for Grumman Wildcats placed by the French. The first Wildcat (known as the Martlet by the Royal Navy) entered service in August 1940. It was clear that some form of coordination of fighter aircraft was required, and this realization led to the development of a fighter direction capability, using ships' radar and a plotting room to direct fighters in defence of the fleet. But most importantly the Norway experience demonstrated that carrier air cover was essential, particularly for expeditionary forces operating beyond the range of friendly land-based air cover. For operations within range of enemy bombers, high-performance fighter aircraft were absolutely essential. Admiral

Fairey Swordfish

ABOVE: Renowned as one of the finest warplanes of World War II, despite its anachronistic biplane format, the Fairey Swordfish achieved some notable victories including the first U-boat sinking and the decimation of the Italian fleet at the Battle of Taranto in November 1940.

Henderson had decreed the armoured deck on the Illustrious-class vessels partly because of the potential threat to carriers operating in the Mediterranean posed by the Italian air force. Although the armoured deck would soon prove its worth, it was far better not to put it to the test.

THE MEDITERRANEAN

Operations in the Mediterranean theatre ensured that 1940, for all its woes, ended on a high note for the Royal Navy's carrier fleet. The entry of Italy into the war – a piece of opportunism by Benito Mussolini that he was to regret – coincided with the fall of France. This meant that operations in the Mediterranean became far more difficult. But Admiral Andrew Cunningham, the Commander-in-Chief Mediterranean, was not overly perturbed, because he had a balanced fleet with the support of at least one, and sometimes two, aircraft carriers. In May 1940, HMS *Eagle* entered the Mediterranean via the Suez Canal, while *Ark Royal* came through the Straits of Gibraltar to join Cunningham's Force H in time to participate in operations to disarm French forces at Dakar.

The first encounter with the Italian fleet came on 9 July 1940. Eagle launched a number of torpedo strikes against the enemy, but spotting for the guns of the fleet proved more profitable. HMS *Warspite* scored a long-range hit upon the Italian battleship *Cesare*, and the Italians turned away, bringing the action to a close. This was a promising start, and matters improved at the end of the month when HMS *Illustrious* arrived. *Illustrious* brought 18 Swordfish and 15 of the new Fairey Fulmar

fighters with her. The Fulmar was an improvement upon the Skua (having twice the number of guns), but was a large two-seater, lacking in speed and manoeuvrability in comparison with land-based fighters. The aircrews made much comment about the fact that the Fulmar had no rear-firing gun, and a whole variety of improvised rear-defence armament soon appeared. Perhaps the most bizarre defensive system consisted of bundles of toilet paper hurled out into the slipstream. Although they stood no chance of damaging a pursuing enemy, they never failed to put the pursuer off his aim.

Despite the fact that *Illustrious*'s fighter aircraft were still not quite up to scratch, the ship herself was much larger than any carrier in Royal Navy service to date. In addition she had a safety barrier, allowing landings to be made while aircraft were parked forward. *Illustrious* greatly increased the effectiveness of the Mediterranean fleet's air force, and this was tellingly demonstrated in November 1940. The operation was to be a classic, and was to inspire the Japanese navy to consider the aggressive use of its carriers against an enemy in harbour.

TARANTO

Plans to attack the Italian fleet in its harbour at Taranto had been made well before the final decision to launch a strike was taken. The attack was authorized in October, and was planned for the 21st of that month. Unfortunately, *Illustrious* suffered a hangar fire, requiring extensive repairs. In addition, *Eagle* had suffered damage to her fuel system from the concussion of a number of bombs dropped by the

Italian air force. *Eagle* therefore transferred some of her aircraft to *Illustrious* to prepare for an attack. On 10 November 1940, photographic reconnaissance showed that the Italian fleet was in the harbour, and 24 hours later *Illustrious* was detached from the fleet so that she could manoeuvre for flying operations.

At 2057 hours, the first 12 Swordfish, led by Lt Cdr Ken Williamson of 825 Squadron, took off, heading for Taranto. Six of them were carrying torpedoes to attack the ships in the outer harbour. Four of the other aircraft carried bombs to attack the vessels moored in the inner dock, and the last two carried some flares to illuminate the area as well as bombs. One of the Swordfish arrived slightly ahead of schedule, alerting the defences. The other aircraft could see the flashes of anti-aircraft guns as they began their run in to the target. The heavy flak claimed Williamson's aircraft (he survived to be taken prisoner), but the strike had already caused serious damage. A second strike, led by Lt Cdr John Hale of 819 Squadron, went in and caused more damage. The Swordfish returned to *Illustrious* to await the results of their efforts. Photo-reconnaissance revealed that the raid had

been a huge success. Three Italian battleships had been put out of action, a cruiser and several destroyers had been damaged, and the bombing damaged some of the shore facilities. The attack gave the first indications of what could be achieved by aggressive use of carrier-based aircraft against an enemy fleet.

The attack on Taranto also marked the beginnings of a change in fortunes for the Fleet Air Arm. The Admiralty's request for a navalized version of the Hurricane had been met by the end of 1940; the first aircraft had been released for service, enabling 880 Squadron to become operational in January 1941. Although the Sea Hurricane was beginning to become outmoded in comparison with the latest German aircraft, it was still good enough – especially in the hands of an experienced pilot – to achieve more than acceptable results. This was extremely welcome, since Taranto had encouraged the Germans to send help to Italy, and the Luftwaffe began to mount a series of bombing attacks against British shipping in the Mediterranean. On 10 January 1941, *Illustrious* was providing air cover to the fleet when a German reconnaissance aircraft

ABOVE: A Fairey Albacore aboard a British aircraft carrier. The Albacore was meant to be the replacement for the Swordfish, but was outlived by its predecessor. The Albacore had an enclosed cockpit for greater crew comfort and a slightly higher performance, but its biplane configuration meant that it became increasingly obsolescent.

was sighted. Admiral Lumley Lister, Rear Admiral Aircraft Carriers, and *Illustrious*'s captain, Captain Denis Boyd, had protested to Cunningham about the positioning of *Illustrious*, claiming that the ship ought to be standing further away from the coast-line, to reduce the danger of enemy air attacks. Cunningham understood their concerns, but rejected them – with unfortunate results. *Illustrious*'s Fulmars shot down one enemy reconnaissance aircraft, but this was not enough to prevent a report of *Illustrious*'s position from being sent. Two Italian air force SM79 torpedo bombers attacked and missed *Illustrious*, but they succeeded in drawing the defensive fighter patrols down to a lower altitude. When Luftwaffe Stukas appeared overhead to launch dive-bombing attacks, the Fulmars did not have sufficient rate of climb to intercept them. *Illustrious* somehow managed to survive being hit for some time, but the inevitable happened: a single 500kg (1103lb) bomb penetrated the flight deck, destroying or damaging every aircraft in the hangar and killing most of the men working there. Fires were started, and six more direct hits and three very near misses by the Stukas hindered the efforts of the

Damage Control parties. *Illustrious*'s steering was crippled, and the aft aircraft elevator and the ammunition hoists were utterly wrecked in the attacks.

The armoured deck, although penetrated, probably saved *Illustrious* from being sunk. Good damage control and careful sailing allowed the carrier to limp to Malta, where she was subjected to further bombing raids. On 23 January *Illustrious* slipped out of harbour, heading for Alexandria. She then sailed through the Suez Canal and headed for the US Navy yards at Norfolk, Virginia, where she was to be repaired (in fact, she was virtually rebuilt). This left only *Eagle* in the Mediterranean until March, when *Formidable*, another of the new armoured-deck carriers, relieved her. The ship's air group was soon to be involved in action. On 27 March, an RAF Sunderland flying boat reported sighting units of the Italian fleet to the southwest of Crete. *Formidable* left Alexandria that afternoon, accompanied by the battleships *Barham*, *Warspite* and *Valiant*. The carrier embarked 13 Fulmars, and a strike force made up of 10 Fairey Albacores (the aircraft that was supposed to replace the Swordfish in service) and four of the ubiquitous Swordfish.

BELOW: Fitted with a heavy armoured flight deck to protect against enemy bombing attacks, HMS *Illustrious* was the lead ship of the class that shared her name.

The role of carrier aircraft was vital, because Admiral Cunningham needed the aviators to slow down the Italian fleet so he could catch up with it and engage in battle.

The first torpedo attack was made by six Albacores at 1125 the following morning. They arrived just in time to distract the Italians, as the battleship *Vittorio Veneto* and her accompanying heavy cruisers were beginning to make life awkward for the British cruiser and destroyers that had made first contact with the enemy. Three Albacores dropped their torpedoes off the *Vittorio Veneto*'s starboard bow, and when the ship turned to 'comb' the torpedo tracks (ie to run between them), the remaining three aircraft came in from the port bow to release their weapons. All the torpedoes missed their target, but the attack had the effect of forcing the Italians to break off their pursuit of the British ships. This was a promising start, but it soon became clear that *Warspite* was having difficulty with her engines, which increased the need to slow the Italians down. Another torpedo strike was launched by

Formidable at 1220, just as the first strike returned. Landing the first wave of aircraft was made more interesting by the need to evade an attack by Italian SM 79s, which once again failed to score any hits with their torpedoes.

The second group of attacking aircraft sighted the enemy at 1510, just as an attack by RAF Blenheim light bombers arrived over the Italians. This meant that three Albacores were able to approach almost unnoticed. The first Albacore dropped its torpedo, and was shot down almost immediately afterwards. This meant the crew did not see their torpedo hit the *Vittorio Veneto*. The explosion ripped a hole in the side of the ship, flooding several compartments. Two Swordfish then attacked from the opposite side, while two Fulmars from the fighter escort machine-gunned the deck of the battleship to distract the gunners. Although the Swordfish scored no hits, the attack was a success. *Vittorio Veneto* began to slow down, and then came to a stop, apparently dead in the water. This could have been fatal, but after a few minutes, the

ABOVE: An early Supermarine Seafire, with non-folding wings, is carefully manoeuvred in a carrier's hangar. By 1941, the need for high-performance fighters in naval service was so urgent that the Navy was prepared to accept its first Seafires without wing-folding, even though this reduced the number that could be carried on a carrier, and increased difficulties in handling.

USS *Wasp*

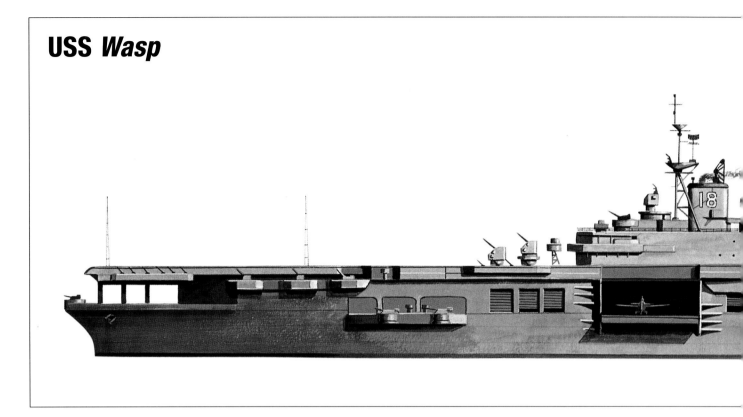

battleship set off again, before any British surface units managed to close in.

At dusk, *Formidable* launched an attack with six Albacores and two Swordfish; their crews were ordered to land at bases ashore afterwards. The strike took place in near-darkness, and it was virtually impossible to ascertain what results had been achieved. In fact, the cruiser *Pola* had been hit, falling out of the Italian formation. When the Italian commander, Admiral Iachino, heard that *Pola* had fallen back, he instructed two cruisers, the *Zara* and *Fiume*, to go to her aid, accompanied by two destroyers. This was a fatal mistake, since this sent the four ships into range of the British fleet. In a surface action later than night, Cunningham's battleships sank both cruisers and the destroyers. The unfortunate *Pola* was sent to the bottom by torpedoes the following morning.

The victory at Matapan once again demonstrated the important role that carrier aviation had to play in naval operations. It is worth noting that air action was normally coordinated with the surface fleet, rather than being sent off independently (as at Taranto). This might have been different had either the Germans or Italians been in possession of their own carriers, with carrier against carrier strikes being conducted. As it was, the carriers gave the Royal Navy a considerable advantage and enhanced the overall flexibility of the fleet. Of course the Germans did not have a large surface fleet, which gave the war in the Atlantic and Mediterranean theatres com-

pletely different characteristics by comparison with the conflict that was to break out in the Pacific in 1941.

SINK THE BISMARCK

The demonstration that carrier aircraft could shape a situation to the advantage of the Royal Navy was to be repeated in May 1941, as the epic pursuit of the 'pocket battleship' *Bismarck* took place. The Admiralty had justifiable concerns about the threat posed by German surface raiders to convoys, and had paid careful attention to the whereabouts of *Bismarck* and the other German pocket battleships. The Germans planned to concentrate a significant naval force to attack allied convoys, but previous damage to the *Scharnhorst* meant that she would be unavailable. On 6 April, the *Gneisenau* was damaged by a torpedo attack by the RAF while in harbour, and this was followed by bomb damage in an air raid four days later. This substantially reduced the possibility of forming a powerful force to attack convoys, but Grand Admiral Erich Raeder, the head of the German navy, decided to go ahead with the two remaining ships, *Bismarck* and *Prinz Eugen*, even though the striking power of the force was far less than had been hoped for. *Bismarck* and *Prinz Eugen* left harbour on 18 May, but this news reached London after a Swedish destroyer spotted them. The Admiralty put together a force including the battleships *King George V* and *Repulse*, the battlecruiser *Hood* and

Displacement	35,438 tonnes (34,880 tons) (full load)	Speed	32.7 knots
Length	265.79m (872ft) (overall)	Armament	12 x 5-inch (127mm) and 32 x 40mm (1.6in) guns, plus 46 x 20mm (0.8in) cannon
Beam	28.35m (93ft)		
Draught	7.01m (23ft)	Complement	2167
Propulsion	Steam turbines; 8 boilers, 4 shafts	Aircraft	91–100

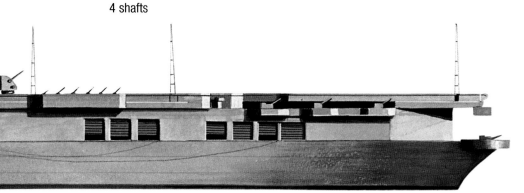

HMS *Victorious*. *Victorious* was carrying a number of dismantled Hurricanes for the Middle East, and her air group was reduced to nine Swordfish and six Fulmars. The chase began, and at 1922 on 23 May, the cruiser *Suffolk* sighted *Bismarck* and *Prinz Eugen*. After losing contact briefly, *Suffolk* located *Bismarck* once more, allowing *Hood* and the battleship *Prince of Wales* to position themselves to intercept.

The *Hood* opened fire against *Bismarck* at just before 0600 on the morning of 24 May. The battle was swift: within eight minutes of the first exchange of fire, *Bismarck*'s fifth salvo plunged into the *Hood*, and the ship was torn apart by an enormous explosion. As soon as the *Hood* began to sink, *Bismarck* and *Prinz Eugen* turned their fire upon the *Prince of Wales*, and forced her to break away. The loss of the *Hood* was an enormous blow to British pride, but a chance to avenge the loss presented itself. Although *Bismarck* sustained light damage resulting in the loss of some fuel, Admiral Lütjens, commanding the German operation, decided to continue with his mission. At 2200 that evening, a strike by Swordfish from *Victorious* scored a single torpedo hit amidships, without causing any damage. Later that evening, the British lost contact with the *Bismarck*, which was now heading for the Bay of Biscay, and thus a considerable way from the British forces. After over a day of concern that *Bismarck* had escaped, an RAF Catalina flying boat located the ship again.

Swordfish from the *Ark Royal* (part of Force H) were soon on the scene and continued to shadow the German ship. Force H steered to within 80.5km (50 miles) of the enemy, and launched a strike with its Swordfish. The attack did not go well. Unknown to the pilots, HMS *Sheffield* was in the same area as the *Bismarck*, and they attacked her in error. Fortunately, the torpedoes on board the Swordfish were unreliable: five of the torpedoes went off prematurely, and *Sheffield* easily evaded the rest. The chastened aircrew returned to *Ark Royal*, where they rearmed, ready to make another attack. The new attack was launched at 1915, and just under two hours later, *Bismarck* was sighted and attacked. One torpedo hit the stern of the ship, and this was enough: *Bismarck*'s steering gear was crippled. This allowed the British battle fleet to close in, and on the morning of 27 May the battleships *Rodney* and *King George V* opened fire. The *Bismarck* was pounded into submission and, by 1000 hours, her guns had fallen silent. Fifteen minutes later the action was broken off, and the destroyer *Dorsetshire* closed in and sank *Bismarck* with torpedoes. Once again, although the surface ships had won the victory, the result could have been very different without the contribution of the carrier-based aircraft.

HUNTING THE U-BOATS

The sinking of the *Bismarck* can be said to have changed the nature of the Fleet Air

Arm's war. The reduced threat from surface raiders, coupled with the increase in sinkings by U-boats, saw the introduction of a very different breed of aircraft carrier: the escort carrier. In September 1941 the first of these, HMS *Audacity*, entered service. *Audacity* was converted from a captured German liner, and had possibly the most luxurious accommodation ever found on board a Royal Navy ship. Within two months, the value of the vessel had been demonstrated. After defending convoy OG76 by shooting down an Fw 200 Condor maritime reconnaissance aircraft in November, *Audacity* joined convoy HG76 at the start of the following month for what was to be a short but intense battle. *Audacity* was alongside the escort group commanded by Captain F.J. Walker, and was almost immediately involved in action. On 17 December, three days after sailing, one of *Audacity*'s Martlets sighted a U-boat on the surface. The pilot attacked, but was shot down. The U-boat had been fatally delayed by this encounter, and was overwhelmed and sunk by the escort group shortly afterward. This began a four-day battle, in which two Fw 200s were shot down, and three U-boats sunk. But there was an unfortunate end: on 21 December, after a misunderstanding in which *Audacity* was illuminated by a flare fired from a destroyer, a U-boat took advantage and crept in to sink the carrier. Despite this disaster, the value of the escort carrier was proved. Although unable to fend off U-boats by itself, the carrier's air group could compel German submarines to

submerge, which dramatically reduced their performance, and made it much more difficult for them to shadow convoys or call other submarines in to join them. Also, the small fighter complement on board the escort carrier could fend off enemy aircraft, thus providing convoys with the sort of cover that they had generally lacked up to that time.

The first escort carrier designed as such, HMS *Archer*, was commissioned on 17 November 1941 and began her career well, her aircraft sinking *U572* when it attempted to attack convoy HX239. From December 1941, the escort carrier building programme began in earnest: 10 Attacker-class carriers based on merchant hulls (and thus quick to build) followed. The 20-strong Ruler class began to arrive in service from April 1942. Although not as plushly furnished as *Audacity*, the ships were fitted out to US Navy standards, which meant that they were more comfortable than British-built vessels: and rather more popular, too.

The introduction of the escort carriers had an almost immediate effect on the safety of convoys, particularly those to Russia. Thirty-two ships were lost to German air attacks in 1942, but the Luftwaffe scored no more successes until 1945. The first success came with convoy PQ18, on 9 September 1942. HMS *Avenger*'s Sea Hurricanes shot down five enemy aircraft, probably destroyed three more and damaged over a dozen others. Another example of successful carrier escort can be drawn from March 1944, when HMS *Chaser* accompanied con-

HMS *Courageous*

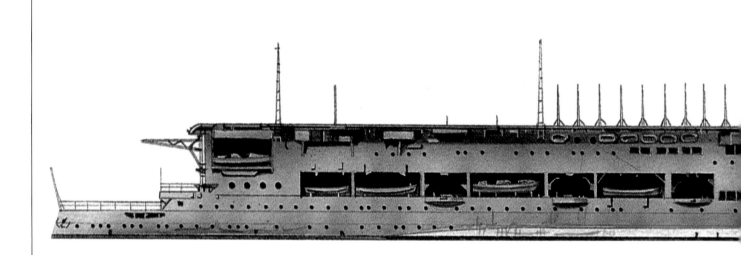

boats – and two more submarines were damaged and forced to break off their attacks. In May 1944, *Fencer* and *Activity* escorted RA59, and sank three U-boats in two days. This work is generally forgotten in studies of British carrier air power, but should not be forgotten: by 1944, the escort carriers were the mainstay of operations. But they were not only used to hunt U-boats and escort convoys – they occasionally hunted larger game. The classic example was in 1944, with the attempt to sink the last serious naval threat presented by the German navy, the *Tirpitz*.

'TUNGSTEN', 'MASCOT' AND 'GOODWOOD'

After *Bismarck* was sunk, the *Tirpitz* became a prime concern of the Admiralty, who were worried that *Tirpitz* might succeed where *Bismarck* failed, wreaking havoc upon convoys. An attack by aircraft from HMS *Victorious* in March 1942 had failed to inflict any damage. This was the only occasion on which the Fleet Air Arm had the opportunity to attack the *Tirpitz* while she was at sea. *Tirpitz* made a further sortie in July 1942, intending to attack convoy PQ17 (which was savagely mauled by air and submarine attacks), but returned to port in Norway when it became clear that *Victorious* was with the Home Fleet, posing a major threat to the battleship. An attack against *Tirpitz* at her moorings at Altenfjord was planned for March 1943, but was called off when the carrier HMS *Dasher* exploded when petrol fumes were ignited.

Twelve months later, another strike was planned, this time using new aircraft. The 9th and 52nd Torpedo Bomber Reconnaissance (TBR) Wings had been

RIGHT: A Supermarine Seafire IIC flies over HMS *Indomitable*. The Seafire was as formidable a fighter in the air as its land-based cousin, the Spitfire, but it proved difficult to land safely on board carriers due to its narrow and somewhat delicate undercarriage.

British Escort Carriers

The threat posed to convoys led to an urgent need for aircraft to accompany the merchant ships that were Britain's lifeline. The solution came in the form of small escort carriers, which embarked a few fighters and anti-submarine aircraft.

HMS *Audacity*

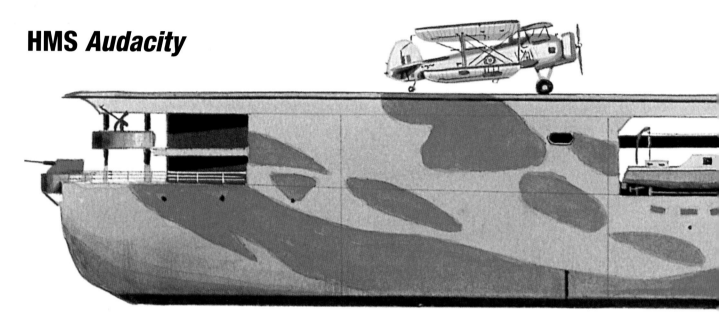

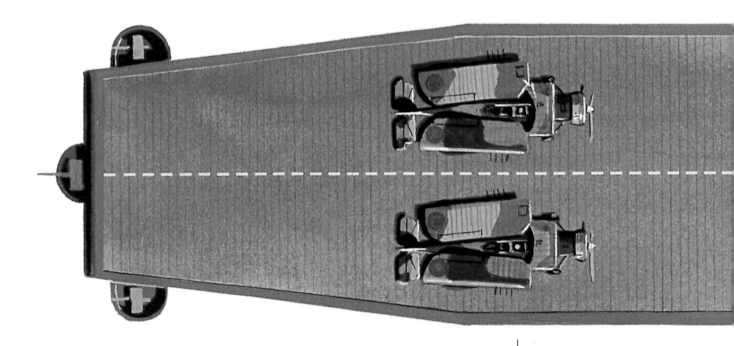

Escort carriers carried Swordfish for anti-submarine work, and Martlets in the fighter role. On patrol, *Audacity* did not carry Swordfish to maximize the number of fighters.

SPECIFICATIONS

HMS *Audacity*

Displacement	10,395 tonnes (10,231 tons) full load	**Propulsion**	one 8-cylinder MAN diesel, driving one shaft
Length	142.2m (467ft 3in) overall	**Speed**	15 knots
Beam	17.07m (56ft)	**Armament**	1 x 4-inch (102mm), 4 x 2-pounder and 4 x 20mm (0.8in) guns
Draught	6.58m (21ft 7in)	**Complement**	480
		Aircraft	6

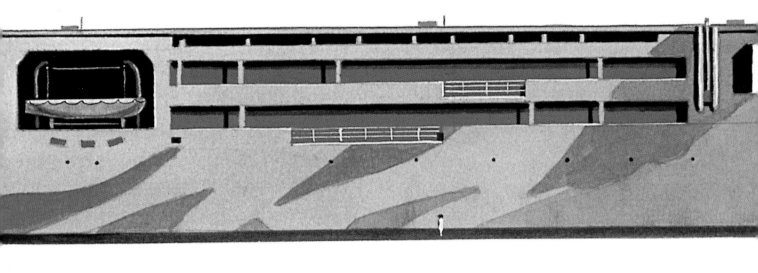

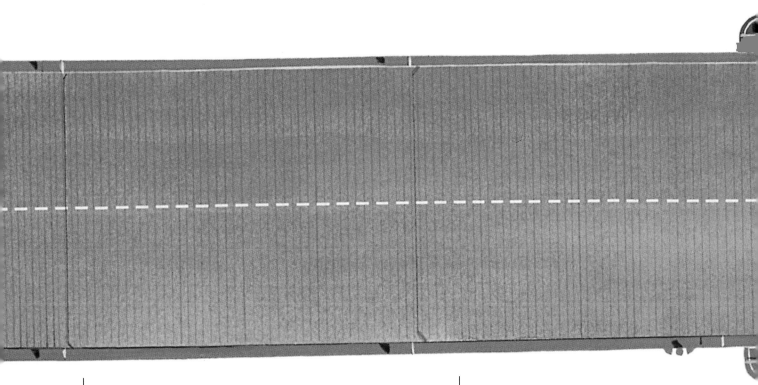

As well as the arrester wires, the safety barrier on the rudimentary flight deck prevented collisions with parked aircraft, and stopped damaged aircraft from leaving the deck after landing.

As an austere conversion, *Audacity* was fitted with a flush deck, with no island. She did not have a hangar, or any need for a lift, so her aircraft remained on deck.

voy RA57. On 4 March, a Swordfish from the carrier attacked *U472* with rocket projectiles. Although this did not sink the submarine, the damage inflicted prevented her from submerging, and HMS *Onslaught* duly dispatched the U-boat with gunfire. On the following day, another rocket attack was conducted, this time against *U336*, which was sunk. Less than 24 hours elapsed

before *U973* was destroyed with rocket projectiles, and the crew of the Swordfish followed up this success by damaging another submarine at dusk.

The next two convoys were accompanied by HMS *Activity* and HMS *Tracker*. The aircraft from these two ships were responsible for the destruction of at least six German aircraft and the sinking of two U-

ABOVE: HMS *Victorious* is seen here in the Mediterranean during World War II with a mix of Hawker Sea Hurricanes and Fairey Fulmars on deck. The large-calibre gun armament is also notable.

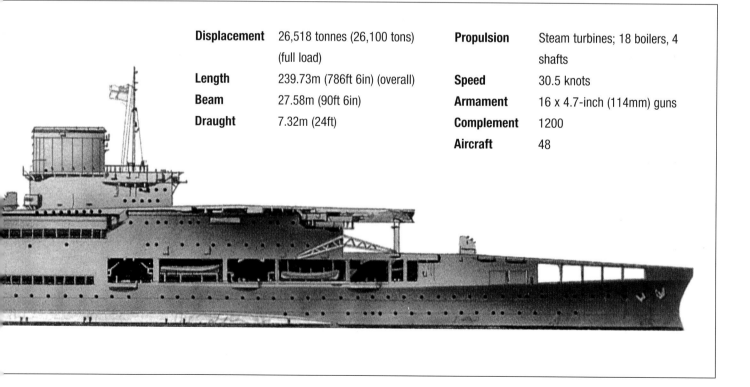

Displacement	26,518 tonnes (26,100 tons) (full load)	**Propulsion**	Steam turbines; 18 boilers, 4 shafts
Length	239.73m (786ft 6in) (overall)	**Speed**	30.5 knots
Beam	27.58m (90ft 6in)	**Armament**	16 x 4.7-inch (114mm) guns
Draught	7.32m (24ft)	**Complement**	1200
		Aircraft	48

LEFT: Three Grumman
Avengers from 846
Squadron Fleet Air Arm are
seen over the Atlantic
during 1943. The Avenger
was a considerable
improvement on the
legendary Swordfish, and
was also used extensively
by the British Pacific Fleet
in the war against Japan.

equipped with the ungainly Fairey
Barracuda. After a number of practice
attacks against dummy targets in Scotland,
the wings embarked aboard their carriers.
HMS *Furious*, drawing to the end of her
illustrious career, embarked 830 and 831
Squadrons, each with nine aircraft, while 24
more Barracudas were divided between
827 and 829 Squadrons aboard HMS
Victorious. *Tirpitz* had been damaged in a
daring midget submarine attack six months
previously when at anchor at Kaafjord, but
had been repaired and moved to Altenfjord

by April 1944. *Furious* and *Victorious* positioned themselves around 193km (120
miles) away from the fjord on the morning
of 3 April. They were accompanied by the
escort carriers *Emperor, Fencer, Pursuer*
and *Searcher*. The first three carried two
fighter squadrons, equipped with a mixture
of Grumman Hellcats, Wildcats (the name
'Martlet' having being dropped) and Vought
Corsairs. The Hellcat and Corsair were
extremely robust and well armed, with the
ability to carry a respectable bomb load in
addition to their six 12.7mm (0.5-inch)

machine guns. *Searcher* carried a mixed squadron of Swordfish and Wildcats to defend the carrier group. At about 0425 hours on 3 April, operation 'Tungsten' began. Forty fighters accompanied the Barracudas. The Wildcats and Hellcats dived in to strafe *Tirpitz*, while the Corsairs provided top cover in case nearby German fighter units should seek to interfere. All the Barracudas from the 9th TBR attacked, making six direct hits on the target. They were followed an hour later by the 52nd TBR Wing, but the element of surprise had been lost: the Germans ignited smoke pots and the target was obscured. Nevertheless, the attack claimed eight more hits. A follow-up attack was called off, since the aircrew were exhausted after the mission. Further attacks were intended, but the next three were all called off because of bad weather.

The next attack therefore had to wait until 17 July, under the codename 'Mascot'. 827 and 830 Squadrons were involved again, this time flying from HMS *Formidable*, while 820 and 826 Squadrons were assigned to HMS *Indefatigable*. Forty-four Barracudas and 48 fighters attacked, but they were spotted by a German obser-

vation post, and a smokescreen was laid over the fjord, making bombing nearly impossible. One near miss was recorded, but that was all. Further strikes were launched in August, under the codename 'Goodwood'. *Furious*, *Indefatigable* and *Formidable* all took part, carrying Barracudas and fighter escort made up of Corsairs, Hellcats, Seafires and the new Fairey Firefly two-seater fighters. The escort carriers *Nabob* and *Trumpeter* carried a mix of Grumman Avengers and Wildcats to defend the carriers. 'Goodwood I' was launched on 22 August, but failed as a result of bad weather; a strike later that evening by Hellcats ('Goodwood II') had similarly bad luck. *Nabob* was torpedoed that evening, and had to limp back to port.

Two days later, 'Goodwood III' took place. Thirty-three Barracudas, each carrying a 726kg (1600lb) bomb and an escort of Corsairs and Hellcats (some of which carried 227kg (500lb) bombs). Despite the smokescreen, a single bomb from one of the Barracudas penetrated the *Tirpitz*'s deck – but failed to detonate. A bomb from the fighter escort also struck home, but did little damage. 'Goodwood IV' on 29 August was again frustrated by bad weather, at

BELOW: Aircrew receive a briefing before the attack against the German battleship *Tirpitz* on 3 April 1944. *Tirpitz* was located in a Norwegian fjord, hence the need for the relief model. The Fleet Air Arm launched several attacks against the ship, scoring a number of hits. Although the ship was damaged, *Tirpitz* was finally sunk by Lancaster bombers from the RAF's 9 and 617 Squadrons.

which point the strikes were called off. Although the attacks were unsuccessful, they clearly demonstrated the ability of the Fleet Air Arm to conduct large-scale attacks. *Tirpitz* did not survive for much longer. On 12 November 1944 Lancaster bombers from 9 and 617 Squadrons RAF dropped 28 'Tallboy' penetration bombs, each weighing 5442kg (12,000lb), against the ship. Two of them hit, and the ship capsized.

With the *Tirpitz* gone, the Fleet Air Arm turned its attention to predominantly escort duties, and to preparations for sending a presence to the Pacific in support of the final assault by the allies against Japan.

THE CARRIER IN EUROPEAN WATERS

The nature of the war in the Atlantic and the Mediterranean militated against any of the great carrier engagements that marked the Pacific war from beginning to end. This was because of the lack of carriers on the German and Italian side, and the fact that the British fleet was not subjected to a stunning blow like Pearl Harbor. As the Royal Navy's battleships were not wiped out at a stroke, this meant that a more traditional approach was possible, with aircraft in support of surface units. Nonetheless, aircraft carriers were of vital importance: they contributed to victories at Taranto, Matapan and against the *Bismarck*; in the first instance, they acted alone. But perhaps their main achievement was in the Battle of the Atlantic, where the smaller, less well known escort carriers accompanied the vital convoys to and from Britain, harrying German submarines and keeping them from attacking merchant shipping. In addition, carriers supported amphibious operations, most notably 'Torch' and 'Husky' in 1942 and 1943 respectively, providing air cover for the invasion of North Africa and Sicily. Although the role of the carriers usually gets less consideration than the part they played in the Pacific war, it must be said that they made a significant contribution to the attainment of victory in Europe, even if they were never around in the sort of numbers that became the norm in the war against Japan.

ABOVE: An aerial view of USS *Bogue*, one of the most successful escort carriers of World War II. Built to provide air power for convoys, aircraft from *Bogue* enjoyed particular success during the Battle of the Atlantic, when she and her support group sank thirteen U-boats. During the last months of the war, *Bogue* was transferred to the Pacific fleet for use as an aircraft ferry.

CHAPTER THREE

FROM PEARL HARBOR TO THE CORAL SEA

The importance of the Pacific to both Japan and the United States meant that a large Pacific fleet was vital. The value of aircraft carriers was recognized by both countries, who had a number of such vessels in service by 1941.

THROUGHOUT THE 1930s, Japan had become a progressively more militaristic society, and the army became the dominant force in politics. Militarism and nationalism were closely related, and this aggressive political background encouraged Japan to embark upon a number of adventures in China, with the aim of gaining territory in Manchuria. It became quite clear to the Japanese leadership that hostility to their actions, particularly from America, which enjoyed a close trading relationship with China, would be problematic. The Japanese government ignored protests from other countries, most notably by leaving the League of Nations. In an attempt to stop Japan, the Western nations placed an embargo on her oil supplies.

There was a solution – the creation of a Japanese empire incorporating

LEFT: A rescue boat approaches the devastated hulks of the USS *West Virginia* and USS *Tennessee* on 7 December 1941. Despite the overwhelming success of the air attack, the Japanese were to suffer heavily for not wholly removing the Americans' ability to strike back.

virtually all of Southeast Asia would give Japan access to immense resources. But this would almost certainly force the United States into war, which could be disastrous, since a war lasting long enough for the Americans to be able to mobilize their industrial capacity to the full would ensure Japanese defeat. The US Navy would present the major threat to Japanese ambitions, but reports from naval officers in Europe had made much of the success of the raid against Taranto by the Fleet Air Arm. It would be unfair to say that Admiral Yamamoto, the Commander-in-Chief of the Japanese fleet, simply copied the idea of Taranto. Rather it confirmed his views, leading him to propose a daring attempt to knock the United States out of the war by sinking the American Pacific fleet in its home port – Pearl Harbor.

A DAY OF INFAMY

While Japanese diplomats embarked on a round of negotiations with the US Government, the aircrew of the Imperial Japanese Navy (IJN) began to practise for the attack. The geography of Pearl Harbor was well known, which meant the Japanese could be reasonably certain of the characteristics of the target. They would use a mix of dive-bombers and torpedo planes to crip-

ple the US fleet while it was at anchor. A lack of suitable armour-piercing bombs was overcome by attaching fins to 356mm (14-inch) naval shells, producing 800kg (1764lb) bombs. Aerial torpedoes were reckoned to be of relatively low lethality by themselves against large targets, so a considerable number would be dropped to guarantee enough hits to sink or cripple enemy targets. By the end of November 1941, all was ready. On the morning of 26 November six Japanese carriers, two battleships and the other warships belonging to Admiral Nagumo's Fast Carrier Strike force left their staging post off the Kurile Islands, north of Japan, and began a journey of 4827km (3000 miles). The carriers carried over 430 aircraft between them, mainly Aichi D3A dive-bombers and Nakajima B5N torpedo planes. Fighter capability was provided by the Mitsubishi A6M (otherwise known as the 'Zero' from its other designation of 'Navy Type 0'). This was meant to swamp American defences.

The force kept to a northern route, concealing itself in thick fog and poor weather to reduce the risk of detection, while submarines were sent ahead to ensure that the force would not inadvertently run into any soon-to-be enemy units. On 1 December, Nagumo received authorization to attack, and two days later he completed the final refu-

BELOW: An aerial photograph of Pearl Harbor, taken on 30 October 1941. The layout of the naval facilities can be seen quite clearly, while ships steam out to sea at the lower right corner. The scene on 7 December 1941 was even more peaceful, until the Japanese began their devastating assault.

LEFT: A flight of Japanese aircraft, headed by a Mitsubishi Zero, warm up in preparation for launch early on the morning of 7 December 1941. The Zero fighters played an important part in the attack, even though they did not carry bombs or torpedoes. They provided air cover to the strike force, although the sheer surprise and ferocity of the attack meant that very few American aircraft managed to get off the ground.

elling of his ships. The force increased speed to 25 knots and moved in. The planning process had been thorough, and the attack was planned for the morning of Sunday 7 December, when readiness was likely to be lower than on other days of the week.

The force began to launch its aircraft 442km (275 miles) north of Hawaii. The first to leave were floatplanes from the cruisers accompanying the force, to provide reconnaissance information. The first strike aircraft left the deck at 0600, and within 15 minutes over 180 aircraft were flown off. The Japanese aircraft did not go undetected. Two mobile radar operators at Opana had shown a little dedication, and had continued to practise with their set beyond 0700, when they had been told that they could pack up. They noted the appearance of a number of mysterious 'blips' on their radar screens, and plotted the approach: it was all good practice, after all. They telephoned this information to their headquarters, just in case it was important, only to be told that a flight of Army Air Corps B-17 Flying Fortresses was expected shortly, and this would explain what they had seen. The plotters dutifully continued to shut down their radar set.

The leader of the strike group, Commander Mitsuo Fuchida, led his aircraft down the west coast of Oahu, attracting little attention from people on the ground. About 10 minutes before 0800, Fuchida could make out 'battleship row' on the eastern side of Ford Island, where seven capital ships sat at anchor in the early morning sunshine. The ships' crews, of course, were not expecting attack. Even if they had been fully appraised of the tension between the United States and Japan, they would not have been too concerned, since negotiations were, apparently, under way. Surprise was complete, and moments before the ceremony to hoist the colours began on the American ships, Fuchida gave the order to attack. The rigorous practice undertaken meant that each Japanese pilot knew what he had to do. The dive-bombers spilt into sections and headed for a variety of shore targets, particularly airfields, while those aircraft assigned to high-level bombing adjusted as they ran in towards their targets. Beneath them, the torpedo aircraft began the long, shallow dive towards their torpedo launching positions.

The first clear indication that Pearl Harbor was under attack came when bombs began falling among the aircraft lined up on the various airfields. Almost simultaneously, the torpedo bombers reached the correct height to drop their torpedoes, and after making sure they were positioned correctly, they did so – the torpedo tracks being clearly visible to the amazed American sailors. Five battleships – *West Virginia*, *Arizona*, *Nevada*, *Oklahoma* and *California* – began taking torpedo hits. High above the melee, Fuchida was still half-expecting some response by American aircraft, but the dive-bombers had done their work well. Nearly 200 aircraft were destroyed and over 150 damaged on six airfields, preventing all but a handful from taking off.

Fuchida's formation began bombing, and the combined effect of the torpedoes and

Shokaku

Displacement	32, 619 tonnes (32,105 tons)	Speed	34.2 knots
	(full load)	Armament	8 x twin 5-inch (127mm) guns
Length	257.5m (844ft 10in) (overall)		and 12 x triple 1-inch (25mm)
Beam	26m (85ft 4in)		cannon
Draught	8.9m (29ft 2in)	Complement	1660
Propulsion	4-shaft steam turbines	Aircraft	72

RIGHT: The Yokosuka D4Y1 'Judy' was a large, powerful dive-bomber, the first of which entered Japanese service in 1942. Some of the first aircraft were used at the Battle of Midway, but it was not until the Battle of the Philippine Sea in 1944 that the D4Y1 saw its first major action; 2033 were built, but this was far from the number required to challenge American supremacy.

armour-piercing bombs was appalling. *Arizona* was hit by a torpedo, and then a bomb penetrated the decks, exploded in the forward magazine, and shattered the ship. Just astern, *West Virginia* took six torpedo hits and began to sink. *Tennessee* was shielded from torpedo damage, but was damaged by a bomb. *Maryland* and *California* were hit severely: *California* took two torpedoes, and began to flood. As the first strike wave departed at about 0825, *West Virginia* was sinking and on fire. *Arizona* had settled on the bottom, taking over a thousand men with her. *Oklahoma* capsized and settled on the bottom, while *Tennessee* was aflame, with a turret pierced by a bomb. The old target battleship *Utah* had sunk, leaving just her upturned keel visible, while the light cruiser *Raleigh* was so deep in the water as a result of flooding and counter-flooding that she appeared to be kept upright by just her mooring ropes.

USS *Nevada* managed to get under way,

but as she did so, the second wave of Japanese aircraft arrived. The defences were, of course, alerted, and put up extremely stiff resistance against this new wave of attackers. Nonetheless, the Japanese hit *California* twice more, sinking her to the level of her upper turrets, while *Nevada* was forced to beach. Two destroyers in the dry dock with *Pennsylvania* were wrecked, while the battleship herself took more damage. At 1000 hours, it was all over. For the loss of just 29 aircraft, the Japanese aircraft carriers had managed to cripple the main ships of the United States' Pacific Fleet – with two notable exceptions.

When the Japanese attacked, the two aircraft carriers *Lexington* and *Enterprise* were not in harbour. In fact, *Enterprise* returned to Pearl Harbor just after the attacks had finished. Had Nagumo followed advice from his airmen and launched a second attack, it is quite possible that *Enterprise* would have shared the fate of

attack had merely aroused a sleeping giant from his slumbers: he was correct.

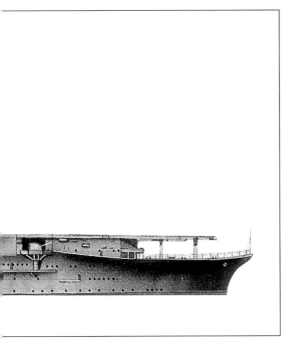

A New Kind of War

The loss of the battleships at Pearl Harbor forced the US Navy to embrace carrier operations in a way that even the most ardent proponent of the aircraft carrier might have been surprised at. Although the Japanese attack did not destroy all the battleships – in fact, most were rebuilt – even the least heavily damaged would take around six months to repair. This meant that if the United States were to undertake any offensive naval action, it would have to do so with its carriers. As a result, the notion of the fast carrier task force was created. The large size of American carriers was an advantage, since they were able to embark a large and potent force of dive-bombers and torpedo aircraft that could serve as highly effective substitutes for the big guns of the battleships. This change appears easy on paper, but was in fact rather more difficult. While the standard US Navy scout and dive-bomber, the Douglas SBD Dauntless, was a superb aircraft, the TBD Devastator torpedo-bomber from the same firm was virtually obsolete. Another scout/dive-bomber, the Vought SB2U Vindicator, was similarly outdated. The

the battleships. Fortuitously, the attacks had not damaged the huge oil tank farm: had they done so, the American fleet would have been forced to retire to bases on the west coast of the United States, well out of range of the area of operations. When congratulated by some of his subordinates, Yamamoto had expressed his fears that the

LEFT: Three days after the attack, an overhead photograph shows the devastation caused by the Japanese air assault on Pearl Harbor. The *Oklahoma* has turned turtle; the *West Virginia* has her decks awash, while the *Arizona* has been utterly destroyed.

Aichi D3A 'Val'

ABOVE: One of the two main attack aircraft to take part in the assault on Pearl Harbor in December 1941, the Aichi D3A 'Val' was the mainstay of the Japanese navy in the early months of World War II. By 1943 the type was obsolete, however, and many were expended in *kamikaze* attacks on Allied shipping.

position with regard to fighter aircraft was slightly better. The Grumman F4F Wildcat was a match for Japanese fighters if handled properly, but the Brewster F2B Buffalo was barely able to survive, no matter how good the pilot, and was soon withdrawn from use. Replacements for these aircraft types were already well advanced, but would not enter service for some time.

The first major action by an American carrier was in fact an audacious raid against Japan itself. By mid-April 1942, the Japanese had enjoyed a wave of unbroken success. They had conquered huge amounts of territory, including Malaya, Singapore, the Philippines and the Dutch East Indies. Corregidor Island was under threat of invasion, and the British were on the brink of being pushed out of Burma. In addition to this indignity, the Royal Navy had lost *Prince of Wales* and *Repulse* to air attack in December 1941, while the aircraft carrier *Hermes* had been sunk on 8 April, sailing without aircraft embarked. The Japanese soldier was regarded with awe, and there were those who feared that Japan's advance was unstoppable. Unsurprisingly, this had serious connotations for morale amongst the Allied nations.

One of the solutions for raising the spirits of both the United States and Britain seemed to be an attack against Japan. For the British, this was out of the question, since the resources and equipment to do so were not available. For the United States, the picture was almost as bad, but there was a feasible way to raise morale, and to deliver a blow – albeit a small one – to the Japanese.

THE DOOLITTLE RAID

The plan was audacious, but simple in outline. The recently commissioned carrier

Hornet would embark a force of US Army Air Corps B-25 Mitchell bombers, convey them to within range of Japan, and then fly them off to attack Tokyo. The aircraft would then head for friendly territory in China. Although this sounded simple, it was not. The Mitchell was far heavier than any other aircraft that had been operated from a carrier before, and was not capable of using the catapult (strictly speaking an accelerator) on the *Hornet*. They would have to make a free take-off and hope that they managed to achieve sufficient speed to leave the deck. The commander of the attack force, Lieutenant-Colonel James Doolittle, was confident that this could be done. Intensive trials and practice showed he was correct, so on 2 April 1942, *Hornet* left port, carrying 16 Mitchells. Accompanied by the *Enterprise*, *Hornet* steamed to within 998km (620 miles) of Japan, and on the morning of 18 April, Doolittle led his aircrew onto the deck. They paused briefly for photographs, and then boarded their aircraft. The Mitchells were loaded to a gross weight of 14,059kg (31,000lb), and rumbled down the deck, watched by a variety of curious onlookers. Within a matter of minutes, the 16 aircraft had left the deck, and were heading for Japan.

The Mitchells reached Japan with little incident and bombed Tokyo, causing considerable consternation, but relatively little damage. Inflicting damage was hardly the point of the raid, since the morale aspect was more important. All the aircraft were lost (either to enemy action or forced landings), but most of the aircrews survived and returned to the United States; Doolittle went on to high command in the US Army Air Forces in Europe later in the war. As intended, the raid had a positive effect upon morale in America, while it compelled the Japanese to take the defence of their homeland far more seriously than they had done before. Within two weeks, American aircraft carriers had struck another blow against Japan in the Battle of the Coral Sea.

THE BATTLE OF THE CORAL SEA

Although the Doolittle raid was a rude shock to Tokyo, it did nothing to disguise the fact that Japan was in a commanding position by April 1942. The successes gained to that point left the Japanese military planners with a variety of options as to how to proceed. The first was the Army's suggestion to launch an offensive against Port Moresby, continuing through the Solomons, New Hebrides, New Caledonia, Fiji and Samoa in an attempt to isolate Australia, and effectively put her out of the war. The Navy advocated either attacking India and Ceylon, or striking directly against Australia. Finally, Admiral Yamamoto called for an operation against Midway and the Aleutian Islands, to precipitate what he

intended to be a decisive battle against what remained of the US fleet. In the end, a plan combining elements of several of the suggestions was adopted: Port Moresby would be attacked and occupied at the beginning of May, to be followed by operations against Midway and the Western Aleutians in early June.

A naval force under Vice-Admiral Inouye headed towards the Coral Sea at the end of April. Under his control, Inouye had three carriers, around 180 aircraft and six cruisers. These were split into three distinct groups – the Port Moresby invasion group, a covering group including the carrier *Shoho* and a striking force under Vice-Admiral Takagi, which contained Rear-Admiral Hara's carriers, the *Shokaku* and *Zuikahu*. Takagi's force was detailed to prevent any interference with operations by the Americans.

The Commander-in-Chief of the US Pacific Fleet, Admiral Chester W. Nimitz, knew the Japanese intended to attack Port Moresby because the Japanese naval code

BELOW: One of the B-25s on the Doolittle raid leaves the deck of the *Hornet* on 18 April 1942. The attack on Tokyo caused little damage, and all the aircraft were lost, either to enemy action or forced landings. These bare facts suggest that the mission was a failure: it was not. The Japanese were alarmed by the bomber attack, and, as intended, the American public were greatly encouraged.

RIGHT: B-25 Mitchell bombers lined up on the deck of USS *Hornet* in preparation for the famous 'Doolittle' raid against Tokyo on 18 April 1942. At a time when the Japanese were enjoying success after success, the raid was intended to show that America could strike back.

had been broken. Nimitz assigned every available ship to meet the enemy in the Coral Sea. A force containing *Yorktown* and *Lexington* was placed under the command of Rear-Admiral Frank Fletcher, and headed toward the Coral Sea area. Reports of Japanese landings at Tulagi in the Lower Solomons reached Fletcher on 3 May, and he took the *Yorktown* force north to launch an attack the next day. Dauntlesses and Devastators from the carrier took off at around 0630, and in a brief action sank an enemy destroyer, three minesweepers and a

number of smaller vessels for the loss of three aircraft. This action was followed by a lull as the Americans and Japanese positioned themselves, with neither side detecting the other. On the evening of 6 May, the Port Moresby invasion group was beginning to approach its objective, covered by the *Shoho* on its left flank. Further out to sea, Takagi's strike group was preparing itself to provide support for the invasion group as and when required. Early the next morning, Hara advised Takagi that an aerial reconnaissance should be conducted

Soryu

Displacement	20,117 tonnes (19,800 tons) (full load)	**Speed**	34.5 knots	
Length	227.5m (746ft 5in) (overall)	**Armament**	6 x twin 5-inch (127mm) guns and 12 x twin 1-inch (25mm) cannon	
Beam	21.3m (69ft 11in)			
Draught	7.6m (25ft)	**Complement**	1100	
Propulsion	4-shaft steam turbines	**Aircraft**	63	

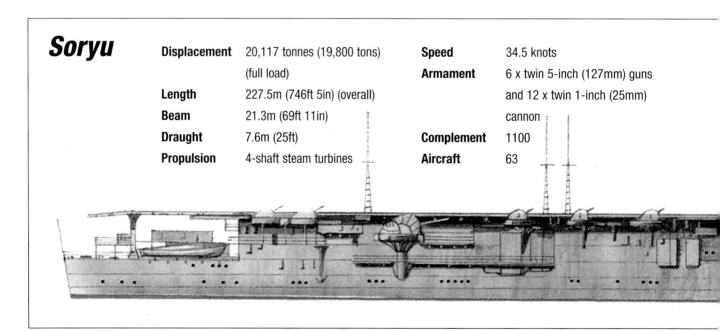

LEFT: The Grumman F4F Wildcat was the prime US naval fighter at the outbreak of war. Although outperformed by the Japanese Zero fighter, the Wildcat was a tough, well armed aircraft, and more than able to match the Japanese aircraft if it was flown correctly.

before the strike group moved to support the invasion group. At 0735, one of the reconnaissance aircraft reported sighting an aircraft carrier and a cruiser at the eastern edge of the search area. Hara had no reason to doubt the report, and launched a maximum effort strike against the two ships. In fact, the two vessels were the destroyer *Sims* and the oiler *Neosho*. The first Japanese aircraft attacked at 0900, followed by 15 high-level bombers about half an hour later. These failed to hit either ship; and at 1038, *Sims* skilfully manoeuvred to avoid nine bombs dropped simultaneously against her. By midday, though, her fate was sealed, as three dozen dive-bombers pounded *Sims* to destruction. Three bombs struck the destroyer, and sent her to the bottom stern first. Twenty more dive-bombers attacked *Neosho*, scoring seven hits. Incredibly, she did not sink, and drifted westwards for four days until a destroyer recovered the crew.

The attack against *Sims* and *Neosho* diverted the Japanese efforts, and they did not have the chance to interfere with Fletcher's attack against the *Shoho*. Fletcher had taken a considerable risk in ordering his support group to attack the Port Moresby invasion group – this meant that the ship-based anti-aircraft support was dramatically reduced, while the support group lost the air umbrella it had enjoyed. The Japanese, however, misread the situation. They concentrated their land-based air power against the support group, without success. While the Japanese air effort was failing to hit the carriers, aircraft from *Shoho* were attempting to locate the American carriers. By 0830, they had done so, and an attack was prepared. Other aircraft had spotted the support group, and this caused Inouye to

worry about the safety of the invasion group, which he ordered to turn away until his aircraft had dealt with the carrier threat, and the American support group.

Fletcher had launched reconnaissance aircraft of his own, and at 0815, one of them had reported two carriers and four cruisers about 362km (225 miles) northwest of the American carriers. Fletcher assumed that this was the striking force, rather than the covering group, and launched a strike of 93 aircraft against it at 0925. But shortly after the last aircraft had left the deck, at about 1030, the scout aircraft returned, and it became clear that the report of the carriers was erroneous: the aircrew had been given an incorrectly printed code pad. This meant 'carrier' should have read 'cruiser' when decoded. Fletcher was disappointed, but allowed the strike to continue, on the grounds that there might be profitable targets near the four ships reported.

The attack group from *Lexington*, well ahead of the aircraft from *Yorktown*, was nearing Misima Island when the commander of one of the Dauntless squadrons spotted an aircraft carrier some 40km (25 miles) to starboard. This was the *Shoho*, and it was easy to redirect the attack. The first attack by the Dauntlesses only managed to blow five aircraft off *Shoho*'s deck and into the water, but this was closely followed by the rest of the strike. Ten more Dauntlesses attacked at 1110, followed seven minutes later by the *Lexington*'s Devastators with their torpedoes. At 1125, *Yorktown*'s attack group went in, and under such a concentrated attack, the *Shoho* stood little chance. She took 13 bombs and seven torpedoes, and sank shortly after 1135.

THE LULL

Fletcher decided to call off further strikes after the *Shoho* was sunk, since he knew

Hiryu

from radio intercepts that the Japanese knew where he was. Bad weather would also present a serious obstacle to searches for remaining Japanese ships, and Fletcher steered a westerly course.

The Japanese were determined to find and sink the American carriers, and Hara sent out a strike from *Shokaku* and *Zuikaku* just after half-past four that afternoon. Thanks to the bad weather, the strike failed to locate the American ships, but ran into an American combat air patrol sent out to meet them. The American F4Fs shot down nine of the 27 aircraft in the Japanese strike group, which headed for home. About an hour later, some of the Japanese aircraft passed over the American carriers, which they mistook for their own: they were recognized, but managed to escape. At 1920, three more Japanese aircraft attempted to join *Yorktown*'s landing pattern, and one was shot down. By the time the surviving Japanese aircraft had landed, only six of the original strike force were left, 11 having ditched when attempting night landings.

BELOW: The A6M 'Zero' rightly remains the most famous of all Japanese warplanes of World War II, and was the first carrier-borne fighter to achieve a performance equal to that of its land-based contemporaries. A staggering 11,280 aircraft were built from 1940 onwards.

Mitsubishi A6M 'Zero'

341-S-51

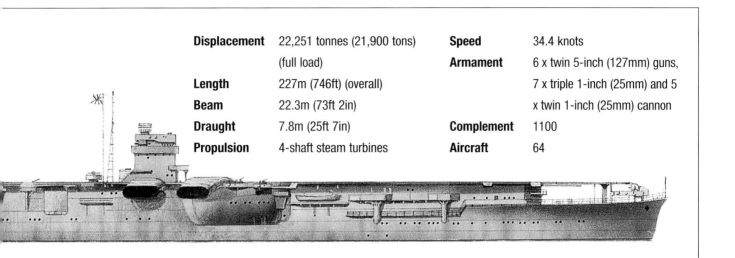

Displacement	22,251 tonnes (21,900 tons)	Speed	34.4 knots
	(full load)	Armament	6 x twin 5-inch (127mm) guns,
Length	227m (746ft) (overall)		7 x triple 1-inch (25mm) and 5
Beam	22.3m (73ft 2in)		x twin 1-inch (25mm) cannon
Draught	7.8m (25ft 7in)	Complement	1100
Propulsion	4-shaft steam turbines	Aircraft	64

THE JAPANESE RETALIATE

Reconnaissance by both sides next morning managed to locate the opposing carrier forces almost simultaneously. This marked the start of the first ever carrier against carrier battle. The first sighting of the Japanese carriers was made at 0815, followed by another at 0900. The Americans launched a strike between 0900 and 0925, *Yorktown*'s aircraft leaving the deck ten minutes before those from *Lexington*. The Dauntlesses spotted the Japanese carriers first, and circled in the cloud cover above the ships to await the arrival of the Devastators. While they were waiting, *Zuikaku* moved into a rain squall, which meant that only one of the two ships was attacked. The torpedoes dropped by the Devastators were too slow to be effective, and were outmanoeuvred, and only two bombs hit the *Shokaku*. But these did significant damage, since they set light to fuel, making it impossible for the *Shokaku* to launch aircraft. The dive-bombers from *Lexington* failed to find the carrier, leaving only the Devastators and four accompanying reconnaissance bombers to attack. The torpedoes again failed, but one bomb hit. The fires aboard *Shokaku* were soon under control, while the majority of her aircraft transferred to *Zuikaku*.

While the Americans were approaching the Japanese carriers, the Japanese had sent a

LEFT: A Nakajima B5N 'Kate' Torpedo bomber leaves the deck of the *Hiryu* on the morning of 7 December 1941. The 'Kate' entered service in 1937, and was a highly effective aircraft. As well as successes at Pearl Harbor, the type was responsible for the destruction of three American carriers during the course of the war.

strike against the Americans. Although it was picked up by radar, the Americans did not have enough aircraft available to intercept, and had to rely on anti-aircraft fire. Just after 1115, the Japanese attack began. *Yorktown* managed to avoid eight torpedoes launched against her, and then evaded a number of bombs. At 1127 a single bomb penetrated the ship, but did not impair flight operations.

The *Lexington* suffered an attack on both bows at 1118, and took a single torpedo hit on the port side forward two minutes later. Almost simultaneously, two small bombs from dive-bombers hit the ship. Twenty minutes later, the battle was over. It appeared that both sides had managed to inflict some damage on each other, but in fact, the Americans were to suffer a major blow. It seemed that *Lexington*, although listing, was only lightly damaged, and her air group landed with little fuss.

At 1240 hours, the damage control officer told the captain that the ship would soon be back on an even keel, jokingly adding that it would probably be best to take any further torpedo hits on the starboard side to even things up. Minutes later, a tremendous explosion caused by the ignition of fuel vapours rocked the ship from bow to stern. A series of further explosions then occurred, causing serious damage. At 1445, another huge explosion tore through the ship, and it became clear that the fires that had started could not be controlled, even with the destroyer *Morris* assisting, and that the only course of action was to abandon ship. At 1630, *Lexington* had come to a dead stop, and the evacuation began at 1710. The ship's dog was among the last of the crew to be rescued, and the captain followed him shortly afterwards. With the ship abandoned, the destroyer *Phelps* was called upon to despatch the crippled carrier, which she did with five torpedoes. The Battle of the Coral Sea was over.

THE BALANCE SHEET

The Japanese had lost one small carrier, and suffered significant damage to a large one. In terms of losses to shipping, the Americans had come off worst, since *Lexington*, *Neosho* and *Sims* outweighed the loss of the *Shoho*. On the other hand, the Japanese felt compelled to call off the invasion of Port Moresby, which meant that they failed in their strategic objective. The damage to *Shokaku* kept her in dock for some time, removing her from the war – and the air group on the *Zuikaku* had been badly mauled, costing a number of experienced aircrew. The need to re-form the air group meant that *Zuikaku* was temporarily removed from the fray also.

There were other significant outcomes from the battle. The Japanese pilots reported that they had sunk both *Lexington* and *Yorktown*, and this was accepted as fact. It meant that Japanese plans for further action were based on the erroneous assumption that the Americans had one carrier less than they actually did. The Americans learned a number of important lessons. They appreciated that the carriers needed more fighters, and duly increased the number embarked with the air groups. Furthermore, improvements were made in the coordination of attacks, since Coral Sea demonstrated that well coordinated strikes stood a good chance of swamping enemy defences, greatly hindering the ability of the ships under attack to escape damage. Perhaps the most significant aspect of the Battle of the Coral Sea was that it marked a first in naval warfare. For the first time in history, no ship on either side had made visual contact with an enemy ship. It was a portent of things to come.

Although the Japanese felt that they had achieved some success in sinking, they believed, two American carriers, Admiral Yamamoto was disappointed that Takagi had chosen to withdraw and postpone the

BELOW: The *Hiryu* is seen here on trials in April 1939. The *Hiryu* was an improved version of the design of the *Soryu*, but was unusual in having an island on the port side, instead of starboard. This was meant to allow operations side-by-side with a carrier with a conventional island, but was not a success: *Hiryu* had far more deck accidents. The *Hiryu* took part in the attack on Pearl Harbor, but the Americans gained revenge at Midway, devastating *Hiryu* in a dive-bombing attack.

invasion of Port Moresby. He ordered Takagi to hunt down the remaining American ships, but by the time the order got through and was acted upon, the Americans were long gone. But Yamamoto was not downhearted, because his plan to engage the American fleet in a decisive battle was accepted. The plan was, once again, simple. The Japanese would launch an attack against Midway Island. Midway was the westernmost outpost of the Hawaiian chain of islands, and the Americans could not ignore a threat there. If the Japanese seized the island, it would give them a base within striking distance of Hawaii itself – Yamamoto reasoned the Americans would simply have to fight. He planned to use a carrier striking force to invade Midway, and when the Americans intervened, their remaining ships would be overwhelmed and sunk. Yamamoto had every reason to be confident: the Americans had lost two carriers at Coral Sea, leaving just two. Yamamoto on the other hand would commit almost the entire strength of the Japanese navy against them. If battles were won simply by the size of forces deployed,

the Americans would have lost. Yamamoto planned to send eight carriers, 11 battleships, 23 cruisers, 65 destroyers and 20 submarines against the Americans. The Americans could muster just three carriers (one more than Yamamoto expected), eight cruisers and 16 destroyers. *Yorktown* was so badly damaged that she arrived back at Pearl Harbor needing an estimated three weeks' worth of repairs. By an almost superhuman effort, 1300 dockyard workers turned the ship around in just three days.

But battles are not decided by numbers alone. The Japanese were quite unaware that the Americans had broken their naval code, and knew their plans. Around 500 BC, the Chinese military philosopher Sun Tzu had remarked upon the need for good, accurate intelligence. Without it, he pointed out, one was at a disadvantage; conversely, knowing what the enemy was up to meant that numerical inferiority could be offset. These basic tenets were just as valid 2400 years later. Midway would not go quite as the Japanese planned it. It would be the turning point of the war in the Pacific.

ABOVE: USS *Yorktown* sits in dry dock early in May 1942 after sustaining severe damage to her flight deck from a Japanese bomb. *Yorktown* was hit on 8 May, during the Battle of the Coral Sea, in which her aircraft sank the Japanese carrier *Shoho*. Despite the severe damage to the deck, the dockyard workers managed to turn the ship around in just four days, allowing *Yorktown* to take part in the battle at Midway.

CHAPTER FOUR

VICTORY IN THE PACIFIC

Aggressive Japanese intentions toward Midway became clearer as the US Navy's Combat Intelligence Office read the Japanese naval code. Decryptions of the code showed that the Japanese were planning a large-scale operation against a target they called 'AF'.

THE HEAD OF THE CIO, Commander Joseph P. Rochefort, was convinced that the Japanese intended to attack Midway, proving this through a simple subterfuge. He asked Midway to send two messages, one encrypted, the other not, to say that their desalination plant was out of order. After some puzzlement at Midway – where the plant was very much in action – the message was sent. As planned, the Japanese intercepted the message, and in their transmissions made reference to the fact that 'AF' was having problems with its desalination plant. The advantage that this gave the Americans should not be underestimated. Admiral Nimitz was able to take pre-emptive action to thwart part of the Japanese plan. He sent a group of ships to the French Frigate Shoals to deny them to the Japanese as a refuelling stop for reconnaissance flying boats, while forces were moved into place before a cordon of Japanese submarines between Midway and

LEFT: A flight of US Navy TBF Avengers seen over the Pacific early in the aircraft's career. After a disastrous debut at the Battle of Midway, the Avenger became one of the most formidable attack aircraft of World War II. Replacing the outmoded Douglas Devastator, Avengers caused havoc amongst Japanese targets.

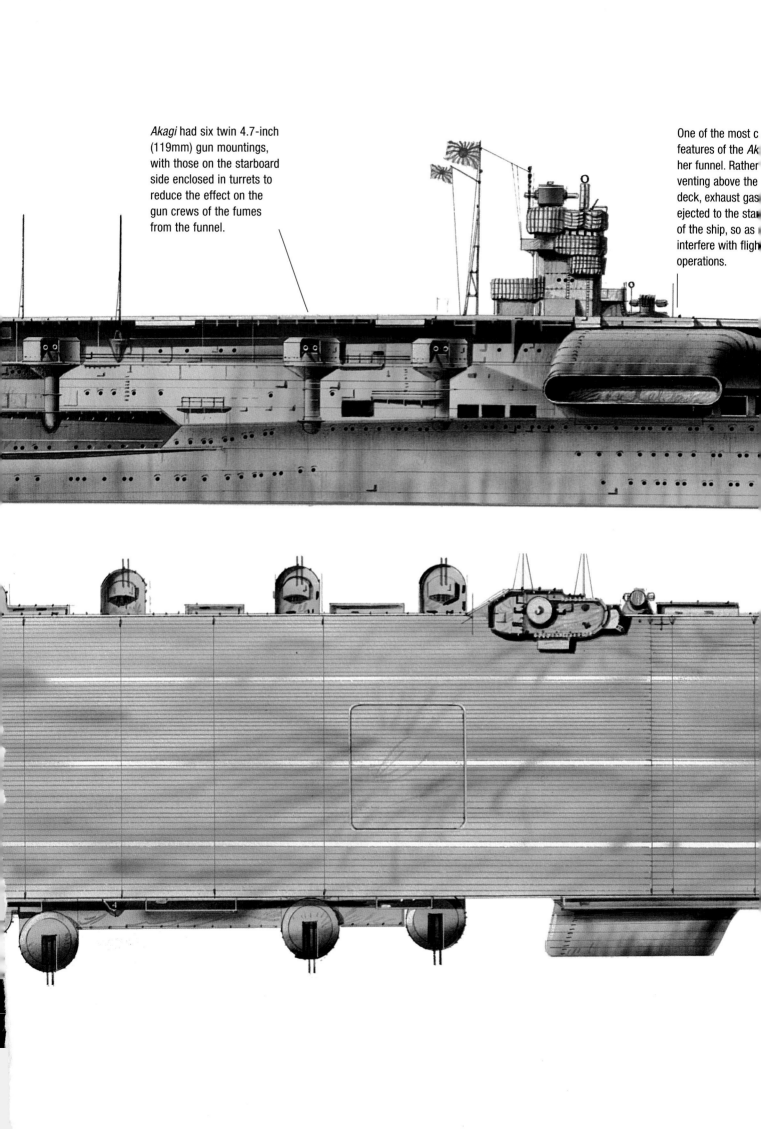

Akagi had six twin 4.7-inch (119mm) gun mountings, with those on the starboard side enclosed in turrets to reduce the effect on the gun crews of the fumes from the funnel.

One of the most c features of the *Ak* her funnel. Rather venting above the deck, exhaust gas ejected to the sta of the ship, so as interfere with fligh operations.

Akagi

Converted from a battlecruiser, the unusually configured *Akagi* led the Japanese carrier forces in the attack against Pearl Harbor on 7 December 1941. The US Navy gained some measure of revenge the following year, sinking *Akagi* at the Battle of Midway.

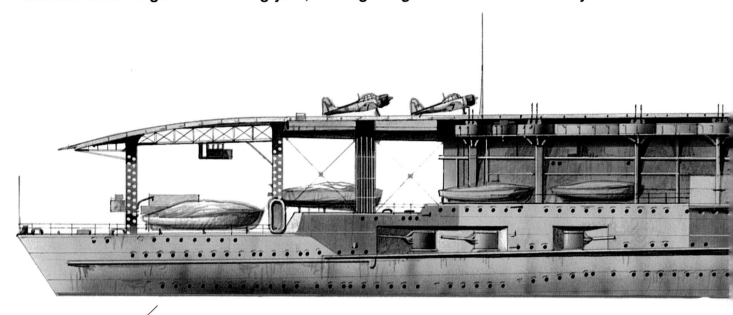

The space between the original deck of *Akagi* and the flight deck added when she was converted to a carrier provided ample space to locate some of the ship's boats.

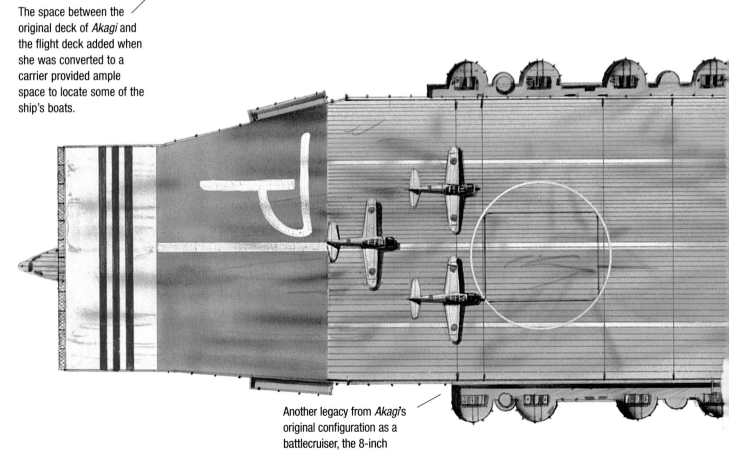

Another legacy from *Akagi's* original configuration as a battlecruiser, the 8-inch (203mm) guns were retained. Their position low down on the carrier's hull meant that they were of limited utility, even for defensive purposes.

Hawaii could be established. In addition, a large number of land-based aircraft were sent to Midway itself to support the fleet, which was moved into position to meet the Japanese. Finally, Nimitz had the huge advantage of knowing which elements of the enemy fleet would attack first.

THE TEST OF BATTLE

The Japanese launched their attack against the Aleutians on 3 June 1942. Knowing the plan in advance, the Americans ensured that no major forces were located at Dutch Harbor – while Japanese aircraft were able to inflict damage on the facilities, they did nothing to hamper American operations. This left the Navy in a strong position to engage the Japanese.

The American forces were divided between Task Force 16 under Rear-Admiral Raymond A. Spruance and Task Force 17 under Admiral Fletcher. Their opposition came in the form of Admiral Nagumo's Carrier Striking Force with four carriers – *Akagi*, *Kaga*, *Hiryu* and *Soryu*. Unaware that the Americans had foreknowledge of what was to come, confidence in the Carrier Striking Force was high: only Nagumo had any doubts, worrying that some of the replacement aircrew who had joined the

fleet were not of the same calibre as their more experienced predecessors.

Spruance and Fletcher joined up on 2 June, and Fletcher took overall command, even though TF16 and TF17 manoeuvred as independent units. Fletcher was confident that the Japanese would be unaware of his presence northeast of Midway. Over the next 24 hours, the two fleets drew nearer to each other, preparing for battle. At around 0430 on 4 June, a flight of Dauntlesses from *Yorktown* set off on the first scouting mission of the day. At about the same time, the Japanese launched their scouts, with one exception. The seaplane on the cruiser *Tone* was unable to launch, because of a catapult defect: this was to have significant consequences. At 0520, the alarm was sounded aboard *Akagi* after a US Navy PBY Catalina flying boat was sighted. Although *Akagi* launched its Zeros to intercept, they lost the Catalina in cloud. The Catalina radioed that it had found the Japanese carriers, and followed up shortly afterwards with a report of large numbers of enemy aircraft heading for Midway. At just after 0600, details of the composition and position of Nagumo's force were transmitted. *Yorktown*'s scouts were recalled, and Fletcher ordered TF16 to head southwest and attack the enemy carriers once they were

BELOW: Admiral Chester Nimitz, Commander-in-Chief, Pacific (centre), chats with Admiral Raymond Spruance (left, Commander of the U.S. Fifth Fleet) and Rear Admiral Forrest Sherman, while aboard the battleship *New Jersey*. Nimitz and Spruance used naval air power to telling effect during the Pacific campaign, and it was appropriate that Nimitz was later commemorated by having an aircraft carrier named after him.

LEFT: Pilots from US Navy fighter squadron 16 (VF-16) receive a briefing from Lieutenant Commander Paul D. Boie (centre) on the deck of the Essex-class carrier USS *Lexington*, while operating off the Gilbert Islands. The briefing was probably staged for the camera, since squadrons had their own briefing rooms below decks: a carrier deck was not the best place to try to hold a conversation.

definitely located. *Enterprise* and *Hornet* set off at 25 knots, and their aircraft were prepared. Meanwhile, Midway itself was about to come under attack.

The Japanese air attack against Midway was met by a force of Brewster Buffalo fighters, which stood little chance against the Zero. They put up gallant resistance while six brand new Grumman TBF Avenger torpedo-bombers (soon to replace the Devastator) and four US Army Air Force Marauder bombers headed out to attack the Japanese carriers. But their mission was almost hopeless, and only one Avenger and two of the Marauders escaped, scoring no hits. This was

less important. The ferocious American resistance prompted the leader of the Japanese attack to call for a second strike to knock out the American defences. The attack on his carriers convinced Nagumo that this was necessary, and he agreed. He instructed that *Kaga* and *Akagi* should rearm their aircraft with bombs rather than torpedoes, a process that would take some time to complete. As arming was halfway through, Nagumo received a message from the *Tone*'s seaplane, launched 30 minutes late after the catapult had been repaired. The seaplane crew found the American fleet – but sent back just one signal, giving the position and strength of the

LEFT: An Avenger is seen on patrol, at some time between 1942 and 1943. By 1943, the Avenger had all but replaced the Devastator, although it was to be used for bombing far more than torpedo attacks. Demand for the Avenger was such that General Motors opened a production line to supplement output from Grumman.

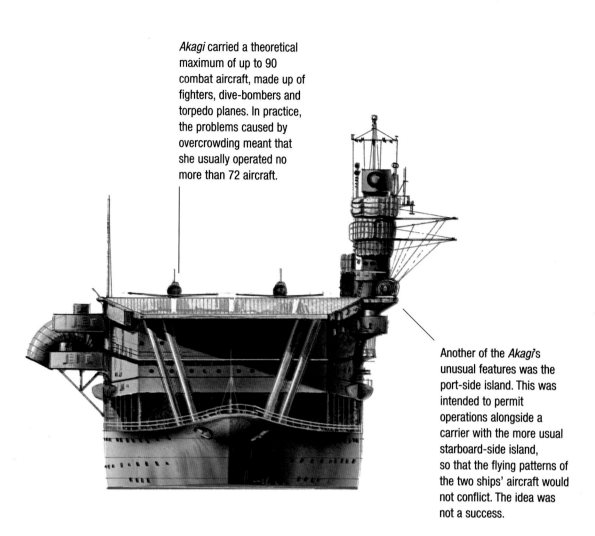

Akagi carried a theoretical maximum of up to 90 combat aircraft, made up of fighters, dive-bombers and torpedo planes. In practice, the problems caused by overcrowding meant that she usually operated no more than 72 aircraft.

Another of the Akagi's unusual features was the port-side island. This was intended to permit operations alongside a carrier with the more usual starboard-side island, so that the flying patterns of the two ships' aircraft would not conflict. The idea was not a success.

SPECIFICATIONS		Propulsion	4-shaft steam turbines
Akagi		Speed	31 knots
		Armament	6 x 8-inch (203mm) guns, 6 x twin 4.7-
Displacement	30,074 tonnes (29,600 tons) full load		inch (120mm) guns and 14 x twin 1-in
Length	260.6m (855ft) overall		(25mm) cannon
Beam	31.3m (102ft 8in)	Complement	1340
Draught	8.6m (28ft 3in)	Aircraft	63

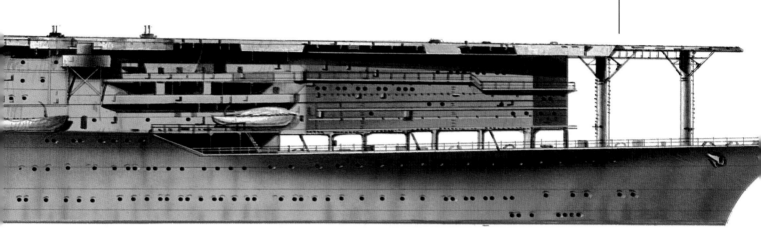

When fitting *Akagi* with a full length flight deck, the end had to be supported by sloping pillars. The only alternatives were a shorter flight deck, or building up the ship's structure, neither of which was practicable.

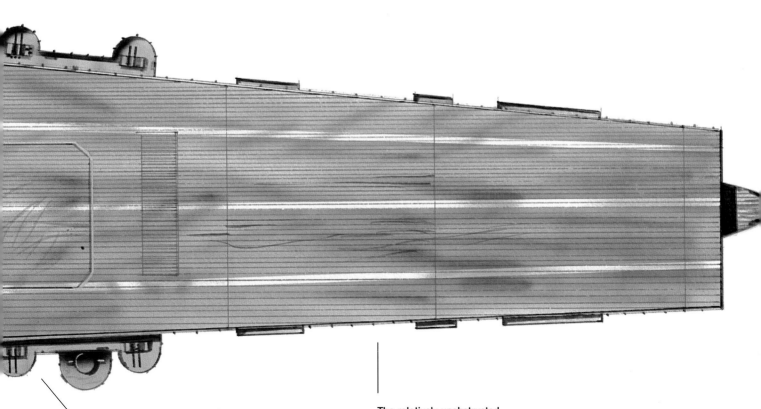

This was one of three lifts on *Akagi*, allowing ready access from the hangar deck to the flight deck.

The relatively unobstructed nature of the flight deck is made clear in this view. The tiny port-side island helped to contribute to this.

USS *Yorktown*

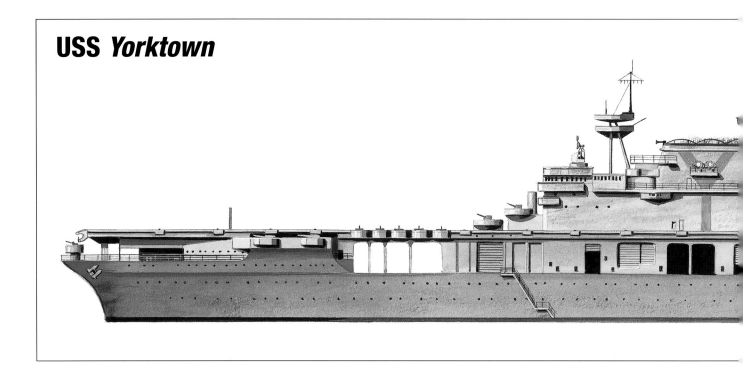

BELOW: The Nakajima B6N 'Jill' torpedo-bomber was used extensively in the later part of the Pacific war, many being expended in *kamikaze* operations. This B6N2 is illustrated as it appeared in IJN service in 1944.

American forces. Crucially, they failed to say what the enemy forces were. Nagumo waited with mounting impatience for this vital information. He had to know if there were carriers in the force, since this would place him in some danger – the Americans were only 322km (200 miles) away. After 15 minutes, Nagumo ordered the seaplane crew to report on the composition of the American forces. While he was waiting, Nagumo ordered the rearming of the aircraft to be suspended, since torpedoes might be needed after all. Only at 0810 did Nagumo receive the information he wanted (a further 25 minutes after it had been called for). 'Enemy ships are five cruisers and five destroyers,' the report proclaimed. This was a relief. At that moment, 16 dive-bombers from Midway appeared over the Japanese, followed minutes later by 15 B-17s. Finally, 11 Marine Corps Vindicator dive-bombers arrived. Every Zero was sent aloft to meet them, and not one hit was scored by the

bombers. This meant that any air strike sent out by Nagumo would lack fighter escort until the Zeros had been recovered, refuelled and rearmed. In the midst of the air attacks, the seaplane crew from *Tone* finally managed to work out that there was a carrier in the American forces and reported the news.

THE FIRST BLOW

Nagumo received this information with concern. He ordered that all the aircraft on deck should be struck below while the strike force from Midway was recovered. While the carriers were at their most vulnerable, the first sighting of the American strike was reported. Spruance had taken the decision to launch every available aircraft against the Japanese carriers, leaving only a bare minimum to defend his own ships. This would have meant that the strike would take about an hour to form up, but when the *Tone*'s seaplane was sighted, Spruance dared not take the risk of

Nakajima B6N 'Jill'

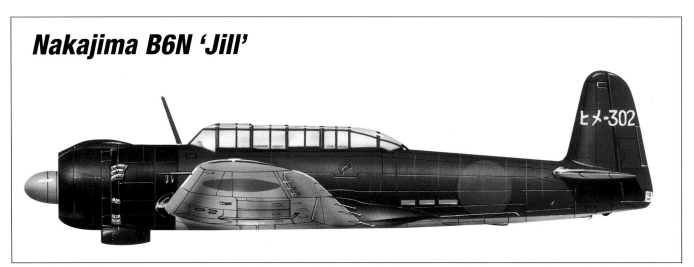

Displacement	20,190 tonnes (19,872 tons) (full load)	Propulsion	4-shaft geared steam turbines
		Speed	32.5 knots
Length	246.74m (809ft 6in) (overall)	Armament	8 x 5-inch (127mm) guns
Beam	25.37m (83ft 3in)	Crew	1890
Draught	6.55m (21ft 6in)	Aircraft	96–100

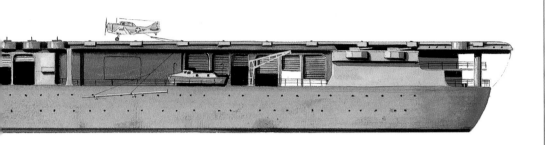

waiting. He did not know about the confusion aboard the Japanese carriers, and feared that the enemy strike would arrive while TF16's aircraft were forming up. The first dive-bombers, commanded by Lt Cdr Clarence Wade McClusky, were ordered to head for their target without waiting for the Devastators to join them; the rest of the aircraft would try to form up on the way. This decision was a risk, but it paid off, albeit at a terrible price. The distance between the different elements meant that the fighters from *Enterprise* took station above the Devastators from *Hornet*, led by Lt Cdr John C. Waldron. They did not manage to make radio contact with the torpedo planes, and thought they were from their own carrier. This left the *Enterprise*'s Devastators without any escort at all. This meant that TF16's strike force advanced in four separate groups: McClusky's dive-bombers, the two torpedo squadrons, and the dive-bombers from *Hornet*, led by Lt Cdr Maxwell F. Leslie.

The Japanese carriers were not at the expected position, and the strike groups had to search for the enemy. While the dive-bombers searched, the two torpedo squadrons sighted smoke over the horizon. Although without fighter escort, they went in to attack without hesitation. They were pounced upon by over 50 Zeros well before they could launch their torpedoes, and only one of the pilots, Ensign George Gay, survived the massacre that followed. Only a few of the Devastators dropped their torpedoes, and none hit. Five minutes later, the Devastators from *Enterprise* led by Lt Cdr Eugene E. Lindsey attacked. By chance, as Lindsey's squadron attacked the *Kaga*, the *Yorktown*'s

Devastators, led by Lt Cdr Lance E. Massey, attacked from the opposite side of the fleet, heading for *Soryu*. The result was the same: no torpedoes hit, and only six out of 26 Devastators survived the flak and the attention of the Zeros. The torpedo-bombers may not have hit their target, but their intervention was vital. While the Japanese fighters hunted at low level, McClusky and Leslie were waiting with their dive-bombers.

The carriers had been forced to manoeuvre to evade the torpedoes, and the separation reduced the concentration of anti-aircraft fire. On the decks of *Akagi* and *Kaga*, the re-arming and refuelling of the strike force were nearly complete, when the sound of incoming dive-bombers was heard. Heads jerked upwards, and eyes concentrated on the black dots tumbling from beneath three attacking aircraft. One bomb struck the *Akagi* amidships, just behind the elevator, and ploughed into the hangar. The effect was devastating. Rearming meant that fuel, bombs and torpedoes were stored on deck and in the hangar, and the flight deck was rent from end to end in the explosion. A second bomb smashed into the torpedo-bombers aft, starting a huge fire. In just seconds, the Japanese flagship had been reduced to a blazing wreck, internal explosions tearing through her as the flames reached more petrol and ordnance. Nagumo reluctantly decided to transfer his flag to another ship, not fully aware of the disaster unfolding around him.

Only three Dauntlesses attacked *Akagi*. The remaining 14 concentrated on the *Kaga*. Four bombs scored direct hits. The first exploded forward of the island, destroying a petrol truck which sent a wall of flame

RIGHT: A Douglas Devastator is seen during a raid against Japanese positions on Wake Island, early in 1942. The Devastator was an advanced aircraft when it entered service, but was outclassed by Japanese fighters. Although they knew the limitations of their aircraft, Devastator crews displayed exceptional courage, particularly at Midway, where whole squadrons were all but wiped out.

sweeping across the bridge, killing everyone there, including the ship's captain. The other bombs wrought havoc among fully fuelled and armed aircraft just as the bombs that hit *Akagi* had done. Within a few minutes, the senior surviving officer saw that the situation was hopeless and ordered that the Emperor's portrait be transferred to a nearby destroyer. This symbolic act told the crew that their ship was doomed, even though she stayed afloat for some time.

While McClusky's squadron attacked *Akagi* and *Kaga*, Leslie's headed for *Soryu*. They attacked in three waves, off the starboard bow, and the port and starboard quarters, released their bombs and climbed away without a single casualty. Three of the bombs hit. The first destroyed the aircraft lift, while the other two landed among the aircraft, setting off huge fires and explosions. Captain Ryusaku Yanaginoto ordered his crew to abandon ship. In five minutes, half of the Japanese carrier force had been destroyed. Although the carriers still remained afloat, they were blazing shells. *Akagi*'s crew fought the fires for nearly eight hours, but the ship was abandoned late in the afternoon, being sunk the following morning by torpedoes from a Japanese destroyer. *Kaga* survived two hits from the torpedoes of an American submarine, but blew up in the early evening. On board *Soryu*, some of the officers headed for the bridge to persuade their captain not to go down with his ship. They stopped as

they entered the bridge, transfixed by the sight of Yanaginoto, sword in hand, looking dead ahead into the distance, awaiting his fate. As the officers left, they heard him begin to sing the Japanese national anthem. At 1913 that evening, ship, captain and 718 crew slipped beneath the waves. By then, further disaster had struck the Japanese.

YORKTOWN

When the American strikes returned to the carriers, they reported that the fourth Japanese carrier had not been seen. Fletcher sent up a defensive patrol in the nick of time, as radar revealed the approach of enemy aircraft. These aircraft were from the *Hiryu*, and charged in to attack. Breaking through the Japanese fighter screen, the defending Wildcats shot down 10 of the 18 dive-bombers that made up the strike. Two more were destroyed by anti-aircraft fire, but this was not enough. The remaining six aircraft, crewed by highly experienced veterans of every operation undertaken by the Japanese navy since 7 December 1941, hit *Yorktown* with three bombs, stopping her dead in the water. Damage control was incredibly effective, and *Yorktown* was soon under way again, building up speed. But just as it seemed the worst was over, another raid was detected on radar. There was just enough time to launch eight Wildcats to support the four still airborne from the first action, but they were unable to penetrate the fighter screen protecting the Japanese torpedo-bombers. They attacked from four different angles, making it impossible for *Yorktown* to evade them all. Two hits on the port side caused serious flooding, inducing a list. All power was lost, making it impossible to counter-flood, and at 1500, the order to abandon ship was given.

While *Yorktown* was being attacked, aircraft from Spruance's TF16 were out again. Twenty-four Dauntlesses arrived above *Hiryu* shortly after the survivors of the attack on *Yorktown* had landed. *Hiryu* circled in a vain attempt to avoid the bombs. Four hit. Rapidly consumed by fires and explosions, *Hiryu* could not be saved. By 2120 that evening, she had come to a stop, while efforts at damage control continued. By 0230 the following morning, it was clear that nothing could be done, and the ship was abandoned. At 0255, Yamamoto ordered a general retirement of his fleet. Spruance had already turned his force eastwards to meet his supply tankers.

Yorktown drifted abandoned throughout the night. At midday on 5 June, a salvage party boarded her, and she was taken in tow. Hopes of getting her to port were dashed when the Japanese submarine *I-168* found her and hit her with two torpedoes. At 0600 on 7 June, *Yorktown* sank. The Battle of Midway was over. So were Japanese chances of winning the war.

THE AFTERMATH

The Japanese lost four key carriers at Midway, but sank only one US carrier. They had also lost a host of highly experienced aircrew, who would take months or perhaps even years to replace adequately. Worse still for the Japanese, American industrial output

was beginning to hit its stride. New, more powerful aircraft for the American carriers were emerging from the factories, and within a month of Midway, the United States had no fewer than 131 carriers building or on order. The carriers would take time to enter service, and the American carrier fleet would be dangerously exposed until the results of the building programme began to appear. Even so, the Japanese could never hope to match American output: with so many experienced naval aircrew lost, forcing a decisive victory in the Pacific was almost impossible after Midway.

The sinking of four enemy carriers at Midway meant that the Americans had an opportunity to make the most of the time the Japanese needed to reorganize their forces. It was decided to capture Rabaul in New Britain, a scheme that necessitated the securing of the Solomon Islands first, most notably Guadalcanal. On 6 August TF61, led by Fletcher and including *Enterprise*, *Saratoga* and *Wasp* along with 69 other ships, entered the Solomon Sea. The carriers fielded 99 fighters (still F4F Wildcats), 103 SBD Dauntlesses, and 41 of the new Grumman TBF Avengers, commencing operations early the next day when the first of 19,000 US Marines went ashore.

THE EASTERN SOLOMONS

Although the landings were successful, the Japanese struck an early blow at the Battle of Savo Island, when their surface ships sank four American cruisers. The presence of a large Japanese surface force prompted Fletcher to take the difficult decision to withdraw his carriers, leaving the Marines to fend

BELOW: USS *Yorktown* lists to starboard, having sustained heavy damage during the Battle of Midway. *Yorktown* was hit by a number of bombs, and nearly sank. Damage control parties nearly succeeded in saving her, but a Japanese submarine managed to creep past the attending destroyers, and sank her with torpedoes.

for themselves. Part of the solution to their problem came in the form of the Marines' own air element, for which an airfield was constructed in the course of a week. The Japanese were determined not to allow the Americans to hold Guadalcanal, and attempted to run supplies to their troops, supported by the carriers *Shokaku*, *Zuikaku* and *Ryujo*. On 23 August 1942, they were sighted by aircraft from TF61, and the Japanese prudently reversed course to avoid an air strike. This was not the end of the confrontation, though. The next day *Ryujo* was spotted by a Catalina while she steamed ahead of the rest of the Japanese fleet. *Enterprise* and *Saratoga* launched their aircraft against her. Just as they did so, another reconnaissance flight sighted *Shokaku* and *Zuikaku*, which had just launched a strike of their own. Attempts to divert the strike against the *Ryujo* to the new target failed. *Ryujo* was sunk by a mixture of Dauntlesses and Avengers. The Japanese response hit *Enterprise* with three bombs, and she had to withdraw. *Enterprise* sent her Dauntlesses ashore to the new airstrip on Guadalcanal (Henderson Field), then retired for repairs. While the Japanese withdrew, their submarines torpedoed both *Saratoga* and *Wasp*, sinking the latter on 15 September. There was one further battle in the Solomons campaign, at the Santa Cruz islands, between 24 and 26 October 1942. The Japanese sent a large fleet, including *Shokaku* and *Zuikaku*, along with *Zuiho* and *Junyo*. They could muster over 200 aircraft, while the Americans had only *Enterprise* and *Hornet* available, with around 170 aircraft aboard.

At 0658 on 26 October, the Japanese launched a strike against the American carriers. As they were preparing to launch their second wave, Dauntlesses from *Enterprise* arrived overhead, and a single bomb fell in the centre of *Zuiho*'s deck. This created a 15.2m (50ft) wide crater, and prevented the operation of aircraft, forcing *Zuiho* to withdraw. At 0822, the Japanese assailed the American carriers, concentrating on *Hornet*. Two torpedoes and six bombs hit her, and despite valiant efforts to get her under way again she was crippled. A measure of revenge was obtained when a strike recently launched by the American carriers seriously damaged *Shokaku*, but this was little consolation. A further Japanese strike damaged *Enterprise* and finished *Hornet*. *Enterprise* withdrew for repairs, while attempts to sink the *Hornet* failed. American concerns that the Japanese might try to capture the ship were well founded, but the heavily waterlogged hulk was impossible to tow, so the Japanese sank her in the early hours of 27 October. The Battle of the Eastern Solomons marked a tactical victory for the Japanese, since it reduced the Americans to one operational carrier in the Pacific. The fighting on Guadalcanal continued for seven months, but the Japanese failed to dislodge the Marines. On 31 December 1942, the Emperor gave his approval for the withdrawal of Japanese

USS *Enterprise*

Displacement	20,190 tonnes (19,872 tons) (full load)	**Propulsion**	4-shaft geared steam turbines
		Speed	32.5 knots
Length	246.74m (809ft 6in) (overall)	**Armament**	8 x 5-inch (127mm) guns
Beam	25.37m (83ft 3in)	**Crew**	1890
Draught	6.55m (21ft 6in)	**Aircraft**	96–100

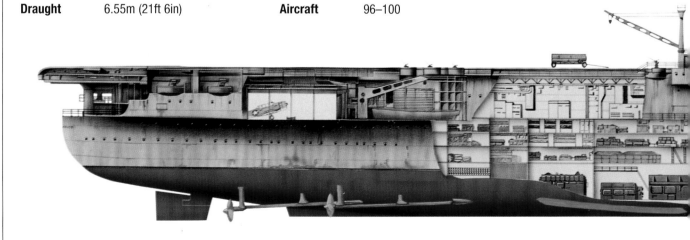

forces from the island. The two carrier fleets did not engage one another in this period: neither side could risk losing what it had.

The difference was that within six months the American carrier fleet started to add large Essex-class carriers, the smaller Independence-class carriers (CVLs), and escort carriers (CVEs) to their arsenal, along with the Grumman Hellcat, a fighter that could master the Zero. They also produced thousands of well trained aircrew. The Japanese, on the other hand, only added as many carriers to their fleet in the period 1943–1945 (five) as the Americans did in April 1944 alone. Of these five Japanese carriers, none deployed operationally. Although the Japanese carriers could not be ignored, in 1943 the American carrier fleet adopted

LEFT: A Grumman Hellcat sits on the deck of an American aircraft carrier, in mid-1943. The scene suggests a training mission, since the deck activity is less hectic than would be expected during operational flying. The Hellcat, although less manoeuvrable than the Zero, was far more robust, and was responsible for gaining air superiority over the Japanese.

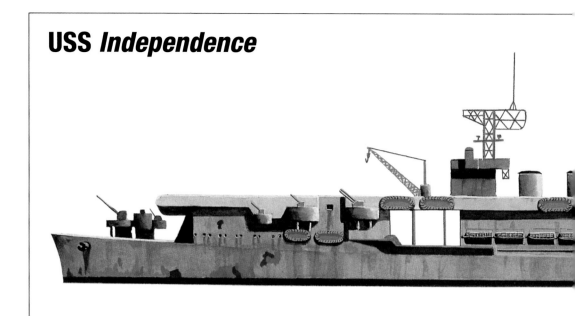

USS *Independence*

entirely new tactics in support of the strategy of 'island hopping'.

ISLAND HOPPING

The Americans realized from their experience at Guadalcanal and elsewhere that the Japanese would fight tenaciously, tying down thousands of men for months at a time. This could reduce the pace of American operations, potentially causing enormous American casualties, and sapping the will to fight. The solution to this difficulty originated in a Naval War College study from 1940, when a strategy of bypassing islands was proposed. This would, in effect, render certain islands irrelevant – American control of the sea would ensure that the Japanese on the bypassed islands could do little, if any, harm, while the Allies thrust for Japan itself.

While some islands were left under Japanese control, others in geographically important locations would be captured by amphibious assault. These islands would then be used as air bases, enabling further operations. To achieve this, command of the sea was essential, and for that, aircraft carriers. In addition, air support for amphibious assaults would have to be provided from carrier decks. The first operations under this plan took place in late 1943, at a time when the American carrier fleet was gaining strength almost monthly.

'GALVANIC'

The first of the island hopping operations was Operation Galvanic, the assault on the Gilbert Islands. This involved the ships of Task Force 50, under Rear Admiral Charles A. Pownall. TF50 contained no fewer than 11 carriers, and over 30 supporting ships, divided between four Task Groups. They began

their attack on 19 November 1943, striking Jaluit and Mili in the Marshall Islands. The attacks were intended as part of a counter-air campaign, designed to prevent Japanese air units from interfering with operations. While attacks were underway on 20 November, the US Army assaulted Makin, with air support from the carriers. Another Task Group attacked airfields on Bougainville in the Solomons, again to prevent interference. The attacks destroyed over 30 Japanese aircraft and a number of ships.

The Americans did not have things all their own way, since the escort carrier *Liscome Bay* was sunk by a Japanese submarine – the carrier exploded after the torpedo hit the bomb store, and sank with the loss of 643 crewmen, including the Task Group commander, Rear Admiral Henry M. Mullinnix. *Liscome Bay* was the only American ship lost in this phase of operations, which continued with the assault on Tarawa. Tarawa was taken in three days of intense fighting. New Britain was taken in December 1943, by which time it was clear that the Pacific war was not going as Japan had hoped – the Gilbert Islands were secured by the end of the month, and the Marshalls became the target for American assault in January 1944. This was the start of a disastrous year for Japan, one in which American carriers played a full part. Those of the Japanese navy were far less evident, and the difference proved telling.

1944

The Japanese carrier force had been forced out of battle by the loss of experienced pilots from the Battle of Midway onwards. Japanese carriers spent much of 1943 training replacement air groups, and their distance from the combat zone encouraged the Americans. The

Displacement	14,986 tonnes (14,750 tons) (full load)	Speed	31 knots
		Armament	2 x 5-inch (127mm) guns, 16 x
Length	189.74m (622ft 6in) (overall)		40mm (1.6in) cannon and 10 x
Beam	21.79m (71ft 6in)		20mm (0.8in) cannon
Draught	6.4m (21ft)	Complement	1569
Propulsion	4-shaft geared steam turbines	Aircraft	30

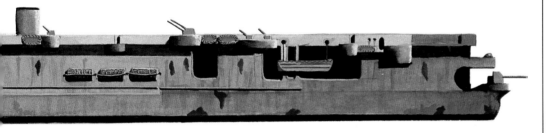

attempt to seize the Marshalls, Operation Flintlock, was postponed for a month as a result of the lack of troop transports, with the new day for the assault being 31 January 1944. There was some debate as to where to attack first, Nimitz finally settling upon Kwajalein. Task Force 51, with 297 ships, was to lead the assault, supported by the 12 carriers from Vice-Admiral Marc Mitscher's Task Force 58. The carrier force provided overwhelming air superiority in the two days before the landings, when they destroyed virtually all of the local Japanese air strength. By 1 February, 11,000 American troops were ashore, attacking in methodical fashion, using air support and artillery to destroy Japanese positions before advancing. Japanese resistance remained fierce until 6 February, when the island was taken. Almost all the garrison had died – over 20 Japanese soldiers died for every American killed. The mix of intense bombardment from the battleships and heavy air attacks did much to reduce the effects of the ferocious Japanese resistance. The Americans then moved on to Eniwetok atoll, at the northern end of the Marshalls. It was originally intended to take Eniwetok in May, but Nimitz decided that it would be advantageous to strike while the Japanese were recovering from Kwajalein, and not in a position to reinforce. There was a difficulty, in that Eniwetok was vulnerable to intervention from the huge Japanese base at Truk in the Caroline Islands.

Mitscher saw this difficulty as an opportunity, and set TF58 against the island. On 17 and 18 February, TF58 launched 30 massive raids on Truk, the smallest of which had no fewer than 150 aircraft involved. Nearly 300 Japanese aircraft fell victim to US Navy fighters, and almost 200,000 tonnes of Japanese

shipping were sent to the bottom. Had it not been for the decision to withdraw major Japanese units from the area just a week before, the total could have been even more disastrous for the Japanese. Eniwetok was attacked on 17 February, and fell four days later. Another part of the Japanese empire had gone: the next American blow would be even more severe.

ON TO THE MARIANAS

Once again, the Americans decided to gamble: they would bypass Truk and the Caroline Islands, instead landing in the Marianas. The geographical position of the Marianas was perfect – US B-29 bombers could be based there, offering the opportunity to begin heavy strategic bombing raids against Japan. It was considered that operations against the Marianas would bring the Japanese fleet out in force, but the Americans were undeterred: the fear of the Japanese fleet was long gone. Thus, Operation Forager was launched, leading to the greatest carrier battle of the war.

Once again, TF58 was at the heart of the fight. The carrier striking force was made up of seven large carriers, and eight light carriers (the CVLs), along with 90 other ships and two escort carrier groups, to provide close support and anti-submarine protection. The American aircraft were impressive both in quality and in number. The faithful SBD Dauntlesses were fewer in number by 1944, equipping only the dive-bomber squadrons of *Enterprise* and the new *Lexington* (an Essex-class carrier). The other carriers employed the new Curtiss SB2C Helldiver in this role. The Helldiver was not a popular aircraft, and its nickname of 'the beast' stemmed from a mixture of affection and contempt. Some aircrew preferred to take the SB2C

RIGHT: USS *Essex* leads a line of American ships, including at least one battleship. The Essex-class became the dominant carrier class of the Pacific war, embarking large numbers of aircraft. The sheer weight of carrier air power available to the Americans by 1944 ensured that the Japanese were simply unable to thwart the Americans' advance towards Japan itself.

type number, and translate it as 'Son of a Bitch, 2nd Class', leaving no one in any doubt as to their feelings. This was probably a little unfair on the Helldiver, which was robust and heavily armed. The torpedo bombing units (which also increasingly conducted level bombing) were equipped exclusively with the Grumman TBF Avenger (or the almost identical TBM, built by General Motors on Grumman's behalf). After its disastrous debut at Midway, the Avenger had matured into a formidable strike aircraft, which was capable of handling itself against Japanese fighters.

Most significantly, the fighter aircraft aboard the American carriers were more than a match for the Japanese – in addition, their pilots were far more experienced than their opponents. The prime fighter aircraft was the Grumman F6F Hellcat. The Hellcat, although not as manoeuvrable as the Japanese 'Zero', had several advantages. It carried six 12.7mm (0.5-inch) machine guns, which could blast their way through the almost totally unarmoured Japanese aircraft. In contrast, the Hellcat was robust, and capable of surviving heavy damage. There was another fighter available to TF58 in small numbers in the form of the Vought F4U

Corsair (already extensively employed from land bases by the US Marines). The Corsair was a formidable fighter, recognizable by its so-called gull wings. Unfortunately, it had a number of undesirable deck landing characteristics, and aircraft with the necessary modifications to make them acceptable for use from carriers were only just entering service. The escort carriers embarked the faithful Grumman Wildcat, this time the FM-2 version, along with more Avengers.

The assault on the Marianas began with fighter sweeps. At 1300 on 11 June 1944, over 200 Hellcats and Avengers took off on a sweep against airfields on Guam, Saipan, Tinian and Pegan. The intention was to either bring Japanese aircraft up to fight, or if they refused the challenge, to destroy them on the ground. The attacks were devastating. By the end of 11 June, 81 Japanese aircraft had been claimed shot down, with another 29 destroyed on the ground. In return, the Americans lost 21 Hellcats and 15 pilots. The opening day was followed by a lull in operations, but the Japanese were soon to retaliate.

On 13 June, the Japanese launched Operation A-Go, the long-planned battle with the US fleet. All nine Japanese carriers and

Vought F4U Corsair

the world's largest battleships, the *Yamato* and *Musashi*, led the operation. Although the commander of the Japanese fleet, Admiral Jisaburo Ozawa, was confident that he could win a battle with the Americans, he perhaps failed to appreciate just how weak his air element was, and how difficult it would be to overcome American air strength. For any chance of success, Ozawa needed surprise: he did not enjoy it. The Japanese fleet was spotted by American submarines, giving Mitscher the upper hand. Mitscher decided to reduce the threat from land-based Japanese aircraft, and on the night of 14 June, Task Groups 58.1 and 58.4 were sent to attack the airbases on Iwo Jima and Chichi Jima. By the early afternoon of 15 June 1944,

the aircraft from the Task Groups were approaching their targets. The first Hellcats to arrive ran into 38 Japanese aircraft, and swept through them, destroying almost all. In the continuing action, more Japanese aircraft were destroyed both in the air and on the ground, almost wiping out Japanese air strength on the islands. By the time the action concluded, US Marines had been on the ground in the Marianas for over 24 hours.

The two Task Groups rejoined TF58 on 16 June, and skirmishes continued during the next 48 hours. On the evening of 17 June the escort carrier *Fanshawe Bay* was hit by a Japanese air strike and withdrew. Reconnaissances by the Japanese found the Americans at 1514 on 18 June, while

ABOVE: The Vought F4U Corsair did sterling service in the grim battle against the Japanese in the Pacific. Flown by Lt (jg) Ira C. 'Ike' Kepford, leading US Navy ace in the Pacific, during early 1944, this F4U-1A carries Kepford's 16 kill markings in the form of Imperial Japanese rising suns.

LEFT: One of the famous 'batmen' is seen here, signalling to a pilot approaching the carrier for landing. The role of the signal officer was absolutely vital, giving corrections to pilots to ensure that their landing was safe. The signal officer would use large paddles to give direction to the pilot – different signals existed to show whether the pilot should increase or decrease altitude, speed and so on.

ABOVE: A maintenance crew member services the 12.7mm (0.5in) machine guns on a Vought F4U Corsair.

USS *Essex*

Catalinas found the Japanese on radar at 0115 the following morning. American efforts were hampered by the failure of a follow-up search to locate the main body of the enemy fleet, but it was clear that battle would be joined shortly.

THE GREAT MARIANAS TURKEY SHOOT

On the morning of 19 June 1944, fighter sweeps by Hellcats were launched against Japanese airfields, destroying a number of enemy aircraft. But at 1000, they were called back to help meet a new threat – a Japanese attack force was spotted on radar approach-ing TF58;140 Hellcats were launched to meet the raid, while aircraft returning from sweeps and earlier patrols above the carriers were brought down to refuel. To the bewilderment of the Americans, the Japanese force stopped 113km (70 miles) away, and began circling. It later transpired that the leader of the strike was giving a final briefing to his inexperienced men, explaining what they had to do. This gave the Americans the opportunity to

RIGHT: Framed over two Grumman Avengers on a carrier deck, a Japanese aircraft crashes in flames, shot down as it attempts to attack the escort carrier USS *Kitkun Bay* during the 'Marianas Turkey Shoot' in June 1944. By this time, the situation had become so desperate for the Japanese that they were starting to employ *kamikaze* aircraft in a vain effort to stem the tide of the American advance.

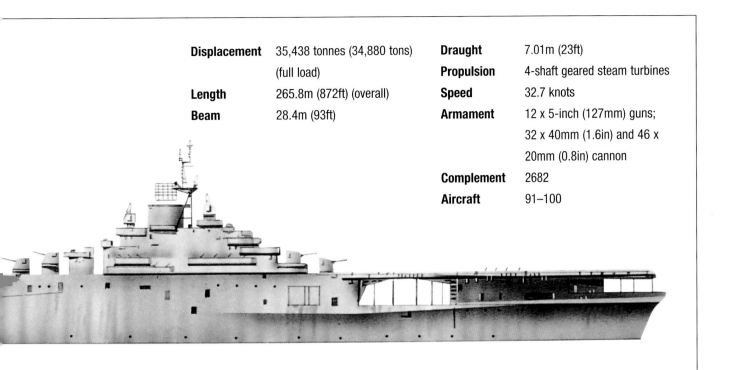

Displacement	35,438 tonnes (34,880 tons) (full load)	Draught	7.01m (23ft)
		Propulsion	4-shaft geared steam turbines
Length	265.8m (872ft) (overall)	Speed	32.7 knots
Beam	28.4m (93ft)	Armament	12 x 5-inch (127mm) guns; 32 x 40mm (1.6in) and 46 x 20mm (0.8in) cannon
		Complement	2682
		Aircraft	91–100

fly out to meet the Japanese before they reached the carriers. At 1035, the first Hellcats met the enemy. In the first pass, 19 Zeros were shot down, and a fierce battle developed. Only 20 Japanese aircraft got through to the fleet, and only one scored a hit – a 250kg (551lb) bomb hit the battleship *South Dakota*. Within minutes of this, the attack was over. The Japanese had lost 42 aircraft; the Americans three.

The second raid was not far behind, but events during the raid's take-off had not been propitious. The American submarine *Albacore* fired two torpedoes at the Japanese carrier *Taiho*, hitting her with one. As if this were not enough, some of the Japanese aircraft had to turn back with mechanical trouble, and 10 aircraft were hit by 'friendly' anti-aircraft fire, two being lost. When the raid finally reached the American fleet, it was ravaged by the Hellcats. Although *Wasp* and *Bunker Hill* were hit by the few aircraft that got through, the damage was minor. In return for this, 96 Japanese aircraft were lost. Worse was to come: as the remnants of the Japanese attack headed for home, *Shokaku* was torpedoed by the USS *Cavalla*. Three torpedoes hit, spreading oil fumes throughout the ship, and at 1500, *Shokaku* blew up. Remarkably, just half an hour later, the *Taiho* followed suit. After a torpedo hit from USS *Albacore*, fuel fumes had been released, and it was decided to open the ventilation ducts on the ship: this allowed the fumes to spread, and at 1532, *Taiho* was ripped apart by a massive explosion. Fighting continued until the early evening: by the end of the day, the Americans had suffered just minor damage to their ships, and had lost 16 Hellcats. But they had sunk two carriers, and claimed 378 enemy aircraft destroyed – seven of them by Commander David McCampbell, the commander of Air Group 15 on USS *Essex*. The Turkey Shoot was almost over, but there was one more major act to come.

The following day, 20 June, Mitscher's aircraft attempted to find the Japanese fleet, but did not succeed until 1540. A strike was launched at 1620, despite the fact that the returning aircraft would have to land in the dark. The strike was not as successful as the American pilots first thought, but was still quite impressive. The Japanese carrier *Hiyo* was sunk, and *Junyo* and *Zuikaku* damaged. The American aircraft reached their carriers at 2245: Mitscher was determined to recover as many men and aircraft as he could, and ordered every ship to turn its lights on, so that the aircrews could find their way home. This led to some alarming incidents in which pilots attempted to land on destroyers, but many aircraft managed to find a carrier, even if it was not the one they had started out from. Even so, 104 aircraft were forced to ditch, but only 49 men were not recovered; most of these had been lost in the attacks on the Japanese carriers.

The Marianas campaign continued until 10 August. The Japanese carrier fleet had been reduced to virtual impotence, and just one more battle was needed to destroy Japan's naval power: it came at Leyte Gulf.

LEYTE GULF

After the Marianas, two offensives were launched, one by Spruance's 5th Fleet, the

RIGHT: A crowded deck aboard a British Pacific Fleet aircraft carrier. The aircraft include Grumman Hellcats, Fairey Fireflies, Grumman Avengers, Vought Corsairs and Fairey Barracudas. The mix of aircraft suggests that this carrier is being used for ferry purposes, since no carrier embarked all of these aircraft simultaneously in its air wing.

other by Task Force 38, under the overall command of Admiral William F. Halsey (while Mitscher retained tactical command of the carriers). Halsey was surprised at the lack of opposition put up by the Japanese, and suggested that Leyte be invaded, preparations beginning on 11 October 1944. The first step was to attack Okinawa and Formosa to remove the threat of air attack. After three days, the Americans had destroyed over 500 Japanese aircraft and wrecked a number of airfields. Japanese retaliation seriously damaged two ships, and lightly damaged a third, the carrier *Franklin*. These minor successes were inflated by Japanese propaganda to the destruction of 11 American carriers and six

other major surface ships. Halsey was infuriated by the Japanese propaganda and sent a pithy signal to Nimitz: 'All Third Fleet ships recently reported sunk by radio Tokyo salvaged and retiring at high speed toward the Japanese fleet'. More significantly, the Japanese truly believed that they had sunk 11 carriers. This prompted them to act as though they had the advantage, which was far from the case.

On 17 October, US Army Rangers began to go ashore on the islands in Leyte Gulf. The Japanese responded, and although the Americans suffered a worrying few hours after Halsey misread Japanese intentions, the result was nothing short of slaughter. On 24

HMS *Indomitable*

Displacement	28,661 tonnes (28,120 tons) (full load)	**Speed**	30.5 knots
Length	226.7m (743ft 9in) (overall)	**Armament**	16 x 4.5-inch (114mm) and 48 x 2-pounder guns
Beam	29.2m (95ft 9in)	**Complement**	1592
Draught	7.32m (24ft)	**Aircraft**	48
Propulsion	3-shaft geared steam turbines		

October, the inimitable David McCampbell and his wingman Roy Rushing came across a formation of Japanese aircraft. McCampbell proceeded to shoot down nine of them (and may well have destroyed two more), while Rushing dispatched a further five. This encounter more than any other demonstrated just how poorly the Japanese now fared in the face of American fighters. Their aircraft could still perform well in isolated cases, however: the carrier *Princeton* was sunk by bombing. In addition, the first *kamikaze* suicide attacks began, with the sinking of the carrier *St Lô* on 25 October.

Although the *kamikazes* were to become a serious problem, they had little influence at Leyte. The mighty Japanese battleship *Musashi* was hit by 19 torpedoes and at least 10 bombs and sunk in an overwhelming air attack; on the same day as the first *kamikaze* attack, carrier strikes accounted for the Japanese carriers *Chitose* and *Zuiho*, while the *Zuikaku*, still leading a charmed life, was damaged and escaped from the Americans once more. This time, though, the respite was brief. The Americans returned and sank her with a second attack by over 100 aircraft which saw her hit with at least seven torpedoes and four bombs. *Zuikako* capsized within minutes, and went to the bottom. As the battle ended, it was clear that the Japanese navy was finished as a fighting force: four carriers, three battleships, nine cruisers and eight destroyers had been lost. The Americans had lost three carriers and two destroyers, but this could be sustained. The Japanese navy's last throw was the *kamikazes*. The original *kamikaze* had turned back an invasion fleet: it would have been even more miraculous if the 1944 version of this 'divine wind' had turned back the might of the American fleet, now joined by the Royal Navy on its return to the Pacific after a long absence.

THE LAST BATTLES

The American carriers, supported by the British Pacific Fleet, now ranged with near impunity against Japanese targets, supporting the landings on Iwo Jima and Okinawa. Attacks by *kamikaze* became a serious nuisance, although the British carriers, with their armoured decks, suffered far less damage than their American counterparts. By spring 1945, the situation was desperate, and on 1 April, the Japanese launched operation 'Ten-Go', a virtual suicide mission. Despite immense losses, the Japanese mustered 4500 aircraft, while the *Yamato* was sent to attack the invading transports off Okinawa. *Yamato* was spotted as she left port, and once in range was assailed by 280 US aircraft. The result was inevitable; the American aircraft swarmed all over the battleship, and dispatched her with ten torpedoes and a number of bombs.

American carriers were subjected to numerous assaults by *kamikazes*, with *Hancock, Enterprise, Essex* and *Bunker Hill* taking hits. The battles were fierce: when Okinawa fell on 2 June, the Americans had lost 790 aircraft – the Japanese over 2000. The Americans were now within range of Japan and able to plan for invasion. This did not happen. The island-hopping campaign provided bases for B-29s, which began ravaging Japanese cities with huge fire raids. Yokohama was all but destroyed in one such raid, and it was estimated that over 500,000 Japanese civilians were killed. The greatest demonstration of American power was yet to come. On the early morning of 6 August 1945, the citizens of Hiroshima were alerted to the presence of a single B-29 overhead. The aircraft was flown by Colonel Paul Tibbets, who had chosen to name the aircraft in honour of his mother: *Enola Gay*.

Moments after the aircraft was spotted high above the city, Hiroshima was utterly destroyed by the first atomic bomb. Nagasaki followed three days later, and the Emperor announced Japan's capitulation on 15 August 1945. General MacArthur presided over the formal surrender ceremony on the deck of Halsey's flagship, the battleship *Missouri*. Although a fitting ship on which to take the surrender, an aircraft carrier might have been more appropriate: after all, without them, the war in the Pacific could not have been won.

MacArthur concluded the ceremony with the words 'Let us pray that peace be now restored to the world'. The prayer went unanswered. Five years later, MacArthur would be at war again, and aircraft carriers would be his key tool for the new war, in Korea.

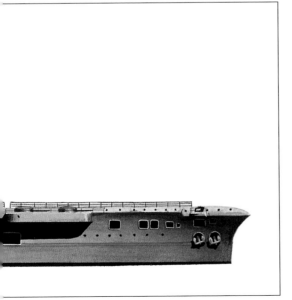

CHAPTER FIVE

JETS AT SEA: NEW TECHNOLOGY

The use of the atomic bomb to end the war with Japan appeared to call into question the future of the aircraft carrier. Given that carriers had been one of the key instruments of victory, this was more than a little ironic. But the appearance of atomic weapons threw all traditional models of war into confusion.

THE VIEW THAT CARRIERS were obsolete was not shared by the US Navy, which argued that they gave the Navy the ability to tackle land targets from the sea, particularly in support of an amphibious invasion. Although the US Navy was confident that carriers would be useful, this did not prevent them from cancelling a number that were building, while others were retired after their wartime service. In Britain, a similar process occurred. The large

LEFT: HMS *Ark Royal* on patrol at some time during the early 1970s, the deck crowded with Buccaneers, Fairey Gannets and Phantoms. *Ark Royal* was withdrawn from service in 1978, Britain's carrier capability subsequently being provided by Sea Harriers embarked upon much smaller ships.

Malta-class carriers ordered from 1943 were cancelled before construction properly began (with hindsight, an unfortunate decision), while cancellations and delays afflicted other new designs. This was unsurprising given Britain's desperate economic state after the war. Two large carriers, to be named *Ark Royal* and *Eagle*, survived the cutbacks, but took a long time to build. Although laid down in October 1942, *Eagle* (originally to be named *Audacious*) did not enter service until October 1951. By way of comparison, although the American building programme slowed, the last Essex-class carriers and the new Midway classes were not cancelled and were in service less than three years after being laid down. The Royal Navy instead relied upon the newly built light fleet carriers of the Colossus class, and considered modifications of some of the Illustrious-class vessels to make them suited for operation of modern aircraft. Finally, the carriers from the Centaur class would help to modernize the British fleet, but these ships did not begin to enter service until the early 1950s.

The problem facing both the Americans and the British was the fact that the jet aircraft had arrived, and was undoubtedly going to be the future of military aviation. Carriers could not afford to carry fleets of propeller-driven aircraft that would be totally outclassed by jets. Jets were heavier than their piston-engined counterparts, and demanded much larger carriers. For the Americans, this was less of a problem, since the Essexes, even without modifications, were more than able to handle up-to-date aircraft. The British carriers, however, would prove far less adaptable, and as aircraft technology advanced, the Royal Navy became painfully aware that its carriers could not handle the most up-to-date aircraft.

CARRIERS IN THE POST-WAR WORLD

The US Navy employed two carriers in 1946, including the three Midway-class ships, each of 45,000 tons. The Midways had an armoured deck, drawing upon experience against *kamikazes* in the Pacific, a formidable gun battery (slowly removed over the coming years) and an air group of no less than 137 aircraft. The *Franklin D. Roosevelt* deployed to the Mediterranean between August and October 1946, carrying 123 aeroplanes. The aircraft were all familiar: 65 Vought F4U Corsairs (but the newer F4U-4 variant), four dozen of the little-loved S2BC Helldiver (again in the form of the latest model of that design), along with eight F6F-5 Hellcats and two Grumman TBM Avengers. This made a formidable air group: the only serious threat to the supremacy of the Corsairs came in the form of jet aircraft. As the only nation outside the United States to have these in any number was Britain, it meant that the *FDR* could patrol safe in the knowledge that it could handle almost any air threat thrown against it. But the US Navy had not been complacent about jet aircraft. In March 1945, the Ryan FR Fireball entered limited service. The Fireball was a composite power aircraft, using a piston engine and a jet engine. Three

USS *United States*

(All figures projected)

Displacement	79,756 tonnes (78,500 tons) (deep load)
Length	331.6m (1088ft)
Beam	39.52m (130ft)
Draught	10.5m (34.5ft)
Propulsion	4-shaft steam turbines
Speed	33 knots
Armament	8 x single 5-inch (127mm) guns; 8 x twin 3-inch (76mm) guns and 20 x 20mm (0.8in) cannon
Complement	4217
Aircraft	72

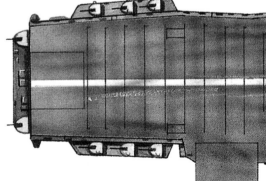

a formidable array of weapons. As well as two (later four) 20mm (0.8in) cannon, the Skyraider had 15 underwing pylons for ordnance and fuel tanks: it was still in service 20 years later. The Americans also began to deploy the first specialist aircraft aboard carriers in the form of the Grumman AF-2 Guardian. The AF-2W carried search radar and equipment for hunting submarines, and the AF-2S carried the weapons to destroy them. In addition, special versions of the Skyraider were developed for electronic warfare and airborne early warning. There was another wholly new aircraft type – the helicopter, useful for transport and for rescuing ditched pilots. Along with the special mission aircraft, they began to add even greater flexibility to aircraft carriers.

THE NUCLEAR CONTROVERSY

Despite all these developments, the thorny issue of nuclear weapons remained key to early post-war thinking. In 1947, the United States Air Force (USAF) was formed as an independent arm. The new force was particularly confident in itself, and immediately insisted that it should have complete control of the nuclear (then known as 'atomic') role. Some senior officers were uncertain as to whether the US Navy should be involved

in atomic warfare at all, while others loudly promoted the virtues of carrier aircraft by comparison with land-based bombers. Rear-Admiral Daniel Gallery, the Assistant Chief of Naval Operations (Guided Missiles), was perhaps the strongest advocate of the nuclear role, producing a memorandum in which he urged the US Navy to prove it could deliver atomic bombs better than the USAF could. Gallery pointed out that carriers could be positioned much closer to an enemy's homeland than land-based bombers, and (unlike the B-29s) did not require airbases in foreign countries. The new Convair B-36 bomber could carry nuclear weapons considerable distances (it already appeared that the Soviet Union was the most likely threat to the United States), but would require fighter escort: the fighters would need overseas basing too. This problem could be overcome by aircraft carriers, which could attack the enemy much more easily, with fighter escort close at hand. Gallery's contentions were rebutted by the Secretary of the Navy, John L. Sullivan, and the Chief of Naval Operations, Admiral Louis Denfield, but their opposition did not quell debate. The Secretary of Defense, James Forrestal (a former Secretary of the Navy himself), took the view that the

BELOW: An atmospheric picture of HMS *Bulwark* at night, while visiting Cherbourg in December 1958. The aircraft on deck are Hawker Sea Hawks, a light and effective fighter bomber that was used until 1960 by the Royal Navy, and until the late 1970s by the Indian Navy.

HMS *Eagle*

Eagle joined the Royal Navy in the 1950s, after a prolonged construction period caused by uncertainties in the aftermath of World War II. She took part in the Suez crisis in 1956, where her aircraft performed impressively, and remained in service until 1972.

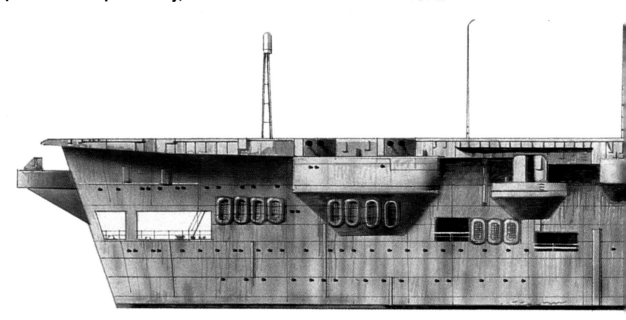

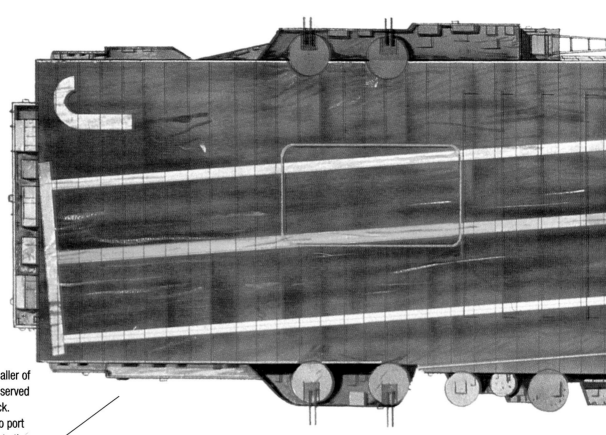

The aft lift was the smaller of the two elevators that served the *Eagle*'s hangar deck. Both lifts were offset to port slightly, to accommodate the boiler trunking on the starboard side of the ship.

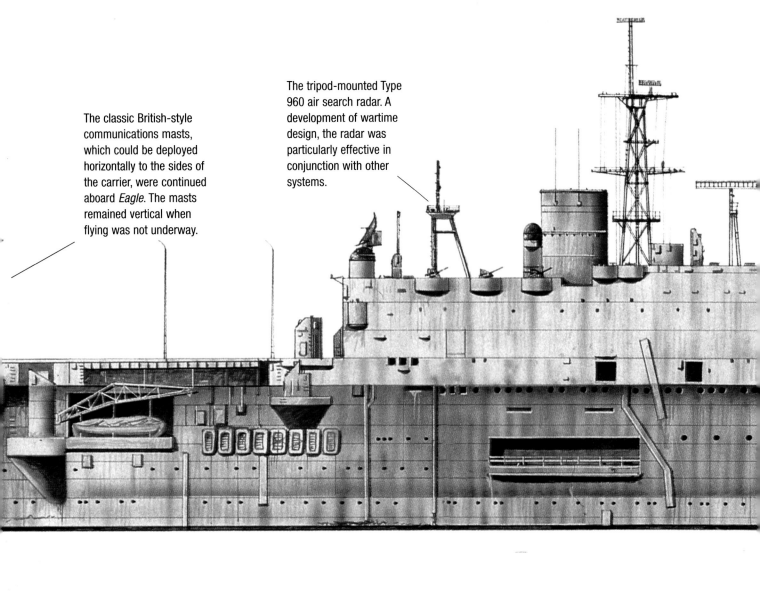

The classic British-style communications masts, which could be deployed horizontally to the sides of the carrier, were continued aboard *Eagle*. The masts remained vertical when flying was not underway.

The tripod-mounted Type 960 air search radar. A development of wartime design, the radar was particularly effective in conjunction with other systems.

In 1954, *Eagle* was given an interim 5° deck by building a small extension to the port side of the deck and re-aligning the arrester wires and safety barrier.

days of carrier trials in May 1945 demonstrated that the aircraft was viable, but it saw little service. The first landing of a true jet aircraft aboard an aircraft carrier came in December 1945, when Lieutenant Commander Eric Brown of the Royal Navy landed a de Havilland Vampire aboard HMS *Ocean*. Brown conducted a number of take-offs and landings both that day and three days later. The problem was that the Admiralty were not convinced by jets, and were very slow to act. The Sea Vampire (a Vampire with arrester hook and launching equipment) was ordered for the Royal Navy soon after Brown's pioneering flight, but the first production model did not fly until 1948. Only 18 were built and they were used only for second-line duties. The Admiralty was more impressed by the Supermarine Attacker, a relatively simple machine armed with four 20mm (0.8in) cannon and some 454kg (1000lb) of bombs. Supermarine had designed the aircraft with the Royal Air Force in mind, but found that their projected customer was not interested. A naval version of the aircraft flew in June 1947 and conducted trials aboard HMS *Illustrious* four months later. Although these tests were successful, it took the Admiralty three years to decide an order, and nearly another 12 months passed before the aircraft entered service. By this time, the US Navy had streaked ahead, and took a lead in carrier aviation that it has never since surrendered.

Even before the Second World War was over, the US Navy had placed orders for three prototype jet aircraft: the McDonnell FD-1 (later FH-1) Phantom, the Vought F6U Pirate and the North American FJ-1 Fury. The Phantom flew on 26 January 1945, and went on carrier trials in July 1946. There were few difficulties in operating the Phantom, but the slow response of the jet engine to throttle movements (a common problem with early jet engines) brought some interesting moments. A year after the trials VF-17A, a fighter squadron, began to equip with the Phantom. The squadron completed carrier qualifications in May 1948, becoming the first operational naval jet unit. The F6U proved a disappointment and was not proceeded with, but the FJ-1 Fury proved a more than adequate machine, and entered limited service shortly after the Phantom. Although the USN was far-sighted enough to begin developing jets, it was not blind to their faults. They consumed fuel at a much greater rate than piston-engined aircraft, and could not carry the same weight of armament. This meant that production of piston-engined aircraft continued. The Vought Corsair was further developed through the F4U-4 ('Dash-4') and F4U-5 ('Dash-5') versions, which carried 20mm (0.8in) cannon – as opposed to the 12.7mm (0.5-inch) machine guns of the wartime models – and an array of bombs and rockets. The Dash-4 and Dash-5 Corsairs soon replaced the Helldivers in the attack role, and were soon joined by another aircraft that was to achieve legendary status: the Douglas AD Skyraider. The Skyraider entered service just after the war ended, and carried

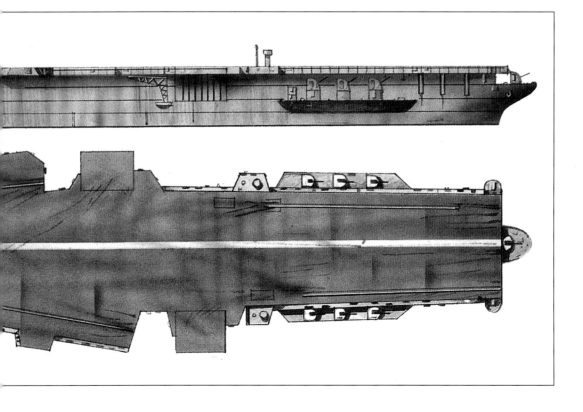

HMAS *Melbourne*

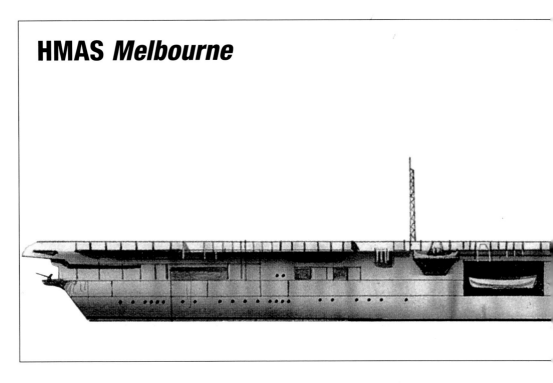

designed as a maritime patrol aircraft rather than a strategic bomber. Tests with Neptunes were conducted from the deck of USS *Coral Sea* in April and May 1947. The Neptunes had to be fitted with Rocket-Assisted Take-Off Gear (RATOG) to help them leave the deck, since the hydraulic catapults fitted to carriers at that time were simply not powerful enough for such heavy aircraft. Furthermore, the Neptunes could not land on the carriers, having to land at friendly airbases. This dramatically reduced the flexibility of the carriers, which were also disadvantaged by the inability to operate the rest of their air group. The large carrier was needed to make the navy nuclear delivery role practicable, even when the purpose-designed Savage entered service. This large carrier would be the first of the 'supercarriers' – but would never enter service.

THE REVOLT OF THE ADMIRALS

The USAF remained resolutely against the Navy's involvement in strategic bombing, but this was not enough to prevent permission for a new carrier, the USS *United States* (CVA-58) being granted. The *United States* was to be a formidable ship: she was designed to displace 83,249 tons at full load, to operate 18 bombers and over 50 fighters. To allow the bombers to operate without risk of their wings clipping the carrier's island, *United States* was to be a flush-deck design. She would have four deck-edge aircraft lifts and four catapults. She would also be enormously expensive, and this was to be the cause of her downfall. Although the Americans perceived a major threat from the Soviet Union – particularly after

the Soviets exploded their own atom bomb in 1949 – this threat did not at first lead to vast increases in defence spending. The B-36 cost around $6,000,000 per aircraft, and the USAF wanted a lot of them. This meant that the B-36 fleet and the carriers (four United States-class carriers were planned) would cost a phenomenally large amount of money to do the same job. The USAF made great efforts to point this out, but ran into the difficulty that Forrestal was in favour of the carrier. Forrestal was not well, however, and resigned in March 1949. His successor, Louis Johnson, was more convinced by the arguments put forward by the USAF, and in April, *United States* was cancelled. This began an unseemly inter-service squabble that became known as the 'Revolt of the Admirals'. Questions about the vulnerability of the B-36 to fighter aircraft were raised as the US Navy retaliated, seemingly bent on getting the B-36 cancelled as well.

The process began when Captain John G. Crommelin held a press conference on 25 May 1949, in which he lambasted the Secretary of Defense for cancelling the *United States*, claiming that this left the United States vulnerable to attack. Although Crommelin's actions were highly controversial, he was supported by almost all the admirals in the US Navy. Crommelin then released copies of supportive letters from a number of admirals to the press (ignoring their 'confidential' security marking), although he insisted that he not be revealed as the source. The sensational headlines produced by the release of the letters prompted Congressman Carl Vinson, the Chairman of the House Naval Affairs Committee, to

The so-called hay rake antenna served the Type 983 fighter direction radar. The Type 983 had a range of 11km (6 nautical miles).

Eagle carried the full range of British naval aircraft, including Sea Venoms, seen here. During the 1956 cruise in which Eagle took part in the Suez conflict, a mix of Sea Venoms, Hawker Sea Hawks and Westland Wyvern fighter bombers was carried.

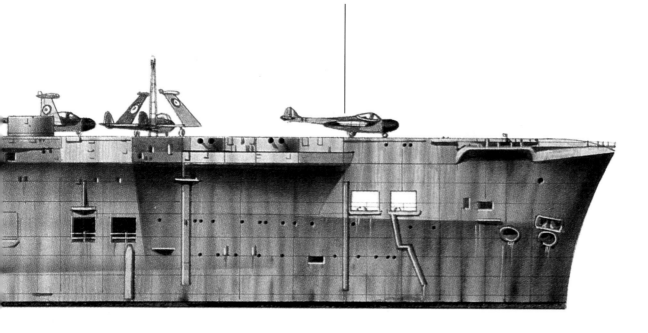

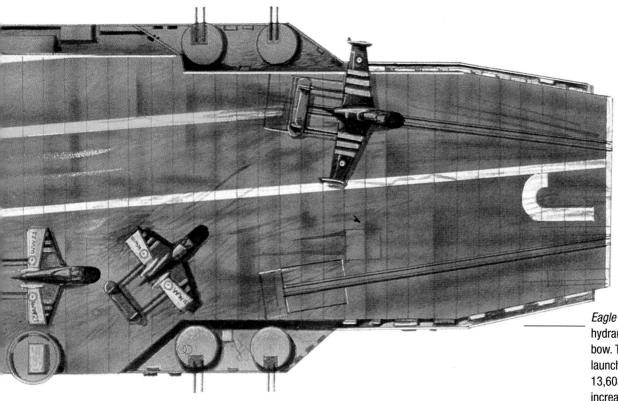

Eagle mounted two BH5 hydraulic catapults at the bow. These were capable of launching aircraft weighing 13,608kg (30,000lb), but the increasing weight of combat aircraft meant that they were replaced by steam catapults when Eagle was given a major refit in 1959.

ABOVE: HMS *Eagle* is seen here in her heyday. At the bow, a Supermarine Scimitar, an early model Blackburn Buccaneer and a Fairey Gannet can be seen, with another Scimitar behind them. By the island, the carrier's squadron of De Havilland Sea Vixen all-weather fighters are visible, while another sits on the waist catapult. At the stern, a single Westland Wessex helicopter can be seen.

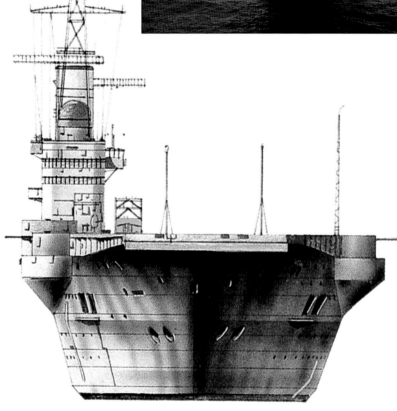

Eagle continued the practice of mounting heavy defensive armament. Sixteen 4.5-inch (114mm) guns were carried in eight turrets. The forward gun turrets were removed in the 1959 refit.

SPECIFICATIONS		Propulsion	4-shaft geared steam turbines
HMS *Eagle*		Speed	31.5 knots
		Armament	16 x 4.5-inch (114mm) guns, 32 x 40mm
			(1.6in) cannon; guns later removed and
Displacement	46,452 tonnes (45,720 tons) full load		replaced by Seacat surface-to-air missiles
Length	244.98m (803ft 9in) overall		
Beam	34.37m (112ft 9in)	Complement	2250
Draught	10.13m (33ft 3in)	Aircraft	82 (as built); 42 (1972)

United States should have a considerable nuclear capability, including carriers. He endorsed proposals for the development of a large aircraft carrier and bombers to carry nuclear weapons from her deck. This presented a difficulty, since early atomic weapons were large affairs that required suitably large aircraft to carry them. This resulted in an order for the North American AJ Savage, a three-engined aircraft, driven by two piston engines and a turbojet. The Savage would not enter service until 1949, so it was decided to improvize, using the Lockheed P2V Neptune, which had been

LEFT: These two photographs show the last-resort means of recovery for a carrier aircraft. In the first picture, a Royal Navy Sea Vixen approaches the deck, its starboard main undercarriage leg clearly not deployed. This would prevent successful engagement of the arrester hook, leaving the crew with no option but to eject. The nylon safety barrier has been deployed to catch the fighter. In the second photograph, the Sea Vixen has been stopped by the barrier, which has wrapped itself around the aircraft. The deck crew (safely out of the way while landing takes place) will soon emerge to disentangle the Sea Vixen from the barrier.

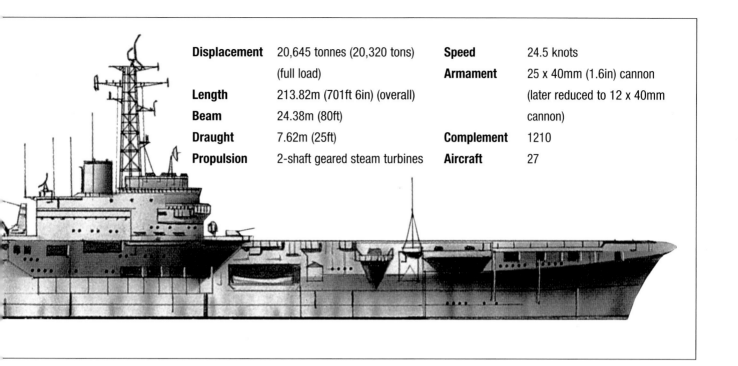

Displacement	20,645 tonnes (20,320 tons) (full load)	Speed	24.5 knots
Length	213.82m (701ft 6in) (overall)	Armament	25 x 40mm (1.6in) cannon (later reduced to 12 x 40mm cannon)
Beam	24.38m (80ft)		
Draught	7.62m (25ft)	Complement	1210
Propulsion	2-shaft geared steam turbines	Aircraft	27

begin hearings into national defence policy. Crommelin then revealed his involvement and was suspended from duty. His career was effectively over, and he was retired the following year (having been promoted to Rear-Admiral, which says a great deal about how the US Navy viewed his actions). The hearings were explosive, with a series of distinguished figures such as Chester Nimitz, Raymond Spruance and Ernest J. King testifying in favour of the carrier. Admiral Denfield was removed as Chief of Naval Operations on 1 November, bringing the 'revolt' to an end. More importantly, when the hearings were over, the House sided with the Navy, supporting the notion of the supercarrier. This did not lead to a change in policy – the *United States* was not reinstated, but it helped release funds to modernize the Essex-class carriers to better suit them for jet operations. A little over six months later, events in Korea would prove how useful carrier aviation could be.

BRITISH DEVELOPMENTS
While the carrier controversy gained momentum in the United States, the Royal Navy began considering some of the problems facing carrier aviation as jet aircraft became larger. The hydraulic catapult (strictly speaking an accelerator) was not designed to propel heavy aircraft from the carrier deck. It was often used to launch just those aircraft ranged at the front of the deck, to give them enough momentum to take off safely. The aircraft behind had enough room for free take-offs. This was simply not possible with jets, so a solution had to be found. A number of interesting

ideas were suggested, and the first was probably the most interesting of them all – and with hindsight the most impractical.

It is obvious that one of the major components in an aircraft, by both size and weight, is the undercarriage. This is particularly so for naval aircraft, which need sturdy landing gear to cope with pitching decks and the violence of arriving at some speed on a carrier deck. To some creative minds this immediately suggested that one of the ways to reduce the weight of jet aircraft would be to remove their undercarriage entirely, and provide a soft surface for them to make belly landings upon instead. A sprung landing surface – officially a 'flexible deck' but ever after known as the 'rubber deck' – was laid down at the Royal Aeronautical Establishment's (RAE) airfield at Farnborough, complete with conventional arrester gear. In December 1947, the inimitable Eric Brown made a landing attempt with a de Havilland Vampire. The Vampire was unmodified for the tests – Brown simply left the undercarriage in the 'up' position when he came in to land. The landing went badly. Brown encountered problems as the aircraft sank towards the ground more quickly than planned. The slow throttle response meant that he was unable to save the situation and the poor Vampire landed very hard. Although the aircraft was damaged, Eric Brown was not. In conjunction with the scientists at the RAE, he worked on modifications to the landing approach, and made a successful landing on the flexible deck in March 1948. This led to a similar deck being fitted to HMS *Warrior*, for trials in November. The trials were a success, but it soon became clear that the rubber deck was not the way forward. Aircraft with wheels were easily marshalled out of the way of aircraft coming into land, but those without needed to be hoisted from the deck. The wheeless aircraft could not land at conventional airfields if forced to divert as a result of bad weather, and launching the aircraft would be an interesting proposition, requiring some sort of trolley arrangement. Despite these problems, the idea was not abandoned immediately, and more thought was given to the issue. While this was done, an old idea was resurrected to deal with the question of launching heavy aircraft.

In 1936, C.C. Mitchell, an engineer at MacTaggart, Scott & Co, the suppliers of catapults to the Royal Navy, suggested using steam rather than hydraulics. The Navy were interested, but did not fund any tests. Mitchell was not deterred, and patented his design in 1938. During the war, he worked for the Royal Navy, and resumed his thoughts on steam catapults when it became clear that the Germans were using a similar idea to launch their V-1 flying bomb. Mitchell obtained captured German equipment for testing at Shoeburyness, and found that the Navy were more interested. The need for more powerful launch systems had begun to dawn. In 1946 the Admiralty decided to adopt slotted-cylinder steam catapults, and began the process of building a prototype. Before this could be tested on the maintenance carrier HMS *Perseus*, British carriers had joined those of the US Navy, off Korea.

KOREA

On 25 June 1950, North Korean forces invaded South Korea. President Truman immediately ordered air and sea forces to the region, under the command of General Douglas MacArthur, then leading the occupation forces in Japan. The US Seventh Fleet had only one carrier in the area at the time, the USS *Valley Forge*. The 'Happy Valley' had over 80 aircraft on board, including over 40 Corsairs and Skyraiders, and 30 recently introduced Grumman F9F Panther jet fighters. The Panther was a robust aircraft, armed with the customary four 20mm cannon, and could carry up to 1361kg (3000lb) of bombs and rockets (although a lesser amount was usually carried for operations from carriers). Although like earlier jets it did not having the range of piston-engined machines, the margin had been narrowed. *Valley Forge* sailed for Korea on 27 June, and was crucial to the response made by the United Nations. The USAF had a number of Lockheed F-80 Shooting Star fighter-bombers based in Japan, but their endurance did not permit them to loiter for long over the battlefield, which denied friendly troops the necessary air support. This problem could have been overcome by basing the F-80s in South Korea itself, but the airfields there were not suitable for the operation of jets. Carrier-based aircraft could thus increase the amount of support provided by remaining in the area much longer, and without any basing problems.

When *Valley Forge* arrived off the coast of Korea, she was accompanied by HMS *Triumph*, one of the Royal Navy's light fleet carriers. *Triumph* had a much smaller complement of 24 aircraft – Seafire Mk 47s of 800 Squadron and Firefly Mk 1s from 827 Squadron. The Seafire 47 was the final version of that aircraft, and suffered from the same problems as every other mark of Seafire. Although a delightful aircraft to fly,

BELOW: Flying from the USS *Oriskany* in November 1952, this Grumman F9F-2 Panther was flown by Lt (jg) J.D. Middleton. US Navy F9F-2s were credited with eight MiG kills during the Korean War.

Grumman F9F Panther

the Seafire was a nightmare to land. Pilots had little difficulty in getting the Seafire on deck, but they had more difficulty in ensuring that their aeroplane was in one piece by the time the landing was over. The flimsy airframe was prone to buckling and developing prominent creases: once these reached a certain number or prominence, the aircraft was grounded. In addition, the narrow tracked undercarriage made landing on a pitching deck a challenge – aircraft would nose forwards, shattering their propellers on the deck, scrape a wing as the aircraft toppled to one side, or smack inelegantly onto the deck as the undercarriage gave up under the strain. Happily, the Seafire 47 was extremely good at its prime task of fighting, so the pilots largely forgave these faults. The Firefly had no such problems – but the Mark 1s aboard *Triumph* were of World War II vintage (some may have fought in that conflict). Although this summed up some of the procurement problems facing the Royal Navy in the immediate aftermath of World War II, it does not detract from the skill with which the aircrews went about their business.

The two carriers launched their first strikes on 3 July. *Triumph* sent her aircraft against the airfield and bridges at Haeju,

causing considerable damage. *Valley Forge* flew off 16 Corsairs armed with rockets, a dozen bomb-laden Skyraiders and eight Panthers against the North Korean capital Pyongyang. The Panthers, although launched last, arrived over the target first by dint of their greater speed. They strafed the airfield, shot down two North Korean Yak-9 fighters, and caused general mayhem before the Corsairs and Skyraiders arrived to make their contribution to the destruction. Serious damage was inflicted, and all the aircraft returned safely. After 10 days of operations, *Triumph* withdrew to Japan for maintenance (and to replace some bent Seafires), leaving *Valley Forge* to continue with her tasks until she too left the area to replenish supplies. The two carriers soon returned to resume operations. The North Koreans were rampaging southwards, driving American and South Korean forces back, until they held only the southeastern corner of Korea, around Pusan. The need to support the defence of the Pusan perimeter dictated that the carriers would fly mainly close air support and interdiction operations, moving around the coast so as to reduce the transit time to and from the target for the aircraft. While *Valley Forge* and *Triumph* undertook these tasks, the carriers *Philippine Sea* and

ABOVE: Two Grumman F9F Panthers can be seen on the wooden deck of the Essex-class carrier USS *Leyte*. The large size of the Essex-class carriers meant that they were able to operate the new jet aircraft after the war.

USS *Forrestal*

Displacement	79,248 tonnes (78,000 tons) (deep load)	**Armament**	Three octuple Sea Sparrow SAM launchers (no reloads); 3 x 20mm (1.6in) Phalanx CIWS added later
Length	331m (1,086ft)		
Beam	39.5m (129ft 6in)		
Draught	11.3m (37ft)	**Complement**	2790 plus 2150 in air wing
Propulsion	4-shaft geared steam turbines	**Aircraft**	up to 90
Speed	33 knots		

Boxer disembarked their air groups to allow them to work up to operational readiness, and ferried large numbers of aircraft to Japan. The escort carrier *Badoeng Strait* embarked a small group of Marine Corps Corsairs to boost air strength, and *Philippine Sea* re-embarked her air group to join *Valley Forge*. *Boxer* raced across the Pacific, collected her air group from the US, and then raced back.

With three carriers now available and a fourth on its way, the allied forces enjoyed far more air support in their defence of the Pusan perimeter, which began to stabilize in early September. This prompted General MacArthur to propose his daring plan to snatch the initiative from the North Koreans, by landing well behind them at Inchon, while breaking out from Pusan. The amphibious assault at Inchon was risky, but MacArthur was willing to take the gamble. He had three large carriers (*Valley Forge*, *Philippine Sea* and *Boxer*) available, along with *Badoeng Strait* and *Sicily*, each with a

RIGHT: USS *Ticonderoga* is seen underway, demonstrating the dramatic enhancements made to the Essex-class carriers during the 1950s. *Ticonderoga* is carrying two A3D Skywarrior heavy attack aircraft, while the bow is crammed with a mix of Vought F8U Crusaders, Douglas A-1 Skyraiders, Douglas A4D Skyhawks and McDonnell F3H Demons.

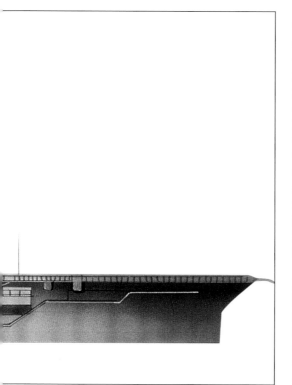

INCHON

The landings at Inchon began at 0633 on 15 September, and met with little initial resistance. Close air support enabled the Marines to secure their beachhead in the first 24 hours, while earlier interdiction operations against North Korean airfields had prompted the North Koreans to withdraw their aircraft further north, so they were unable to play much part in opposing the landings. North Korean forces were soon in full retreat. Those attacking Pusan found themselves trapped between two bodies of allied troops, with their supply lines cut. The allies drove towards Seoul, and liberated the South Korean capital.

On 25 September, *Triumph* left the area, having completed the first operational tour by an aircraft carrier in the Korean War. By this stage, she was down to one operational Seafire, while a number of her Fireflies were also suffering serviceability problems. She was replaced by HMS *Theseus*, which carried a similarly sized air group, but with different aircraft. Although *Theseus* still carried Fireflies, they were the later Mark 4; and instead of Seafires, Hawker Sea Furies were embarked. The Sea Fury was far more robust, and would go on to claim at least one enemy MiG-15 jet shot down.

It appeared that the Korean War would

single Marine Corps Corsair squadron aboard. Finally, HMS *Triumph* was also available, but was stationed off the east coast of Korea, staging a diversionary attack while the amphibious force made its way round the west coast, to position off Inchon.

BELOW: HMS *Ocean* heads for another patrol in Korean waters. The straight, axial deck is shown to advantage here, packed with a mixture of Hawker Sea Furies and Fairey Fireflies. *Ocean* and her fellow light fleet carriers were the only British carriers employed in the Korean conflict, and their air operations were highly successful.

McDonnell F2H Banshee

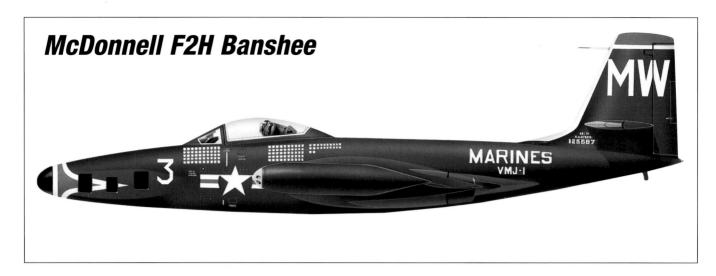

ABOVE: The McDonnell F2H Banshee proved an effective escort fighter during the Korean War. The aircraft shown above is a photo-recce variant, F2H-2P, of the US Marine Corps.

not last much beyond Christmas 1950, if that. By October, South Korea had been cleared of communist troops, and the Allies began advancing across the 38th Parallel in accordance with the directive to MacArthur that he was to destroy the North Korean army. With hindsight, it is easy to say that the thrust into North Korea went too far, because it worried China and eventually brought this formidable new enemy into the conflict, completely changing its nature. By the end of October 1950, the United Nations' forces had captured Pyongyang and were pursuing the remnants of the North Korean army toward the Yalu River. But they could see Chinese troops at the front line – a major new threat. On 8 November, carrier aircraft were tasked to bomb the 17 bridges across the Yalu River, across which the Chinese troops were being supplied. There were

problems. For political reasons, only the Korean ends of the bridges were to be attacked, and they were all heavily defended by anti-aircraft fire.

The first sorties were launched on 9 November, each strike being made up of between 24 and 40 aircraft. Panthers provided top cover, while a mixture of Corsairs and Skyraiders attacked the bridges. Between 9 and 21 November, nearly 600 sorties were flown against the Yalu bridges in the face of fierce flak and enemy aircraft. The enemy fighters were more formidable than before, since they included MiG-15s. On 9 November the commanding officer of VF-111, Lt Cdr William T. Amen (flying an F9F Panther), shot down a MiG-15, becoming the first navy pilot to make a jet vs. jet 'kill' in the war. Although the attacks were successful, the Chinese countered them by using pontoon bridges.

USS *Midway (1945)*

Displacement	55,882 tonnes (55,000 tons) (full load)	**Speed**	33 knots
		Armament	14 x 5-inch (127mm), 21 x
Length	295m (968ft) (overall)		quadruple 40mm (1.6in) and 82
Beam	34.44m (113ft)		x 20mm (0.8in) cannon
Draught	9.98m (32ft 9in)	**Complement**	Over 3000
Propulsion	4-shaft geared steam turbines	**Aircraft**	137

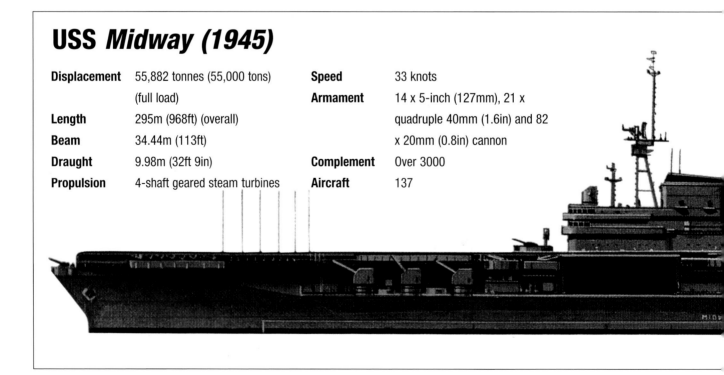

Shortly afterwards the river froze and supplies simply went straight across the ice. On 26 November, the Chinese mounted a huge ground offensive.

As the overwhelming numbers of the Chinese compelled the allies to retreat, carrier aircraft launched maximum-effort operations in support of their ground forces. As the nature of the war changed, it was clear that more carriers were needed. *Valley Forge* had returned home, leaving *Leyte* and *Philippine Sea. Sicily* had disembarked her Marine Corsair squadron and gone to Guam to take on board her AF–2 Guardians (to provide anti-submarine cover). As soon as she arrived in Japan, the AF-2s were sent ashore, and more Marine Corsairs replaced them. *Badoeng Strait* turned around and headed back toward the fray, while *Theseus*, replenishing in Hong Kong, made ready to return to the war zone at full speed. The USS *Bataan*, having ferried two wings of USAF fighters to Japan, took Corsairs aboard and reached Korean waters on 15 December 1950. She had been preceded by the *Princeton* (an Essex-class carrier that had been taken out of reserve), which arrived on 5 December, largely crewed by called-up reservists. Finally, *Valley Forge* was ordered to continue to the United States, send her air group ashore and take on that of *Boxer*, then return to Korea. By 1 January 1951, there were nine aircraft carriers off Korea.

The carriers launched wave after wave of close air support missions. On one of these, a Corsair piloted by Ensign Jesse L. Brown, the first coloured American naval pilot,

crash-landed near Chosin reservoir. Members of his squadron circled anxiously overhead, and saw that Brown was trapped in his burning aircraft. Lt Thomas L. Hudner deliberately crash-landed his aircraft nearby, unstrapped himself and ran to help Brown. He could not free Brown, and radioed for a helicopter to bring cutting tools. While he was waiting, Hudner packed snow around the cockpit of Brown's aircraft in a bid to keep the flames away. Although the helicopter arrived soon afterwards, Brown died before he could be released from his aircraft. Hudner was awarded the Congressional Medal of Honor, the first to be awarded to a member of the US Navy in the war.

THE INTERDICTION WAR

By late January 1951, the Chinese offensive began to lose momentum. The carriers continued interdiction missions, switching to more close support when a Chinese offensive began in late April. On 30 April Skyraiders from Princeton made an attack against the Hwachon dam to deny the Chinese the ability to control the water level to their advantage. The first attack holed a sluice gate, but did little other damage, so the next day, an attack was made by Skyraiders carrying torpedoes: six out of eight exploded, and destroyed the dam. As May progressed, the Allies began a counter-offensive, while the US Army asked for air attack to be used to prevent all communist supplies from reaching the battlefield. The plan became Operation Strangle, launched on 5 June 1951, but it was a disappointment. Although hundreds of trucks were

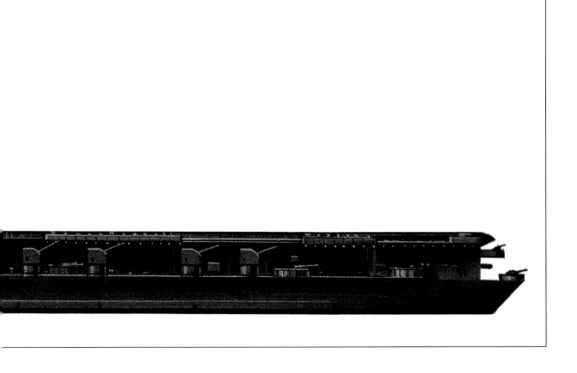

destroyed and bridges and roads cut, the
Chinese simply used manual labour instead
of the vehicles, and formed highly effective
repair teams to overcome the damage
inflicted by air attack. Once again, naval aircraft played a major part, including the new
McDonnell F2H Banshee, which joined
operations when USS *Essex* reached Korean
waters late in August. By this time, the war
was settling down to a stalemate, since
armistice negotiations had begun in July. It
would take another two years for them to
bear fruit.

STALEMATE
Once the negotiations had begun, the carriers settled down to a familiar routine of
interdiction and close air support where
required. This continued for the rest of the
war, with carriers spending some months
on operations before returning to the
United States as other carriers arrived to
replace them. Negotiations to end the conflict finally led to an armistice on 27 July
1953, but technically speaking the war still
continues, since no peace treaty has ever
been signed.

HMCS *Bonaventure*

Displacement	20,320 tonnes (20,000 tons) (deep load)	Propulsion	2-shaft geared steam turbines
		Speed	24.5 knots
Length	214.8m (704ft 8in) (overall)	Armament	4 x 3-inch (76mm) guns
Beam	24.38m (80ft)	Complement	1370
Draught	7.62m (25ft)	Aircraft	21–24

LESSONS FROM KOREA AND NEW DEVELOPMENTS

The Korean War clearly demonstrated the value of carriers. Congressional approval for modification to Essex-class carriers was readily forthcoming, with 15 of them being modernized for jet operations. This was greatly enhanced by use of the steam catapult, which had undergone successful testing in 1951, just in time to allow incorporation in the Essex-class modifications. Another British invention, the angled deck, was to have even greater importance. At a conference to discuss the flexible deck concept at the RAE at Bedford on 7 August 1951, Captain Dennis Campbell, RN suggested that the deck ought to be angled, allowing aircraft landing on it to be pulled off to one side, and others to land quickly behind. The conference concluded that angling the deck would be useful on conventional carriers as well. Axial-deck carriers had a major problem in that the deck park was at the bow, straight in the path of landing aircraft. This necessitated the installation of a safety barrier, so that an aircraft that missed all the arrester wires would crash into the barrier rather than the aircraft. This was fine in theory, but there were many cases where the aircraft jumped the barrier and ploughed into the deck park, often with fatal results. Angling the deck would allow aircraft to have a clear path; if they missed the wires, the pilot could simply open up the throttle and go round again. The significance of this idea was immense, and the angled deck was adopted with great alacrity. The Royal Navy was only able to angle its decks gradually, while the US Navy seized the opportunity to put the new type of deck (complete with the companion mirror landing aid that made the task of judging an approach much easier for pilots) onto the Essex conversions and into the plans for the new supercarriers that Congress had authorized. If the prospects for new carriers had been bleak before Korea, events there had changed matters decisively. The carrier had been shown to be a key tool in limited war; the next demonstration of this would be given by the British and the French as they disengaged from their colonial empires and fought one major action at Suez.

BRITISH AND FRENCH CARRIERS

In the aftermath of Korea, the Royal Navy's carrier fleet began to enjoy the benefits of new innovations, particularly the angled deck. By 1955, new carriers were beginning to enter service, supplanting the light fleet carriers. *Ark Royal, Centaur, Albion, Bulwark* and *Hermes* joined *Eagle* as the main components of the carrier force. Financial difficulties meant that the Illustrious-class ships were pensioned off, apart from HMS *Victorious*. *Victorious* suffered delays from being converted at a time of labour shortages and new innovations: she was not to emerge from the dockyard until 1958. Although the carrier fleet was modernized, there were a number of problems, not least the fact that only *Ark Royal* and *Eagle* would be large enough to operate later generations of aircraft. The introduction

of the excellent Hawker Sea Hawk and the de Havilland Sea Venom helped – both were capable machines (if outdated in comparison with American designs), and could be accommodated on board British carriers without difficulty.

The French Navy faced a major disadvantage with its carriers in that *Arromanches, Lafayette* and *Bois Belleau* were outdated. *Arromanches* had begun life as HMS *Colossus*, and had been loaned by Britain before being bought outright, while *Lafayette* and *Bois Belleau* were American Independence-class light carriers. They operated only piston-engined aircraft, mainly the F4U-7 variant of the Corsair, and the F6F Hellcat. In the context of the operations the carriers conducted this was not a major problem. Both types of aircraft proved extremely useful in the fight against the Viet Minh as France struggled (and failed) to retain her colonies in Indochina, and later in operations against Algerian rebels in a similarly fruitless effort to retain Algeria.

SUEZ

The French and British carriers faced their major test in response to the Suez crisis of 1956. Egypt's President, Gamal Abdel Nasser, decided to nationalize the Suez Canal to gather funds for the building of

the Aswan Dam. This decision was met with outrage in London and Paris, since the canal was controlled by Anglo-French shareholders. The French and British governments decided to use force to recover the canal, and colluded secretly with Israel: Israel would attack in the Sinai and Britain and France would call for a ceasefire. When the ceasefire was rejected (as it almost certainly would be) by Egypt, the French and British would intervene to 'protect' the Suez Canal. In fact, they would invade to retake the waterway, not just 'protect' it. As well as land-based aircraft, five aircraft carriers were assigned, as shown in the table opposite.

The Israelis began their assault on 29 October 1956, and the Anglo-French ultimatum for a ceasefire was duly ignored. On the 31st, the British and French began attacks, with aircraft based in Malta and Cyprus attacking Egyptian airfields. The next morning, the five carriers launched strikes of their own. The first attack was made by 40 Sea Hawks and Sea Venoms from the British carriers, again against airbases. The Corsairs from the French carriers, accompanied by Wyverns from *Eagle*, hunted for targets of opportunity. There was little opposition from Egyptian aircraft (Nasser decided to withdraw them from the battle area rather than risk losing his air force), and the greatest interference came from American carrier aircraft. President Eisenhower had been outraged by the invasion, and ordered the US Sixth Fleet to close up to Anglo-French naval forces as a means of applying visible pressure. It seems unlikely that Eisenhower would have risked destroying NATO by actually ordering his forces to conduct operations against Britain and France (after the crisis, America's lack of support led to many British shopkeepers refusing to serve American servicemen for a while).

The air assault continued for six days, before paratroops were dropped on Port Said on 5 November. The next day, the amphibious assault force arrived, and began landings. The Royal Navy introduced a new element to amphibious warfare, using Whirlwind and Sycamore helicopters from the decks of the carriers *Ocean* and *Theseus*. The air assault was successful, if rather ad hoc: the Whirlwinds could only carry five Marines, and the Sycamores only three. The Sycamores had to have their seats and doors removed to save weight, while the passengers sat on the floor. The passenger sitting in the middle had to hold on tight to the other two to ensure they did not fall out.

Opposition from the rest of the world,

Aircraft Carrier	Air Group
HMS *Eagle*	17 Sea Venom (all-weather fighter-bomber); 24 Sea Hawk (fighter-bomber); 9 Wyvern (strike); 4 Skyraider (Airborne Early Warning); 2 Dragonfly helicopters
HMS *Albion*	8 Sea Venom; 19 Sea Hawk; 2 Skyraider; 2 Dragonfly
HMS *Bulwark*	30 Sea Hawk; 2 Avenger (anti-submarine); 2 Dragonfly
FNS *Arromanches*	14 F4U-7 Corsair; 5 Avenger; 2 HUP-2 helicopters
FNS *Lafayette*	22 F4U-7 Corsair; 2 HUP-2

most notably America, led to the Suez operation being called off at midnight on 7 November 1956. It was a political disaster, but once again demonstrated the utility of carriers. Their presence close to the operational area enabled them to generate a large number of sorties, in contrast to the aircraft based on Malta and Cyprus. The campaign showed that aircraft carriers and land-based aircraft complemented one another perfectly: it also demonstrated that larger carriers with larger air groups were more effective. This was something that the Americans already appreciated, and were acting on with the development of their 'supercarriers'. The first demonstration of what these carriers could do was provided in the long-running and bitter conflict in Vietnam.

BELOW: The powerful Westland Wyvern, which operated from HMS *Eagle* during the Suez crisis of 1956, was the only turboprop-powered naval fighter ever to see operational service.

CHAPTER SIX

VIETNAM: CARRIER COMBAT

American involvement in Vietnam began even before the French had given the country independence. Anxious to prevent communism from spreading throughout Southeast Asia, President Eisenhower provided limited support to the French as they sought to re-establish control over Indochina.

WHEN THE OUTPOST at Dien Bien Phu was besieged by the Viet Minh, the French appealed to the Americans for air support from the carriers operating in the South China Sea. It was politically impossible for the Americans to agree, and on 7 May 1954, Dien Bien Phu fell. Peace negotiations between the French and the Viet Minh took place at Geneva later that year. Vietnam was partitioned, with the North and South being separated

LEFT: Although this photograph was taken just after the conflict, it gives a good idea of the nature of carrier operations and the make-up of an air wing towards the end of the Vietnam War. A Grumman EA-6B Prowler sits on the catapult of the USS *John F. Kennedy*, with A-6 Intruders, an E-2 Hawkeye and A-7 Corsairs also visible.

BELOW: A Vought F-8 Crusader from VF-33 'Tarsiers' sits on the deck of USS *Enterprise*. The Crusader was hugely popular with its pilots, who claimed 'when you're out of F-8s, you're out of fighters'. The Crusader was highly prized for having guns, while the Phantom was forced to rely upon missiles.

by a Demilitarized Zone (DMZ) at the 17th Parallel. The partition was meant to be brief, ending once elections had been held. The Americans were all too aware that the leader of the Viet Minh, Ho Chi Minh, was likely to win, and this appeared to present a problem. Ho was thought to be a Marxist, and the prospect of allowing a communist to take control of all Vietnam was too much for the Americans, who prevented the elections from taking place. Historians have long since debated whether or not the American view of Ho was correct – he was above all else a nationalist. What is more, he had asked the Americans for help in removing French colonialism at the end of the Second World War. The intriguing notion that American

assistance to Ho could have led to a Vietnam well disposed to the United States remains just a notion, however. From the mid-1950s, America and North Vietnam became implacably opposed.

TONKIN GULF

American aircraft carriers began their involvement in the conflict in the early 1960s, as reconnaissance aircraft gathered information about North Vietnamese activity, particularly in support of guerrillas around the DMZ. By 1964, carriers and other naval units were patrolling the Tonkin Gulf on a regular basis as they sought to gather intelligence and provide support to operations against the communists. Carrier air-

LEFT: Three A-4E Skyhawks on the deck of the USS Ranger. Aircraft numbers 204 and 206 are carrying AGM-45 Shrike anti-radiation missiles for attacks against North Vietnamese SAM sites. These attacks, code-named 'Iron Hand', were amongst the most dangerous of the war as pilots dueled against enemy anti-aircraft artillery and missiles.

craft provided photographic intelligence, and surface units conducted electronic eavesdropping missions as part of what was known as the Desoto Patrol. On 2 August 1964, the destroyer USS *Maddox* was in the middle of such a patrol when she picked up three high-speed surface contacts on her radar, heading towards her. *Maddox* identified these as being North Vietnamese PT torpedo boats, and began to take evasive action. As the PT boats came within range, a warning shot was fired at them, but they continued, two of them launching torpedoes. *Maddox* evaded the torpedoes and returned fire. At the same time, four Vought F-8 Crusader fighter aircraft on routine training flights from the carrier *Ticonderoga* were sent to assist. Although the Crusader was designed as a fighter, it could also carry a variety of ground-attack weapons. It so happened that the Crusaders were carrying 127mm (5-inch) Zuni rockets, which came in useful. They strafed the PT boats with their 20mm (0.8in) cannon, and launched a number of rockets as the torpedo boats headed back for North Vietnam. One of the boats was reported sunk.

The United States chose not to respond directly to the attack, but reinforcements were sent to the area in the form of the carrier *Constellation* and the destroyer *Turner Joy*. Two nights later, the radar operators on *Turner Joy* and *Maddox* reported surface radar contacts approaching from the east. The destroyers increased their speed, but the contacts resolutely maintained pursuit of the two ships. When the contacts were estimated to be within 5485m (6000 yards) of *Maddox*, the destroyers opened fire with their main armament. Air support was dispatched, and over the next four hours, torpedo tracks were reported in close proximity to the destroyers. It appeared that the North Vietnamese had again attempted to attack shipping in international waters, but the second contact remains shrouded in confusion: the aircraft sent from *Ticonderoga* were directed towards the enemy, but saw nothing. There is now some suspicion that the radar contacts were spurious returns caused by atmospherics, which led to understandably tense crews misinterpreting them – the torpedo tracks being caused by nerves and imagination rather than real torpedoes. But these suspicions are by no means universally accepted. Whether the second attack took place or not, President Johnson authorized a series of reprisal raids against the PT boats' bases: 64 sorties from *Constellation* and *Ticonderoga* targeted five bases. The attack force was made up of a mixture of venerable Skyraiders, Douglas A-4 Skyhawks and more Crusaders. The attacks succeeded in destroying a number of PT boats and many of their associated shore facilities. Two American aircraft were lost: the pilot of one Skyraider was killed, and Lt (junior grade) Everett Alvarez ejected from his Skyhawk and was captured. He remained a prisoner of war for the next eight and a half years. On the same day, President Johnson received support for his Vietnam policy from Congress, which passed the Tonkin Gulf Resolution, giving Johnson immense executive powers to conduct the war against

RIGHT: An A-1E Skyraider drops napalm against Viet Cong targets in South Vietnam. The Skyraider proved to be an immensely versatile attack weapon during the conflict, and was employed by both the US Navy and the US Air Force. Although the Navy withdrew its last attack Skyraider in 1968, the air force continued to use the aircraft until the end of the war.

communism in Vietnam. As is well known, these powers led to 'micromanagement' of the war, with the American armed forces operating in circumstances where political expediency overrode military objectives. For example, some key targets were denied to American air attack, including the proliferation of Surface to Air Missile (SAM) sites developed as the war went on.

THE CARRIER COMMITMENT

In September 1964, USS *Ranger* was sent to bolster the carrier force in the Tonkin Gulf, but there was little action for the carriers for the remainder of the year. This changed in February 1965, when guerrillas attacked the US military advisors' compound at Pleiku, killing nine men and wounding 75 others, as well as destroying a number of helicopters. The American response was to launch an attack by over 100 aircraft against targets just north of the DMZ, under the codename 'Flaming Dart One'. Aircraft from USS *Coral Sea, Hancock* and *Ranger* formed the largest strike force launched from US carriers since the Korean War. *Ranger*'s aircraft were unable to reach their target, but those from *Hancock* and *Coral Sea* inflicted serious damage.

ROLLING THUNDER

The policy of only launching retaliatory strikes against North Vietnam was changed in March 1965, as a sustained bombing campaign, Rolling Thunder. These strikes marked an enormous intensification in the effort made by American carriers. Two geographic points off the coast of Vietnam were used as stations for carriers. North of the DMZ, in Tonkin Gulf, Yankee Station was established, enabling strikes to be undertaken against targets in North Vietnam. Off the south of Vietnam, Dixie Station was set up, giving carrier aircraft the ability to attack targets south of the DMZ, as well as in Cambodia. As the war intensified, carriers arriving in the war zone would be sent to gain experience of air operations from Dixie Station, developing their weapon-delivery skills in a relatively benign operating environment, before heading to Yankee Station where they would conduct operations in the far more hostile conditions to be encountered over North Vietnam.

The first Rolling Thunder bombing mission was launched by aircraft from *Coral Sea* and *Hancock*. Skyhawks and Skyraiders, accompanied by a few A-3D Skywarriors, attacked a variety of targets. Despite the professionalism of the aircrews, Rolling Thunder was fatally flawed by political micromanagement of the list of permissible targets. This meant that a number of key objectives were not attacked for political reasons. In addition, the North Vietnamese substantially increased their air defences with the assistance of the Soviet Union and China. The most sophisticated threat came from surface-to-air missiles (SAMs), but these were not as lethal as the staggering amount of anti-aircraft artillery possessed by the North Vietnamese. This was not all, since the North Vietnamese population was liberally equipped with small arms. Although low-tech, it only took one lucky shot with a rifle to inflict serious damage on a low-flying aircraft. Additional defences came in the form of combat aircraft, most notably the MiG-17 and MiG-21.

To meet these defences, the US Navy evolved what became known as the Alpha Strike. This was a group or package of carrier aircraft, with different elements of the package assigned to different tasks. While the main body of the package would be tasked with attacking a particular target, the other aircraft in the strike would provide support. Some would be detailed for flak-suppression duty, using cluster bombs or rockets, while fighters would conduct combat air patrols (CAP) to protect against the threat of enemy aircraft. The package would be tightly coordinated, and arrived over the target with the intention of saturating the defences by sheer weight of numbers. The coordination also allowed the use of electronic countermeasures (ECM) against enemy fire-control radars (the close proximity of aircraft increasing the jamming power). The Alpha strike thus became the main element of carrier warfare against North Vietnam. The missions were never easy, and the multiplicity of threats from the enemy increased as time went on.

THE AIRCRAFT

When the Americans began the conflict in Vietnam, there were four major types of combat aircraft aboard the carriers. Attack missions were largely in the hands of the pilots of A-4 Skyhawks and veteran A-1 Skyraiders. They were accompanied by A-3 Skywarriors on some carriers, although the Skywarrior – affectionately known as 'the whale' – was difficult to operate from the smaller carriers. Designed to carry nuclear weapons, the A-3 was a large aircraft, and displaced a number of the smaller machines from the deck. Within two years, however, the Skywarriors were conducting fewer attack missions, being used instead for vital support tasks like refuelling and electronic warfare. The first Skyhawks to see combat were the A-4C model, which had only three underwing pylons to mount their ordnance. When underwing fuel tanks were carried, this meant that the Skyhawk might be left with just one pylon for carrying bombs. Although use of a multiple ejector rack could increase the number of bombs carried, it was not an ideal solution: the A-4E model was soon introduced with two extra ordnance stations to enhance flexibility.

Two types of fighter aircraft were embarked aboard the American carriers. These were the Vought F-8 Crusader and the McDonnell Douglas F-4 Phantom. Both aircraft were the product of 1950s design, but varied enormously. The Crusader was a single-seater air-superiority fighter, much loved by its pilots. The F-8 carried four 20mm (0.8in) cannon and up to four AIM-9 Sidewinder infra-red (IR) homing missiles mounted on fuselage pylons. The aircraft could also carry a variety of ground attack ordnance on two underwing stations, while the Sidewinder rails could be replaced with special launchers for 127mm (5-inch) Zuni

BELOW: The Skyraider was among the most hardworking and versatile aircraft to be deployed over Vietnam. This A1-H Skyraider was the personal mount of Commander Bill Phillips during his time as the head of VA-52 aboard USS *Ticonderoga* between 1964 and 1966.

Douglas A1-H Skyraider

In addition to her 20mm (0.8in) cannon, *Lexington* carried up to sixty 40mm (1.6in) cannon, most in quadruple mountings as shown here. The number of 40mm (1.6in) guns was raised after the 20mm (0.8in) cannons proved less effective than hoped against *kamikaze* attacks.

…rican carriers in the …fic faced a notable air …t, particularly after the …nese began *kamikaze* …ions. Up to eighty …m (0.8in) cannon were …l to *Lexington* and other …x-class ships to provide …firing, last-ditch anti-…aft weapons.

The American reliance upon sizeable deck parks as well as a hangar was in contrast with the Royal Navy's initial policy that a carrier's complement of aircraft was the number that could be fitted into the carrier.

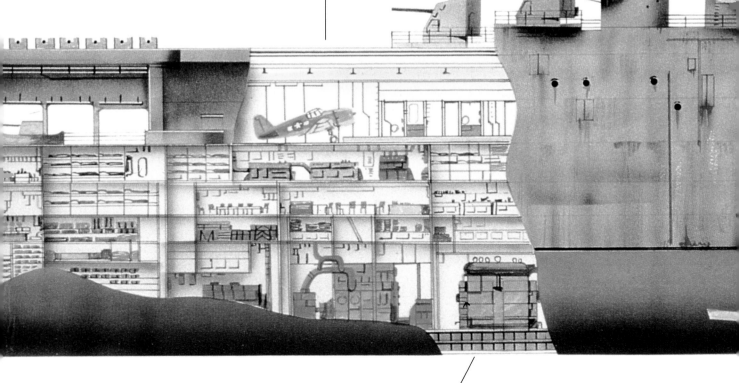

The Essex-class ships were powered by four geared steam turbines, employing eight Babcock & Wilson boilers.

USS *Lexington*

The second carrier to bear the name, *Lexington* was the longest-serving of America's World War II carriers. After distinguished service in the Pacific, *Lexington* was rebuilt and became an anti-submarine carrier. She was then employed for deck landing training, finally retiring in 1992.

Lexington, in common with other Essex-class carriers, could carry over 100 aircraft. Well suited to post-war operations, their size meant that they could accommodate the new generation of carrier aircraft.

The *Lexington* had four shafts, driven by her steam turbines. These produced over 111MW (150,000 shp), and gave the ship the ability to reach 61km/h (33 knots).

rocket projectiles. The F-8s that had supported the *Maddox* in the Tonkin Gulf incident had been so equipped on the night of that action. The Phantom, on the other hand, was a large, twin-engined, two-seat interceptor, capable of twice the speed of sound. The Phantom was too large for operation from the Essex-class carriers, and was confined to the decks of the Midways and the supercarriers (USS *Forrestal* onwards). Unlike the Crusader, the Phantom did not carry a gun, but relied entirely upon missiles. The chief weapon (designed to destroy attacking aircraft well before they came within range of the fleet) was the radar-guided AIM-7 Sparrow. The Sparrow used semi-active radar homing (SARH) to give a beyond visual range capability. The theory was that the enemy would be located on the Phantom's powerful radar, and a missile (or more than one) would be fired and guided to the target by the radar, destroying the target before the Phantom's crew saw it. The practice was rather different. Political constraints meant that aircrew were usually required to make a positive visual identification of their target before engaging it, thus reducing the effectiveness of the weapon system. In combat, the Sparrow suffered from a number of reliability problems, and

BELOW: An F-4J Phantom of VF-102 leaves the catapult of the USS *America* during the carrier's 1968 cruise off Vietnam. The Phantom was an excellent interceptor and attack aircraft, but found itself at a disadvantage in close-in air-to-air combat, as it was less manoeuvrable than North Vietnamese MiGs.

did not work as well as had been hoped. This was largely because it was being fired in an entirely different set of circumstances to those for which it had been designed. Over the oceans, against large Soviet bombers, the Sparrow would have stood a good chance of success. Against nimble North Vietnamese fighters that could break radar lock or out-manoeuvre the missile, the Sparrow fared less well. Although the Phantom could also rely upon four Sidewinders, it was at a disadvantage in that it was far less manoeuvrable than the North Vietnamese MiGs. Furthermore, the US Navy (just like the US Air Force) had not provided much training for air-to-air combat for the Phantom crews because this had not been foreseen as their role. This omission would later become a major cause for concern.

FIRST KILLS

While the Phantom may have been at a disadvantage against the smaller North Vietnamese aircraft, it scored the first air-to-air victories for the US Navy fighter force. The first encounter was not against the North Vietnamese, however, but the Chinese. Two F-4Bs from the USS *Ranger* were conducting a CAP on 9 April 1965, and went close enough to China to provoke a

McDonnell Douglas F-4 Phantom II

response by MiG-17s. One of the Chinese aircraft was shot down, but one of the Phantoms also failed to return. The Chinese did not claim the victory, but reported that the aircraft had been hit by a missile fired by the other Phantom. After this inauspicious start, on 17 June F-4s from USS *Midway* ran into two North Vietnamese MiG-17s. The Phantom crews (Cdr Louis Page and Lt John C. Smith, and Lt Dave Batson and Lt Cdr Robert Doremus) promptly shot them down and returned to the carrier. *Midway* was carrying a mixed fighter force at the time: VF-21, with its Phantoms, was accompanied by VF-111 with F-8Ds. It is interesting to speculate how the Crusader pilots (usually dismissive of the Phantom for its lack of

aesthetic appeal, lack of guns and lack of manoeuvrability) responded to this success.

Three days later, an even more spectacular 'kill' was achieved. Two Skyraiders, flown by Lts Charlie Hartman and Clint Johnson, were attacked by enemy MiGs. The MiGs made the fatal mistake of trying to turn with the Skyraiders, which were far more manoeuvrable than any jet. The two Skyraiders poured 20mm cannon fire into one of the MiGs, and it went down in flames. This marked the last victory scored by carrier-based aircraft until 1966.

CARRIER AIR WINGS

To conduct the array of missions demanded, the aircraft carriers deployed to Vietnam

ABOVE: The McDonnell F-4 Phantom II was first deployed aboard USS *Enterprise* in 1962. The aircraft pictured above made four deployments to the Gulf of Tonkin between 1964 and 1969 aboard USS *Constellation*.

LEFT: Three A-4E Skyhawks from attack squadron VA-56 formate for the camera in the early part of the Vietnam War. The white shape behind the pilots' heads is a nuclear flash screen, designed to protect pilot vision from the blinding light of a nuclear detonation. This was installed because the A-4's prime initial task was as a nuclear weapons carrier. As Vietnam progressed and the Skyhawk became involved in conventional warfare, the screens were removed.

SPECIFICATIONS

USS *Lexington*

Displacement	35,438 tonnes (34,880 tons) full load
Length	265.8m (872ft) overall
Beam	28.4m (93ft)
Draught	7.01m (23ft)

Propulsion	4-shaft geared steam turbines
Speed	32.7 knots
Armament	12 x 5-inch (127mm) guns; 32 x 40mm (1.6in) and 46 x 20mm (0.8in) cannon
Complement	2682
Aircraft	60–70

Lexington had three aircraft lifts. One of these was mounted at the deck edge to port, while the others were in the centre of the flight deck. The forward lift, indicated here, brought the aircraft out between the hydraulic catapults.

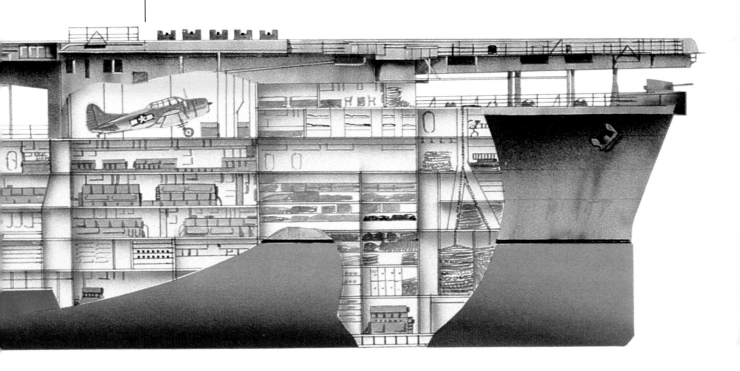

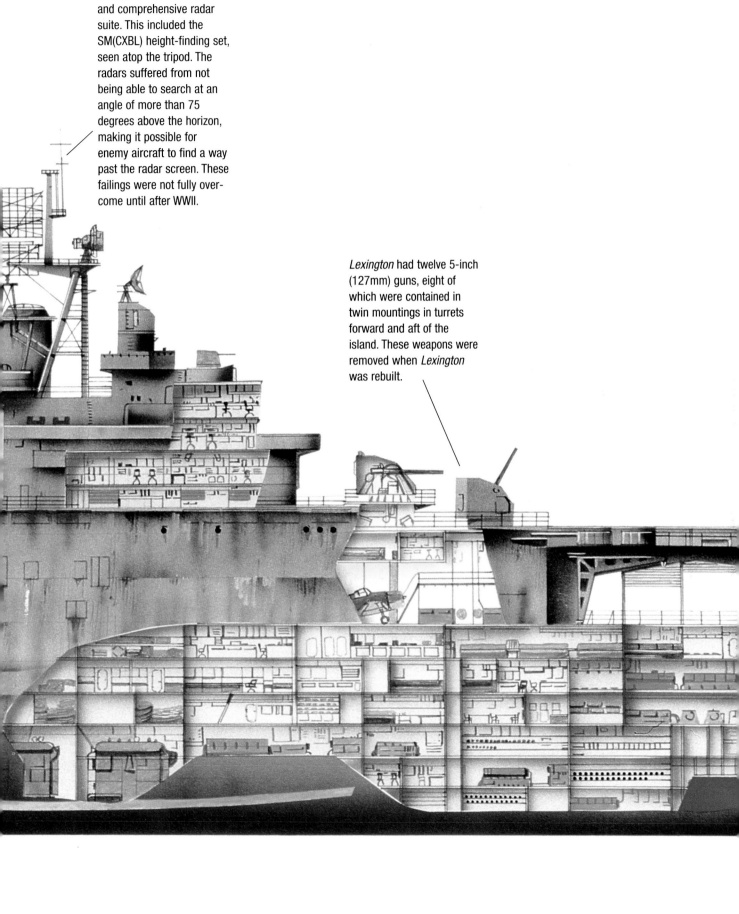

Lexington had a complex and comprehensive radar suite. This included the SM(CXBL) height-finding set, seen atop the tripod. The radars suffered from not being able to search at an angle of more than 75 degrees above the horizon, making it possible for enemy aircraft to find a way past the radar screen. These failings were not fully over-come until after WWII.

Lexington had twelve 5-inch (127mm) guns, eight of which were contained in twin mountings in turrets forward and aft of the island. These weapons were removed when Lexington was rebuilt.

RIGHT: An RA-5C Vigilante prepares for take-off. The Vigilante began life as a nuclear bomber, but problems with the unique weapon launching system (the bomb was ejected from between the jet pipes) meant that the 'Vigi' was soon re-roled into a reconnaissance aircraft par excellence.

carried an impressive variety of aircraft. The Essex–class vessels fell into two categories: the CVA (attack) and CVS (anti-submarine). The anti-submarine carriers usually carried a mixture of S-2 Trackers and helicopters, also embarking some A-4s for attack missions and to provide some fighter cover (the A-4 was more than adequate for this task, even though this was not its primary role). The attack carriers carried a wider range of aircraft. The air wing carried by the USS *Oriskany* (the most updated Essex) on her tour in 1966 gives a representative example of the nature of the air wing on the smaller decks. *Oriskany* had two fighter squadrons

with F-8s, and three attack squadrons (two with Skyhawks and one with Skyraiders). A detachment from VAH-4 operated a few Skywarriors in the heavy attack role, and a detachment from VAP-61 – which was not embarked for the whole cruise – flew some RA-3s on photo-reconnaissance tasks. Another detachment flew RF-8 Crusaders, again for reconnaissance work, and the air wing was completed by a detachment of E-1 Tracer airborne early warning aircraft and a few UH-2 helicopters for search and rescue duty. This sort of air wing could comprise up to 70 aircraft, although this meant that the carrier was very crowded. The

North American RA-5C Vigilante

401

120

Midways carried around 75 aircraft (and could operate the Phantom), while the supercarriers carried anything up to 90 aircraft. On her first cruise to Vietnam, the USS *Enterprise* carried one of the largest air wings seen aboard a carrier operating jets. As well as no fewer than four Skyhawk squadrons, *Enterprise* carried two squadrons of Phantoms and around a dozen Skywarriors. She also embarked the customary mix of helicopters and airborne early-warning aircraft as well as a squadron (RVAH-7) flying the formidable RA-5C Vigilante. Designed as a supersonic nuclear bomber, the Vigilante found its forte as a reconnaissance aircraft, operating in squadrons of six to eight aircraft. As the war progressed, the aircraft on board the carriers changed as new types entered service. Although these increased the capability offered by the carrier air wings, the new types did not help to make the prosecution of the war easier, since the strategy imposed from Washington was a serious impediment to success.

PROBLEMS

The American carrier force faced several practical difficulties in 1965, in addition to the political restrictions they had to deal with. The pace of operations made it clear that there were going to be shortages of aircrew, aircraft for them to fly and weapons for them to fire or drop. This could be addressed by increasing the throughput of trainee pilots and increased production by the defence industry, although aircraft such as the Skyraider were out of production and would have to be replaced by new types if

their numbers dwindled. The major problem came in the provision of carriers for operations off Vietnam. Several of the Essex-class vessels were nearing the end of their operational lives or needed refitting: some of the newer carriers also needed overhauling. *Midway*, for example, completed her 1965 deployment and went into dock for a refit that lasted until 1970. It was obvious that the Pacific Fleet would not be able to provide enough carriers for the war unless it was to deploy its assets on a more regular basis (changing the crew and embarked squadrons each time). But this risked that the lack of maintenance that would result from increased deployments would reduce the effectiveness of the ships and, eventually, their service lives. The solution was to decree that carriers assigned to the Atlantic fleet should conduct operations off Vietnam as well, and this began with the deployment of the USS *Independence* in June 1965. *Enterprise* was reassigned to the Pacific Fleet in 1966 when she returned from her cruise. Five other Atlantic fleet carriers were temporarily redeployed to Vietnam to offset some of the shortages that would otherwise have resulted. There was little doubt that naval aircraft made a major contribution to Rolling Thunder and there was a strong need to get as many as possible operating in the area.

BOMBING PAUSES AND ESCALATION

Rolling Thunder continued throughout 1965, with further developments in the command and control arrangements affecting the area of operations for the carriers. To permit effective coordination of forces,

LEFT: Flying at near supersonic speeds, the RA-5C was difficult to intercept, and produced some of the most accurate reconnaissance information ever obtained: on one practice mission, a Vigilante's sensors proved that an American football field was a few feet too short. The aircraft was retired in 1979, and the US Navy has still not found a reconnaissance system of similar capability.

USS *Oriskany*

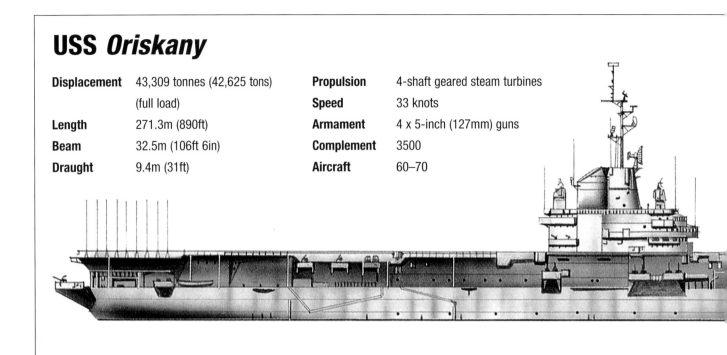

Displacement	43,309 tonnes (42,625 tons) (full load)	**Propulsion**	4-shaft geared steam turbines
Length	271.3m (890ft)	**Speed**	33 knots
Beam	32.5m (106ft 6in)	**Armament**	4 x 5-inch (127mm) guns
Draught	9.4m (31ft)	**Complement**	3500
		Aircraft	60–70

North Vietnam was divided into 'Route Packages' (or 'Route Pacs') designated by Roman numerals. Route Package VI was subdivided into Route Pacs VIA and VIB. The carriers had responsibility for targets in Route Pacs II, III, IV and VIB. These included targets in the urban areas of Dong Hoi, Haiphong and Nam Gai. Although this offered a means of coordination, it was later regarded as being ineffective (being rejected as a command arrangement in the Gulf War of 1990). The most serious problem with the Route Pacs concerned targeting permissions from Washington. Hanoi was 'off-limits' for attack, along with Haiphong. The North Vietnamese were not slow to exploit this, placing crucial facilities within these restricted areas, safe from attack.

President Johnson ordered a halt to Rolling Thunder for Christmas 1965, but the campaign resumed in late January 1966. The implementation of bombing pauses was extremely controversial, since it gave the North Vietnamese the opportunity to repair damage and re-equip their forces. There is little doubt that the defences were stronger when operations resumed. When Johnson gave the order for bombing to restart, USS *Enterprise, Kitty Hawk* and *Hancock* were deployed 'on the line' as part of Task Force 77. They were sent against communications targets, and encountered formidable anti-aircraft fire, although SAMs and enemy aircraft were conspicuous by their general absence. This changed dramatically in April, as strikes were sent against an increased range of targets in Route Pacs IV and VIB, including bridges and targets of opportunity on major

lines of communication. The MiG threat escalated, and the fighters became particularly busy. On 12 June 1966, the F-8 enjoyed its first success against a MiG.

VF-211, led on this mission by its commanding officer, Cdr Harold L. Marr, had provided fighter cover for an attack by Skyhawks against targets north of Haiphong. Just after the strike group left the target, Lt (jg) Phil Vampatella called a 'Tally Ho' on MiGs approaching the American aircraft. Marr looked in the direction Vampatella called, and saw four MiG-17s about a mile and a half away. He pulled into a hard turn, and fired a short burst with his cannon, more, as he said later, to improve his morale than for any other purpose. A turning battle developed, and Marr took another shot at a MiG, but missed again. As the fight descended, Marr found himself a thousand feet above one of the MiGs. He fired a Sidewinder, but under the high g-forces the missile broke lock, and flew into the ground. The MiG pilot saw his chance to escape, and tried to disengage. Marr selected afterburner to close the distance, and rolled in behind the MiG. At around half-a-mile range, Marr fired his second and last Sidewinder. The missile flew straight and true, and sliced through the MiG's tail and starboard wing, sending it cartwheeling into the ground. Marr reversed course, 'plugged in' his afterburner again, and departed the area at high speed. Nine days later, Phil Vampatella shot down a MiG-17 of his own. Although his aircraft had been seriously damaged and was losing fuel, when a MiG was sighted Vampatella immediately sought

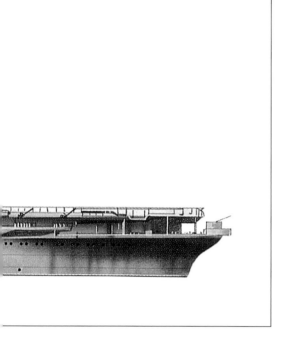

renewed the rivalry between the Crusader and Phantom pilots.

Although it attracted much attention, fighting MiGs was not the most important task faced by carrier aircrews. The policy of escalating the bombing against North Vietnam in an attempt to coerce the Hanoi government into withdrawing support for the Viet Cong guerrillas in the South saw an increase in effort. On 23 June, Washington finally granted permission for petroleum facilities to be attacked: before any strikes could be mounted, though, the news was leaked to the press and the attacks were called off. After some indecision, authority for the strikes was granted once more, and the first attack against petroleum and oil facilities was launched on 29 June 1966, when targets near Haiphong were attacked. Skyhawks from *Ranger* dropped over 19 tons of ordnance on the facility, leaving it in a burning heap.

This success was rather offset by the measures the North Vietnamese were able to take to offset the effects of attacks on petrol and oil targets. The President had been advised that a combined air campaign against transport targets and petrol facilities would cause serious difficulties for the North Vietnamese, but this did not meet with political approval. The North

BELOW: The aftermath of the tragic fire aboard USS *Forrestal*. The grotesque and barely recognizable remains of aircraft destroyed in the inferno can be seen – the nose of an A-7 can be made out to the bottom right of the picture. In all, 134 men died in the fire and the efforts to put it out, after a freak accident when a Zuni rocket, heated by exhaust gases, ignited and slammed into parked aircraft nearby. The fire illustrated just one of the multitude of hazards faced by the crews on a carrier.

to engage it. After a high-speed engagement just above tree-top level, Vampatella dispatched the MiG with a Sidewinder, before heading back to his carrier (the *Hancock*) where he made a safe landing. The increase in the likelihood of air-to-air combat was good for the morale of the F-8 pilots and

Vietnamese correctly read the warning signs, and began construction of underground storage facilities in case the Americans should choose to target their fuel supplies. In addition, since the Americans were doing nothing to prevent supplies from reaching North Vietnam (suggestions that Haiphong harbour be mined had been overruled), the overall effect of the raids was dramatically reduced. The dispersed underground storage facilities, coupled with supply from overseas, meant that the North Vietnamese were able to withstand the assault against their fuel supplies.

The year 1966 ended badly for the American carriers, with a disastrous fire aboard *Oriskany*. As parachute flares were being stowed on 26 October, one of them went off. The intense heat generated started a fire, which set off ordnance. The fire rapidly spread to the hangar deck and into the living spaces of the ship, setting off yet more bombs, rockets and ammunition. Skilful damage control and the courage of the crew brought the fire under control, but at a cost. At the end of the firefighting, 44 men had died. Many aircraft were written off. *Oriskany* limped to Subic Bay in the Philippines for temporary repairs, and then headed back to her home port for more extensive refitting. Within seven months, *Oriskany* was ready for another cruise. Tragically, this was not the last fire to affect the carrier fleet during the Vietnam War.

1967

The bombing campaign continued in 1967, and was significant for several reasons. The threat from North Vietnamese SAMs had been addressed, and a mixture of improved electronic jamming and new weapons had been introduced in an attempt to offset the threat. The US Air Force responded by introducing specialist aircraft – the famed 'Wild Weasels' – modified from F-105 Thunderchief strike aircraft. The Wild Weasels were packed with electronic gear to locate enemy radar emissions, and carried a nasty surprise for the enemy radar operators. A rapid development programme led to the introduction of Anti-Radiation Missiles (ARMs) such as the AGM-45 Shrike and, later, the AGM-72 Standard ARM, with which the Weasels could destroy enemy SAM radars. The US Navy adopted a similar approach, although it did not initially introduce highly specialized aircraft, instead equipping standard squadron aircraft (notably Skyhawks) with improved ECM and the ability to launch Shrikes: these aircraft could fly what were known as 'Iron Hand' anti-SAM missions one day, and then be used to tote bombs against a target the next. Pilots did not necessarily have to destroy the enemy radars. Forcing them to shut down for fear of attack by ARMs was almost as good, since it meant that the SAMs could not be guided to their targets. On an Iron Hand flight on 20 April 1967, Lt Cdr Michael J. Estocin, flying from *Ticonderoga*, neutralized three SAM sites before his Skyhawk was badly damaged while attacking a fourth. Six days later, Estocin undertook a further Iron Hand sortie in a strike against Haiphong. Estocin's aircraft was hit and set on fire. Undaunted, Estocin retained control of the Skyhawk and fired his Shrikes before his aircraft was engulfed in the fireball from another exploding SAM. The aircraft went out of control, but Estocin recovered it and radioed that he was heading out to sea. Before he could cross the coast, the Skyhawk went into an uncontrollable series of rolls, and disappeared inverted into low-

BELOW: The Grumman A-6 Intruder was designed from the outset as a carrier-borne all-weather strike aircraft. During the Vietnam War the A-6 carried out round-the-clock bombing missions that no other aircraft was capable of undertaking until the introduction of the General Dynamics F-111 in 1967.

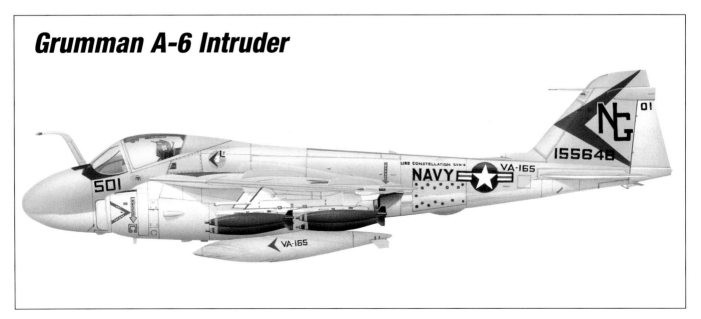

Grumman A-6 Intruder

lying cloud. Estocin did not survive, and was posthumously awarded the Medal of Honor for his work on Iron Hand missions.

As well as this dangerous mission, the carriers were increasingly able to launch effective night attacks against North Vietnamese targets. In 1965, the Grumman A-6 Intruder entered service with VA-75, flying from USS *Independence*. This first cruise for the Intruder was marked by a disastrous start, when in the course of a month three A-6s were lost as the result of bombs detonating prematurely after release, destroying the aircraft. The Intruder's next combat cruise came in the course of *Kitty Hawk*'s deployment between October 1965 and June 1966: six aircraft were lost, after which it was accepted that sending the Intruder against low-value targets was inappropriate. The Intruder was fitted with a highly sophisticated avionics suite which enabled it to conduct extremely accurate attacks at night and in very poor weather conditions. The decision to change tactics first came to fruition in the next cruise made by Intruders, on board *Constellation* between June and December 1966: however, it would be from 1967 that the Intruder really came into its own.

Finally, 1967 was marked by an increase in naval fighter activity. In the early part of the year, navy strikes did not meet many MiGs (the USAF did, shooting down 46 between January and June). Pleas from planners to attack the MiGs on their airfields were met with swift rejection from Washington, until the persistence of commanders paid off. In April, authority to attack the enemy fighters on their home bases (a key principle of aerial warfare since 1918, if not before) was granted. The Navy chose the largest MiG base, at Kep, as their target.

Aircraft from *Kitty Hawk* and *Bon Homme Richard* launched a strike on 24 April. A mixed force of A-6s and A-4s made an attack in daylight, while a further A-6 attack was made that night. The runway was cratered, while a number of airfield buildings and aircraft were damaged or destroyed. The fighter escort for the daylight mission enjoyed some success: F-4s from VF-114 shot down two MiG-17s as they attempted to take off. Once Kep had been authorized as a target, it was visited again by the Navy. On 1 May, Commander Ted Swartz, flying a Skyhawk, managed to shoot down a MiG with his unguided rockets. This was the most unusual of the 12 'kills' against MiGs made by navy aircraft between April and July 1967. These successes were once again offset by tragedy. On 29 July, another catastrophic fire hit Task Force 77.

The *Forrestal* had left home port at Norfolk, Virginia, a month before, and began operations at Yankee Station on 25 July. After four days, disaster struck. Aircraft had been armed, fuelled and 'spotted' on the deck ready for the second launch cycle of the day. As a starter unit was being positioned to allow it to start the engines on an F-4, the hot exhaust fumes blew directly into the Phantom's wing pylon. The heat ignited a Zuni rocket, which raced across the flight deck, smashing into a fully armed and fuelled Skyhawk, which blew up in a cataclysmic explosion. The fire engulfed the stern of the carrier and spread below, setting off bombs and ammunition as it went. Nearby ships rushed to help the firefighting efforts, and after an hour the fire on deck was out, but the fires below took another 12 hours to extinguish. The firefighting efforts were heroic – deck crews ran here and there pulling bombs off the aircraft (some of which were already ablaze), throwing them overboard, while other men sought to move aircraft out of the path of the fire before they were engulfed. At the end of the firefighting, 134 men had died and 62 were injured. Twenty-one of the carrier's aircraft were totally destroyed, while another 43 suffered varying degrees of damage (in some cases enough to ensure that the aircraft were not repaired).

As 1967 went on, the routine of strikes continued, in the face of determined opposition. On 24 October, the airfield at Phuc Yen, the largest MiG base not thus far attacked, was subjected to the attentions of a massive strike by aircraft from the carriers and the US Air Force. At least 30 SAMs were fired as the attack went in, but the runway was badly damaged. The next day, aircraft from *Coral Sea* struck the base again, but resistance was markedly less.

In December, USS *Ranger* returned to the combat zone, carrying another new aircraft type – the Vought A-7 Corsair II. The Corsair bore a family resemblance to the F-8, but was a very different aircraft. It had been designed to supplant the A-4 in the attack role. The A-7 had six underwing hardpoints, which allowed it to carry virtually every weapon in the navy inventory. In addition, it had two fuselage stations for Sidewinders, and two 20mm (0.8in) cannon (later replaced by a six-barrel 20mm Vulcan cannon of Gatling-gun type). The Corsair had far greater range than the A-4, and was equipped with extremely accurate avionics, making it an excellent attack platform. The first Corsairs had a few problems. The low-slung air intake had an appetite for foreign objects (nearly including members of the

ABOVE: USS *Midway*, one of the longest-serving carriers, seen after her modification to embark jets. *Midway* entered service in 1945, when she could carry an air wing of over 100 aircraft. Even though they were capable of operating the new heavy attack aircraft without modification (unlike the Essexes), the three Midway-class ships received progressive modification.

deck crew on occasion) and ingested steam from the catapults, with an adverse effect on the engine's power output. In addition, the TF30 engine was slightly underpowered, and Vought were already searching for a replacement (which they soon found in the TF41). The final 'problem' was the name: although 'Corsair II' evoked memories of the F4U, the pilots did not take to it. Instead, they christened their stubby mount the 'SLUF', which stood for 'Short Little Ugly Fellow' (at least in polite company). This disguised the affection with which pilots increasingly regarded the A-7. It was to see considerable action in the last years of the war.

TET AND BEYOND

The customary Christmas bombing halt was enacted again in 1967. The North Vietnamese used this generosity to move larger than usual numbers of men down the Ho Chi Minh trail into South Vietnam. Although the movement was detected by aircraft, they were not allowed to bomb. On 31 January 1968, the North Vietnamese and Viet Cong launched the Tet offensive, attacking every important city in the South. The adoption of more conventional tactics enabled the Americans to inflict serious casualties on the enemy. Perversely, this success was irrelevant. The media coverage of Tet suggested that the North Vietnamese

and Viet Cong could strike at will, and seemed to show that the Americans were trapped in a war they could not win. Although it is too simple to say that Tet destroyed the American will to fight, it was a significant element in bringing the war to an end (for the Americans), even if this process took another five years. The government was, once more, uncertain. On 31 March, President Johnson addressed the nation, and announced that he had called a halt to bombing against North Vietnam. Johnson's speech was dramatic, but the ending was even more so. The President finished talking about Vietnam and then told the American people that he would neither seek, nor accept, the nomination of the Democratic Party to run for another term of office. The next day, combat operations north of the 20th Parallel were suspended.

THE SKYRAIDER BIDS FAREWELL

April 1968 was significant for the US Navy for another reason, in that the last attack squadron retired its Skyraiders. The A-1 (as the AD had become known after the introduction of the 1962 tri-service designation system) had become operational in 1947, but by 1968 was too vulnerable to radar-predicted flak when used in the attack role. The electronic warfare versions soldiered on for a few more months, but the

US Air Force continued to operate them until 1974 in support of search and rescue helicopters. The Skyraider was replaced by more A-6s and A-7s, giving the Navy considerably more capability – which circumstances prevented them from using. Operations continued south of the 20th Parallel throughout the spring and summer, but this was not to last. Increasing efforts to negotiate with North Vietnam led Johnson to suspend all bombing of North Vietnam on 1 November 1968 at 2100 hours. Rather than bring the war to an end, it merely changed the nature of the conflict, leaving a new President to bring the war to a conclusion.

1968 TO 1972

The suspension of the bombing of North Vietnam did not mean an end to the carrier commitment to Vietnam. Efforts were instead devoted to stopping the supplies being sent to guerrillas in South Vietnam down the Ho Chi Minh Trail. The Ho Chi Minh Trail was not, in fact, a single trail, but a series of routes through Laos. This meant it was almost impossible stop the traffic on it. Aware of the danger from air attack, the supply traffic was light during the day, and reached its peak at night. Every conceivable means of road transport was used to take supplies down the trail – buffalos, trucks, bicycles, men on foot being just some of the methods employed. This meant that even

though the US Navy was employing some of the most sophisticated technology against the trail, stopping the flow completely by air attack was simply not possible.

1972

Although the bombing halt meant a dramatic reduction in air activity against the North, it did not mean that it had stopped. American reconnaissance flights were conducted on a regular basis, under rules of engagement known as 'protective reaction' – this translated as being able to fire only if fired upon.

After a reconnaissance flight had seen ground crews pushing a MiG-21 into a cave at Quang Lang, it was decided to mount a further reconnaissance mission to investigate. Bad weather prevented the follow-up flight until 19 January 1972, when crews from *Constellation* were dispatched. The force sent on the mission was impressive. As well as the RA-5C Vigilante that would take the pictures, an escort of A-7s and A-6s was sent to deal with any attack that was made by anti-aircraft positions. In addition, top cover was provided by fighters from VF-96.

The flight reached Quang Lang, and immediately came under heavy fire. The A-7s and A-6s went in to attack (as permitted by the rules of engagement), and the defences increased their efforts. As well as heavy flak, a number of SAMs were

BELOW: 1975, and the end of the war. A South Vietnamese UH-1 'Huey' is pushed over the side of an American carrier (probably USS *Midway*) to make room for other aircraft bringing the multitude of South Vietnamese refugees seeking to escape Saigon before its inevitable fall to North Vietnam.

launched. The Phantoms then discovered that they had unwittingly managed to position themselves over two SAM sites, which engaged them with alacrity. One of the Phantoms was crewed by Lt Randy Cunningham and his Radar Intercept Officer, Lt (jg) Willie Driscoll. Cunningham threw their aircraft into a series of manoeuvres to defeat one SAM, and then had to repeat the process to beat a second missile. In the course of these manoeuvres, the Phantom ended up with its nose pointing straight down. This enabled Cunningham to catch sight of two A-7s – or so he thought – leaving the scene. A closer look revealed that the two aircraft were in afterburner: the A-7 did not have an afterburner, so Cunningham was moved to look even more carefully. He reversed his turn, and identified the aircraft as MiG-21s.

Cunningham lit his own afterburners and raced after the MiGs, which were flying at less than 150m (500ft). Driscoll locked an AIM-7 Sparrow onto the lead aircraft, but Cunningham, having suffered a number of Sparrow failures during training, selected a Sidewinder instead. He launched the missile, but the MiG broke hard, and the missile lost track. As Cunningham manoeuvred against the MiG, it became clear that the MiG pilot had lost sight of his pursuers. The MiG reversed in front of the Phantom, and Cunningham fired a second Sidewinder, which blew the MiG's tail off. Cunningham's success was the first MiG kill for 18 months. It was not the last for the US Navy – nor was it the last kill for Cunningham and Driscoll.

NORTH VIETNAMESE OFFENSIVE

On 30 March 1972, the North Vietnamese launched a huge offensive against the South, prompting the resumption of bombing against the North. On 8 May, President Nixon told the American public that he was authorizing the mining of North Vietnam's ports and harbours, bringing to fruition a plan that had been available for several years, but had not been accepted by the planners in Washington. The mining of the harbours was carried out by A-7s and A-6s from *Coral Sea, Constellation* and *Midway*. Opposition was intense; between March and 9 May, five MiGs were shot down, including a second by the team of Cunningham and Driscoll.

On 10 May, the most intense air-to-air combats of the war took place. The morning strikes against storage areas north of Haiphong were covered by VF-92 and VF-96 from *Constellation*. As the last of the strike aircraft cleared the target area, two Phantoms from VF-92 swept across Kep, catching two MiG-21s as they took off. The lead Phantom, flown by Lt Curt Dosé and Lt Cdr Jim McDevitt, charged after one of the MiGs. Dosé and McDevitt were frustrated when their first Sidewinder missed the MiG by a matter of feet, the warhead failing to detonate. The second Sidewinder slammed into the tail of the MiG and sent it cartwheeling into the ground. As fuel was low, Dosé turned his aircraft round and headed back to sea. When he returned, intelligence officers on board *Constellation* reported that the action over Kep had prompted some of the most

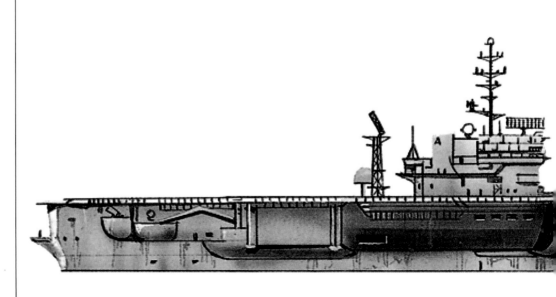

USS *America*

intense radio traffic ever intercepted during the war. It was a precursor for more activity later in the day.

ACES

The second strike of the day was sent against the railyards at Hai Duong. Ground defences were expected to be fierce, and several of the Phantoms assigned to escort duties were loaded with cluster bombs for flak suppression in addition to their air-to-air missiles. Among those assigned to flak suppression duties were Randy Cunningham and Willie Driscoll. As they approached the target area, the enemy defences were surprisingly quiet. The A-7s assigned to Iron Hand duties launched pre-briefed Shrike shots against SAM sites. The flak suppression Phantoms accelerated, and ran in on their targets. The anti-aircraft guns opened up, and the Phantoms released their bombs. At this point, the destroyer on radar picket duty in the Gulf of Tonkin (code-named 'Red Crown') came on air to report that MiGs were airborne. Cunningham was the first to spot them as he climbed back to altitude. Cunningham attempted to drag a MiG-17 in for his wingman, but the MiG pilot made a slashing attack against Cunningham and broke away. Cunningham reversed, and fired a Sidewinder against the MiG. The missile tracked and blew the MiG to pieces.

The dogfight developed into a large-scale melee over Hai Duong as aircraft manoeuvred. Cunningham turned his Phantom back towards Hai Duong and saw an F-4 being pursued by two MiG-17s and a MiG-21. At the same time, a MiG-17 was closing in on Cunningham and Driscoll. The Phantom's speed advantage allowed Cunningham to keep the attacking MiG-17 at bay, and he headed towards the three aircraft that were troubling the other F-4. He managed to get into a clear firing position on one of the MiG-17s, and fired a second Sidewinder. The missile headed straight towards the MiG's tailpipe, entered it and blew up. The MiG pilot immediately ejected. Four MiG-21s were now approaching, and Cunningham decided that it was time to leave the area. As they made their exit, he spotted another MiG-17 ahead of them. Cunningham moved to allow the MiG to pass alongside. Cunningham and Driscoll were graduates of the recently formed Fighter Weapons School (better known as 'Top Gun'), and had made this manoeuvre in training. But this time there was a major difference – the other aircraft could fire back. Cunningham was soon reminded about the MiG-17's heavy cannon armament as the MiG's nose lit up. Cunningham pulled his aircraft into a vertical climb, and was amazed to see the MiG following. It was clear that they were up against a skilled opponent. The two aircraft manoeuvred together until they lost momentum, the MiG falling away first. The fight continued as both pilots sought to gain an advantage, until they were in the vertical plane once more. Cunningham decided that he needed to do something different, and idled the throttles as he put out the speed brakes. He stamped on the rudder pedal to turn the Phantom in towards the belly of the MiG. The enemy pilot, struggling to

Displacement	82,808 tonnes (81,500 tons) (full load)	**Armament**	3 x octuple Sea Sparrow SAM launchers; 3 x 20mm (0.8in) Phalanx CIWS
Length	319.3m (1047ft)		
Beam	39.6m (130ft)	**Complement**	2900 plus 2500 air wing
Draught	11.3m (37ft)	**Aircraft**	up to 90
Propulsion	4-shaft geared steam turbines		
Speed	33.6 knots		

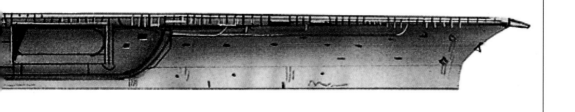

RIGHT: A mixture of aircraft sit at the stern of USS *Constellation*, awaiting the beginning of the day's flying. Nearest to the camera, three RA-5Cs can be made out. In the middle of the Vigilantes, an A-7, carrying an AGM-45 Shrike and a Rockeye cluster bomb unit, sits waiting for its pilot. To the stern, F-4s from VF-92 'Silver Kings' and VF-96 'Fighting Falcons' prepare to move towards the catapult.

keep control at such slow speed, dived for the ground in a bid to escape, but the Phantom was in an ideal firing position. Cunningham fired another Sidewinder, which tracked perfectly. For an instant, he and Driscoll thought that the missile had failed, since there was only a small flash as the warhead detonated: but this was followed seconds later by a larger flash, and the MiG crashed in a fireball.

Cunningham and Driscoll headed back for their carrier, but just as they approached the coastline, a SAM hit them. The Phantom began to go out of control, and Cunningham was forced to roll the aircraft with a combination of afterburner and rudder as he struggled to get out to sea. Shortly after they crossed the coastline, Cunningham and Driscoll were forced to eject as the Phantom's controls burned through. They were rescued by a US Marine Corps CH-46 helicopter and returned to *Constellation* to a heroes' welcome, having become the first 'aces' of the Vietnam War.

DRAWDOWN

Operations against the North continued on a daily basis, as key targets were struck. The more focussed application of air power meant the North Vietnamese were soon suffering from reduced supplies. Peace talks between the Americans and North Vietnamese began in Paris, prompting Nixon to call a halt to the bombing – but the North Vietnamese proved reluctant to negotiate, and on 13 December 1972, they walked out of the peace conference.

Nixon's response was to launch Operation 'Linebacker II' on 18 December. The operation saw massive application of strategic air power in the form of raids by US Air Force B-52s and F-111s, while A-6s flew from the carriers. Linebacker II succeeded in its aim of forcing the North Vietnamese to the conference table again, and on 3 January 1973, all bombing of the North ceased. Twenty days later the peace accords were signed. American prisoners of war began to leave captivity on 12 February, including Everett Alvarez, the first man taken captive nearly 10 years before.

The Paris Peace Accords did not quite mark the end of the involvement of American carriers in the Vietnam War. The North Vietnamese resumed their campaign, and by April 1975, their forces were closing in on Saigon. The American embassy was ordered to evacuate, and *Enterprise, Midway, Hancock* and *Coral Sea* were sent to assist, becoming landing bases for the helicopter shuttle flights that carried American citizens and thousands of South Vietnamese refugees out of Vietnam for the last time. On board *Enterprise*, VF-1 and VF-2 were equipped with the last new type of carrier aircraft to serve off Vietnam, the F-14A Tomcat. The new aircraft flew top cover for the helicopter flights, in case the North Vietnamese air force sought to interfere. Although there was some anti-aircraft fire against the Tomcats, they would have to wait to encounter enemy MiGs. On 30 April 1975, Saigon fell, and was renamed Ho Chi Minh City. The Vietnam War was finally at an end.

LEFT: Randall Cunningham and Willie Driscoll relax aboard USS *Constellation* after their epic mission of 5 October 1972, when they became the first 'aces' of the Vietnam War.

CHAPTER SEVEN

RISE OF THE SUPERCARRIERS

The cancellation of the USS *United States* may have been a serious blow to the US Navy, but it was a temporary setback. Congressional support for *United States*, coupled with the hearings led by Carl Vinson, gave the Navy reason to hope that new carrier building would be authorized. In addition, by 1950, the future role of carriers was being redefined.

IT WAS BECOMING reasonable to assume that technological advances would lead to lightweight atomic weapons that would be suitable for carriage by fighter-sized aircraft. This vision was given strength by events in Korea. On 11 July 1950, less than a month after the Korean War had begun, the Joint Chiefs of Staff decided that they would postpone any further consideration of cuts to the carrier fleet. The next day, Secretary of Defense Johnson, who had gained the enmity of many in the US Navy for cancelling *United States*, told the Navy that he was prepared to authorize the construction of a new carrier.

LEFT: A Catapult Officer aboard the USS *Independence* drops to the deck to signal the catapult crew to launch an aircraft (an S-3 Viking can be seen rushing by). The four catapults aboard an American supercarrier can launch two aircraft every 37 seconds during daylight hours.

On 30 October 1950, Secretary of the Navy Francis P. Matthews agreed to the list of priorities drawn up by the Navy (with conversion of Essex-class ships at number six in the list and the building of a new carrier at number eight). Matthews announced that the new carrier would be named *Forrestal* (CVA-59) after Johnson's predecessor at Defense.

By 1952, the Navy had set the goal of building a new aircraft carrier every year. After some time without an idea about how many carriers the Navy would maintain, the figure of 15 was decided upon. The intention was to retain the three Midways and build 12 new carriers by the end of the 1960s. In fact, only nine 'supercarriers' were completed by the end of that decade, while several of the Essex class remained in service well into the 1970s, both as attack and anti-submarine carriers.

FORRESTAL (CVA-59)

The new carriers needed to be able to operate not only the latest generation of jets, but to be capable of operating the sort of aircraft that might enter service over the next decade or more (much more as it transpired). This meant that the carriers would need to be big, not only to operate the aircraft, but to carry sufficient fuel and ordnance for them too. In addition, two British inventions were adopted to assist in flying operations. The US Navy recognized that the hydraulic catapult would be totally inadequate for launching heavy jet aircraft, and investigated using a powder charge catapult. The explosive catapult was not a success in

trials. Instead, the British-designed steam catapult was adopted, offering lighter weight and the ability to launch larger aircraft. In addition, the angled deck made flying operations far simpler. Although a safety barrier would still be employed, this would be to catch aircraft that were unable to take the arrester wires, rather than to prevent them from ploughing into parked aircraft at the front of the deck. *Forrestal* (CVA-59) was equipped with four catapults to maximize launching rates. The ship was laid down on 14 July 1952, and was commissioned on 1 October 1955. By this time, three sister ships were being built: *Saratoga* (CVA-60), *Ranger* (CVA-61) and *Independence* (CVA-62). A further ship had been authorized, and there was talk of equipping some of the later vessels out of the projected 12 with nuclear power. A team led by Captain Hyman G. Rickover had begun studies into using nuclear power for large ships and submarines in August 1951, and three years later the Large Ship Reactor project was authorized. This would take time to come to fruition in carriers, but when nuclear power was available, it would prove to be a huge enhancement of the already impressive capabilities of the American carriers.

AIRCRAFT FOR THE SUPERCARRIERS

Although designed to enable the operation of a new generation of aircraft, *Forrestal* began her service career employing types that were familiar from the Korean War. The F2H Banshee remained in service, albeit in a larger and heavier variant than had seen action in Korea. While the Banshee was a

USS *Midway* (1973)

Displacement	60,858 tonnes (59, 901 tons) (deep load)	**Speed**	33 knots
		Armament	2 x octuple Sea Sparrow SAM launchers
Length	295m (968ft) (overall)		
Beam	34.44m (113ft)	**Complement**	2615 plus 1800 in air wing
Draught	10.52m (34ft 6in)	**Aircraft**	75
Propulsion	4-shaft geared steam turbines		

capable machine, there was concern that straight-winged aircraft would have difficulty in surviving against well flown MiG-15s and their successors. As a result of these concerns, a redesign of the F9F Panther had begun, and as the Korean War drew to a close, the first F9F-6 models appeared, with swept wings and renamed the 'Cougar'. Although it was capable of carrying a similar war load to the Panther (four 20mm (0.8in) cannon and 1814kg (4000lb) of bombs and rockets) from 1956 the Cougar began to carry the new infra-red homing GAR-83 (later AIM-9) Sidewinder air-to-air missile.

The Cougar was joined by another swept-wing type shortly after the conclusion of hostilities in Korea. The success of the North American F-86 Sabre led the Navy to request a navalized version of the Sabre. This was slightly ironic, since the Sabre had been derived from the Navy's FJ-1 Fury. The FJ-2 was almost identical to the F-86 to the untrained eye, obvious differences being the arrester hook, folding wings and a change in gun armament from six 12.7mm (0.5-inch) machine guns to four 20mm (0.8in) cannon. The first Furies reached the fleet in January 1954. When *Forrestal* entered full service, she was equipped with a later model of Fury, the FJ-3, which had Sidewinder capability, adding greatly to the potential of the aircraft. The FJ-3 entered service just as another model, the FJ-4, was nearing readiness. By the end of 1956, there were 23 Navy and Marine fighter squadrons equipped with the FJ-3.

The Cougars and Furies were soon joined by two new types, the Douglas F4D Skyray

LEFT: A member of the deck crew aboard USS *Independence*, festooned with tie-down chains for the aircraft. The deck crew are essential to the safe operation of the aircraft carrier, and their job is dangerous, dirty and noisy. Different coloured shirts show the job of each man on the deck; the brown shirt on this sailor shows that he is a plane captain, responsible for the care and maintenance of an individual aircraft in the air wing.

and the McDonnell F3H Demon. The Skyray was an incredible, bat-winged aircraft designed by the great Ed Heinemann for fighter duties. The Skyray had impressive performance, and one set an official world speed record in 1953. The Skyray carried a large radar to permit all-weather operations (although the radar was prone to reliability problems), and a mixture of Folding-Fin Aircraft Rockets (FFARs) and Sidewinders to complement the customary 20 mm cannon.

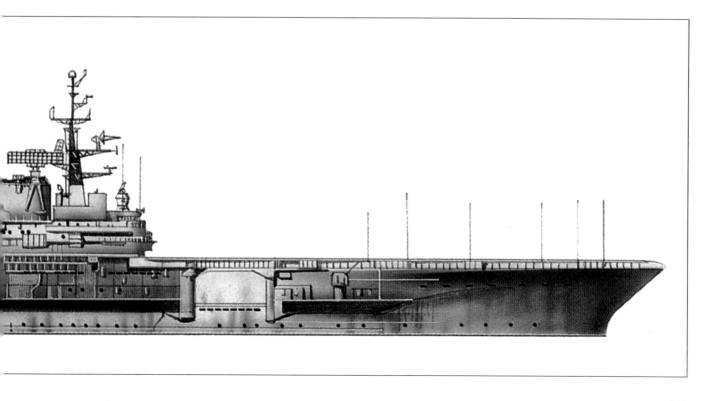

Douglas A4E Skyhawk

ABOVE: This Douglas A-4E Skyhawk was aboard the USS *Independence* while in the South China Sea during May 1965. The Skyhawk was so small that it did not need folding wings to be stowed economically on board a carrier.

The Demon was developed alongside the Skyray, but the engine chosen for it, the Westinghouse J40, proved to be an utter disaster. This meant that the first batch of F3Hs never reached operational service, many being sent straight to maintenance units for use as instructional airframes. The aircraft was re-engined with the Allison J71 after a redesign in 1954, and this solved the problem. Despite the delays, the Demon was able to carry the first versions of the radar-guided Sparrow missile, along with Sidewinders, rockets and air-to-ground weaponry.

As if to demonstrate the pace of aircraft development in the 1950s, a number of other fighter aircraft entered service at about the same time. The first, and least successful, was the Vought F7U Cutlass. The Cutlass was perhaps the most radical-looking aircraft to serve with the US Navy, with swept back wings and no horizontal tail surfaces. The vertical tail surfaces were mounted on the wings, about halfway between wing tips and fuselage. The first F7Us proved to be disappointingly underpowered and extremely difficult to fly. Improved engines (complete with the first afterburners to be fitted to a US Navy aircraft) improved the aircraft, but it was unpopular

with pilots as a result of handling difficulties and the alarmingly high attrition rate. This offset the Cutlass's ability to carry the Sparrow missile, and the type was withdrawn in 1957.

The second significant type came in the form of the Grumman F11F Tiger. The Tiger was the first aircraft to incorporate the new aerodynamic principle known as 'area rule', so as to reduce drag. This meant that the Tiger was faster than its predecessors, becoming the first Navy fighter to break the sound barrier in level flight. The Tiger was regarded with affection by pilots, and carried the respectable war load of four 20mm cannon and up to four Sidewinders. It went on to become an extremely popular mount for the Navy's Blue Angels aerobatic display team, but despite the respect it was held in, the Tiger did not see particularly widespread service.

The reason for this was the third significant naval fighter of the late 1950s, the Vought F8U Crusader. The Crusader was a masterpiece of design. To enable it to operate from the smaller carriers, it was designed with a variable-incidence wing that pivoted upwards by 7 degrees during take-off and landing to provide the necessary angle of attack while keeping the fuselage in the necessary attitude for a successful landing. The Crusader exceeded the speed of sound on its first test flight, and the Navy was justly proud of it. The Crusader was used to set a whole series of records, including a world air speed record of over 1609 km/h (1000 mph). In June 1957, two Crusaders took off from Bon Homme Richard off the California coast, and using inflight refuelling crossed the United States to land on Saratoga off Florida.

CARRIER ATTACK

The carriers also began to adopt a new range of attack aircraft as the supercarriers entered service. While the *Forrestal* (CVA-59) was the first carrier designed to operate jets, this did not prevent the evergreen Skyraider from deploying. Although the Skyraider had over a decade more service at the time of *Forrestal*'s commissioning, the US Navy was concerned by a number of the aircraft's features. Although the Skyraider could carry an impressive war load, it took a long time to get it to the target and return to the carrier. There had been occasions in Korea when pilots had returned from arduous missions lasting eight hours or so, and were so fatigued that they had to be lifted out of the cockpit. There were obvious questions as to whether the Skyraider was appropriate for the nuclear strike mission, and threats from ground defences were a worry too. The Navy was also concerned about the increased weight and size of aircraft, and sought a relatively light machine that could meet their requirement.

The specification was challenging. The US Navy demanded an aircraft that could carry a bomb load similar to the Skyraider, have a radius of action of at least 483km (300 miles) and a maximum loaded weight of 13,605kg (30,000lb). At the Douglas com-

pany the chief designer, Ed Heinemann, had been growing concerned about the increasing weight of combat aircraft, and conducted an in-depth study to see how weight could be reduced. He put in a design proposal for an aircraft that astounded the Navy's Bureau for Aeronautics (BuAer) because it was less than half the weight specified. A number of sceptical officers claimed that Heinemann must have taken leave of his senses, and claimed that the proposal would never work. Despite these views, there were enough people at BuAer who were intrigued. Heinemann's reputation was well established, and it was decided to proceed. When Heinemann produced a prototype aircraft, the YA4D Skyhawk, the doubters were convinced. The A4D-1 began to join fleet squadrons in 1956, providing the US Navy with an aircraft that could carry around 2268kg (5000lb) of bombs, and which, more importantly, could be carried in large numbers aboard aircraft carriers. Indeed, the Skyhawk was so small that it did not have the folding wings customarily fitted to naval aircraft.

While the Skyhawk represented a major step forward, Heinemann was also responsible for one of the largest aircraft to serve aboard a carrier. This was the A3D Skywarrior, which was designed at a time when the lightweight nuclear weapon was just a desire. The Skywarrior had a gross weight of 37,187kg (82,000lb) when loaded, and, like the Skyhawk, entered service in 1956 aboard Midway class ships, embarked in squadrons that were seven to ten aircraft strong. By 1956, it was not just the Midways that could carry the Skywarriors, since the *Forrestal* was ready for her first cruise.

FORRESTAL ENTERS SERVICE

On 24 January 1956, *Forrestal* set off for her first cruise, scheduled to last for three

BELOW: The North American AJ-2 Savage was developed specifically as a carrier-based bomber, and unusually featured a pair of radial piston engines plus a turbojet in the tail.

North American AJ-2 Savage

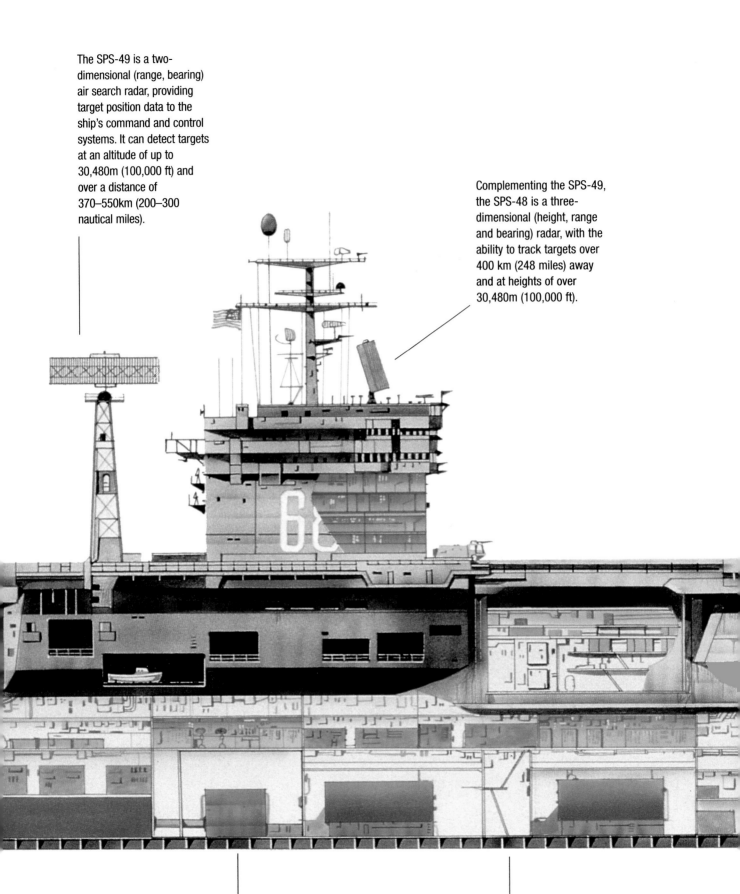

The SPS-49 is a two-dimensional (range, bearing) air search radar, providing target position data to the ship's command and control systems. It can detect targets at an altitude of up to 30,480m (100,000 ft) and over a distance of 370–550km (200–300 nautical miles).

Complementing the SPS-49, the SPS-48 is a three-dimensional (height, range and bearing) radar, with the ability to track targets over 400 km (248 miles) away and at heights of over 30,480m (100,000 ft).

The use of nuclear power means that Nimitz has a theoretical range of over 1.85 million km (1 million nautical miles).

In addition to the nuclear reactors, Nimitz has four diesel engines for use in emergencies.

USS *Nimitz*

With the ability to carry over 80 combat aircraft, *Nimitz* was a powerful example of US military strength during the Cold War. With a smaller air wing tailored for use in the new strategic environment, the Nimitz-class vessels give America unparalleled ability to project air power thousands of miles away from home.

The Nimitz-class carriers each have four deck-edge aircraft lifts, three on the starboard side and one to port. Using deck-edge lifts ensures that flight operations are not affected as aircraft are brought up to the deck or lowered to the hangar.

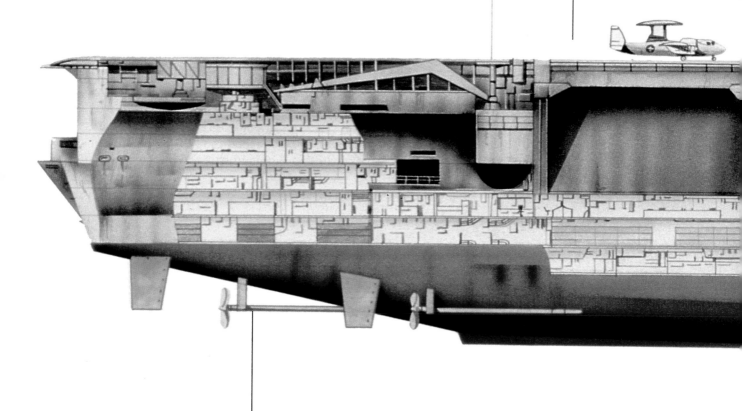

The four shafts, each with five blades, deliver a total output of 208.9MW (280,000 shp), giving a top speed of over 56km/h (30 knots).

months. She embarked an air group of five squadrons. As well as F2H-3 Banshees and FJ-3 Furies in the fighter-bomber role, a squadron of Cutlasses was carried, along with a squadron of Skyraiders. The air group was completed by a heavy attack squadron with AJ-2 Savages, and a detachment of helicopters. This air group was similar to those embarked aboard other carriers, although the introduction of new aircraft meant that there were regular changes in the types of aircraft. By the end of the 1950s, each carrier would embark one squadron of all-weather fighters (either F4D Skyrays or F3H Demons); one day-fighter unit with the F8U Crusader and two or three light attack units. These were initially equipped with either the F2H-3 or -4 model Banshee, the F9F-8 Cougar or the FJ-4B Fury, with the Skyhawk supplanting these types as the decade drew to a close. Finally, another squadron of Skywarriors or Savages completed the attack line-up. Specialist aircraft for photo-reconnaissance (usually the F8U-1P), AEW (the E-1 Tracer or AD-5W Skyraider) and electronic warfare (AD-5Q Skyraiders) were also on board, along with helicopters embarked for a variety of roles. Anti-submarine aircraft, like the S-2 Tracker, were carried aboard the Essex-class ships that had been assigned to the anti-submarine role.

The *Forrestal* was soon followed by sister ships. *Saratoga* commissioned on 14 April 1956, and *Ranger* joined on 10 August the next year. As these supercarriers joined the fleet, the least capable Essex-class ships were relegated to the anti-submarine role. By mid-1958, there were 15 attack carriers in service, with *Coral Sea* being refitted and *Independence* being built (she would join

the fleet in 1959). Two of the supercarriers nearly found themselves at war before 1958 was over.

THE LEBANON CRISIS

By 1958, the Middle East had become extremely volatile. The aftermath of the Suez crisis saw President Nasser's status dramatically increased in the Arab world as he promoted his idea of Pan-Arab nationalism. This appeared to bear fruit in February 1958 when Egypt and Syria merged into the United Arab Republic (UAR), presenting a major threat to Jordan, which had already faced a revolt by pro-Egyptian elements of its army. On 14 July, the Iraqi Government was toppled in a coup d'état, in which the pro-western king was murdered along with the Prime Minister. Lebanon also felt threatened, and the Lebanese leader, President Chamoun, sent a request to President Eisenhower that the United States provide troops to maintain order. He sent similar requests for troops to London and Paris, although negotiations between the NATO allies meant that it was decided that Britain, with its long-standing relationship with Jordan, would send troops there, while only American troops would go to Lebanon.

As a result of the request, Eisenhower ordered the three available carriers *Saratoga*, *Essex* and the anti-submarine carrier *Wasp* to head to Lebanon to support the US Marines who would be landed from 15 July. A mix of FJ-3s and Skyraiders from *Essex* staged through Cyprus to overfly the first landing by the Marines, who met only friendly locals as they landed. *Saratoga* reached the area on the evening of 17 July, and prepared to give support to the Marines

USS *Enterprise*

Displacement	91,033 tonnes (89,600 tons)	**Speed**	32 knots
Length	335.2m (1100ft)	**Armament**	Surface-to-air missiles
Beam	76.8m (252ft)	**Crew**	3325, 1891 air group and 71
Draught	10.9m (36ft)		marines
Propulsion	Quadruple screw-geared turbines, steam supplied by eight nuclear reactors	**Aircraft**	99

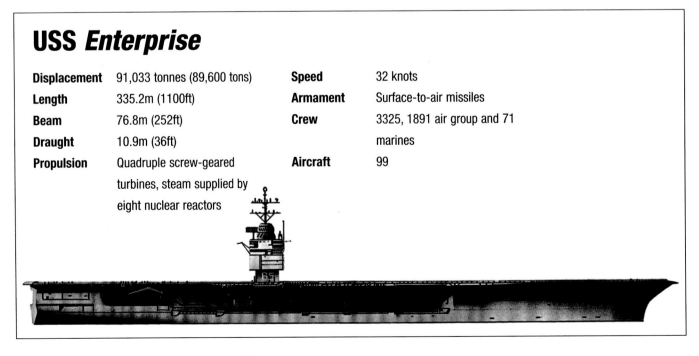

LEFT: USS *Enterprise* underway. *Enterprise* carried one of the largest attack carrier air wings ever on her early cruises. An array of A-4 Skyhawks can be seen at the front of the deck, and these were the mainstay of American efforts in Vietnam.

if it was required. This meant that, within three days of the request coming from Lebanon, the US Navy managed to have three carriers and over 200 aircraft in a position to launch strikes if required. This was an eloquent testament to the virtues of carrier aviation. The lesson was repeated in August when carriers (not including the supercarriers) were sent to meet the apparent threat posed to Quemoy and Matsu by the People's Republic of China as it sought to bring Formosa under commu-

nist control. Although the usefulness of the carrier had been demonstrated once more, the carrier building programme again faced controversy.

THE MOVE TO NUCLEAR POWER

Congressional approval for building carriers became more difficult to obtain as the 1950s drew to a close. One of the key reasons for this was the increasing cost. CVA-63 and CVA-64 were approved and were modified *Forrestal* designs (becoming *Kitty*

SPECIFICATIONS

USS *Nimitz*

Displacement	92,955 tonnes (91,487 tons) full load
Length	332.9m (1092ft) overall
Beam	40.8m (134ft)
Draught	11.3m (37ft)

Propulsion	Two A4w/A1G nuclear reactors
Speed	35 knots
Armament	3 x octuple Sea Sparrow SAM launchers (no reloads); 3 x 20mm (0.8in) Phalanx CIWS
Complement	6300
Aircraft	up to 90

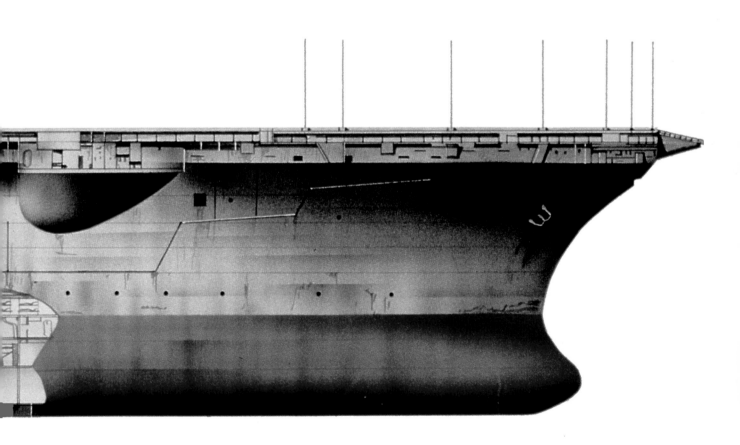

Tomcats from Fighter Squadron 41 (VF-41) 'The Black Aces' await their turn to launch from the starboard bow catapult on USS *Nimitz*, while a Skywarrior leaves the deck from the port 'cat'. Tomcats from VF-41 shot down two Libyan Su-22 Fitters in 1981, and the squadron was the first to use the Tomcat in an air-to-ground role during the air campaign over Bosnia in 1995.

The hangar holds less than
half the carrier's air wing,
with the remainder being
parked on the deck.

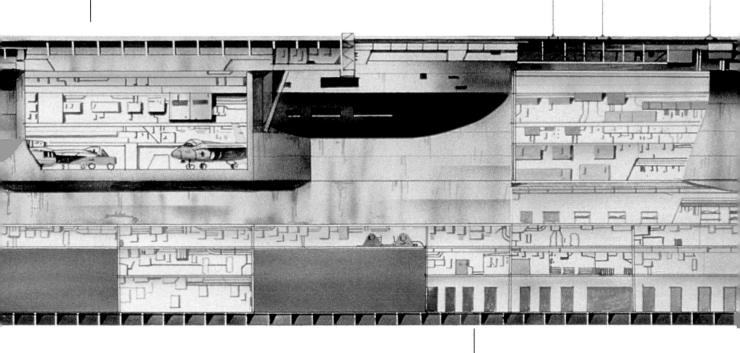

ion fuel is stored below
waterline as a safety
sure. Around 9000
es (8857 tons) can be
d to sustain the air
's operations.

As with the fuel stowage,
the magazines are below
the waterline for safety
reasons – if needed, they
can be flooded to prevent a
catastrophic detonation.

Hawk and *Constellation* respectively). The next carrier, CVA-65, was more controversial because it was to be nuclear-powered. This was reflected in the designator changing from 'CVA' to 'CVAN'. The ship, to be named *Enterprise* (contrary to one urban myth the name was not chosen to honour *Star Trek*) would cost nearly $445,000,000, making her the most costly ship ever built.

Opposition to *Enterprise* and any follow-on ships came from several quarters, not least the head of the House of Representatives' Appropriations Committee, Clarence Cannon. Cannon did not have a great deal of time for aircraft carriers or their proponents, seeing them as irrelevant in the Cold War context. Although the House voted to drop the next carrier (which would have been CVAN-66) from the budget, the Senate restored it. Admiral Rickover testified to Congress that building a carrier without nuclear propulsion would be a retrograde step, but although he was a persuasive advocate, the final decision was to build a conventional carrier, CVA-66. If any more nuclear-powered carriers were to follow, they would have to rely upon *Enterprise* proving her worth.

'BIG E'

Enterprise joined the fleet on 25 November 1961, and was equipped with the latest aircraft. Apart from a squadron of Skyraiders, *Enterprise* carried some of the first F4H Phantom II fighters, and the A3J Vigilante bomber. The Phantom, with its eight air-to-air missiles and all-weather capability, greatly increased the fighting power of carrier air wings (as they became in 1963), even if it was still mocked for being ugly, gunless and lacking in manoeuvrability by Crusader pilots. The Vigilante was designed as a supersonic replacement for the Skywarrior. It was perhaps the most advanced aircraft of its day (employing one of the first computers carried by an aircraft) but its novel mode of bomb delivery meant that it was not a success. A tunnel between the engines was designed to contain a single nuclear weapon sandwiched between two fuel tanks. The idea behind this was that the Vigilante would overfly its target at high speed, jettisoning the fuel/bomb package as it went. Unfortunately, the idea was flawed. There were a number of serious problems in getting the package to leave the aircraft at all. In addition, the fuel tanks (plus dummy bomb) had a nasty habit of flying out of the back of the Vigilante under the stresses of take-off or landing. This left an impressive trail of fire behind the huge bomber as it went – the thought of this occurring with a

nuclear weapon was just too much, and the aircraft was reassigned to reconnaissance. It was a great success in this role, carrying some very sophisticated equipment. The US Navy ultimately retired the Vigilante at the end of the 1970s, and has yet to find anything as good to replace it. *Enterprise* made her first deployment in the Cuban missile crisis in 1962, and then set off on a round-the-world cruise. But before the carrier began full service the decision that the next two carriers (CVA-66 and -67) would be oil-fired was confirmed by the new Secretary of Defense, Robert S. McNamara. Once again, it seemed that there was some doubt in high places about the effectiveness of aircraft carriers – something that was changed by the Vietnam War.

THE SWITCH TO NUCLEAR CARRIERS

Although CVA-66 and CVA-67 (*America* and *John F. Kennedy*) were to be oil fired, the success of *Enterprise*, coupled with the reduced demands on logistics presented by nuclear power (the nuclear reactors obviously did not require the carrier to sacrifice space for fuel oil, or to refuel), meant that there was another shift in opinion about carrier powerplant. The Vietnam War persuaded McNamara that carriers were useful, and instead of reducing the number of carrier battlegroups to 13, as he had once planned, he agreed to increase them to 15. As the new carriers entered service, changes were made to their air wings. The old anti-submarine carriers were to be retired, and their aircraft transferred to the attack carriers. As the attack carriers adopted multi-purpose air wings, they would be redesignated as CVs (or CVNs), losing their attack designator. The next carrier to be built, then still known as CVAN-68, was authorized in 1967, and given the name *Nimitz* after Admiral Chester Nimitz, who had achieved so much in the Pacific War. *Nimitz* entered service in May 1975, at a time when the nature of the air wing was changing dramatically.

THE 1970s AIR WING

The decision to embark anti-submarine aircraft was not the only change to affect the attack carriers in the 1970s. They were also taking on board a new range of combat aircraft. The Skyraider disappeared from the inventory in 1968, and the Skyhawk was quickly replaced on the supercarriers by the A-7 Corsair. The A-6 Intruder provided all-weather attack capability, with its avionics undergoing further updating in the post-Vietnam A-6E model. Airborne Early Warning came from the Grumman E-2 Hawkeye, and a new anti-submarine aircraft, the Lockheed S-3 Viking, entered service in 1975. The F-4 Phantom remained in service as the primary interceptor, but from 1975 began to be replaced by the Grumman F-14 Tomcat. The Tomcat was designed to overcome some of the shortcomings of the Phantom revealed by combat over Vietnam. A swing-wing design, the Tomcat was more manoeuvrable than the Phantom, and carried an M61 20mm (0.8in) Vulcan multi-barrel cannon for close-range combat. As well as the usual Sparrow and Sidewinder missiles, the Tomcat also employed the AIM-54 Phoenix, a long-range radar-homing missile that was coupled to a powerful (and initially unreliable) radar and fire control system. This allowed Tomcat pilots to engage multiple targets detected at over 160km (100 miles) range. The Tomcat was introduced into service in 1975 on board *Enterprise*, covering the evacuation of Saigon, and began to join other naval

LEFT: The island of USS *Enterprise* early in her service life, at some time between 1963 and 1964. The flat sides to the island are radar arrays which were removed in a refit. Beneath the island, the fastest and slowest combat aircraft in US Navy service at the time of the photograph can be seen. The tail of a Vigilante juts into view, while a Skyraider sits at the edge of the deck.

squadrons shortly afterwards. It was even bigger than the Phantom, and proved impossible to operate from the Midway-class carriers – there was some initial concern that even the Forrestals would have to continue to use the Phantom. This led to a requirement for a lighter fighter aircraft, and a programme took shape in the later 1970s as an offshoot from the USAF's lightweight fighter competition (that led to the F-16). The US Navy preferred the unsuccessful candidate, the Northrop YF-17 (largely because it had two engines instead of the F-16's one), and after McDonnell Douglas teamed up with Northrop, a development of the YF-17 became the F/A-18 Hornet. This multi-role fighter began to enter service in 1983.

The normal complement for an American supercarrier from the end of the 1970s until the end of the Cold War was as follows. There would be two squadrons of 12 fighter aircraft (either F-14s or F-4s). These would be accompanied by two light attack squadrons, each with 12 A-7s (or F/A-18s from the mid-1980s) and a medium attack squadron with A-6 Intruders. The Intruder units normally had 10 A-6s and four KA-6D Intruders adapted as tankers. Anti-submarine capability was provided by a squadron with up to 10 S-3 Vikings, while another squadron would embark with four E-2 Hawkeyes for airborne early warning. A four-seat development of the Intruder, the EA-6B Prowler, supplied the radar jamming capability, and were normally four of these aircraft to a squadron. The last squadron on board the carrier would consist of up to eight SH-3 Sea King helicopters for anti-submarine and search and rescue duties. In addition to these squadrons,

detachments of photo-reconnaissance RF-8 Crusaders were carried until the mid-1980s (they were replaced by the TARPS reconnaissance pod carried on the F-14), while small numbers of Skywarriors converted for air-to-air refuelling and electronic warfare were a common sight until the late 1980s. Carriers could also embark a C-2 Greyhound for transport tasks, although these aircraft were not formally assigned to the carrier's air wing.

SUPERCARRIERS IN ACTION

After the end of the Vietnam War, the American armed services went through a period of profound change. Public distrust of the military and the election victory of Jimmy Carter in 1976 meant that the question of military funding was raised once again. In addition to *Nimitz*, CVN-69 (*Dwight D. Eisenhower*) and CVN-70 (USS *Carl Vinson*) were under construction, with the former entering service in 1977. Carter sought to cut back on defence spending, and the idea of what became known as the 'CVV', a smaller, conventionally powered carrier, emerged. This would not be able to carry the 90-strong air wings of either the conventional or nuclear supercarriers, and this lack of versatility led to the US Navy abandoning interest. The election victory of Ronald Reagan in November 1980 was to secure the nuclear carrier's future.

Reagan came to power convinced that the Soviet Union posed a serious threat to the United States and western democracies. He had criticized Carter's stance on defence spending, and was to increase the defence budget to unprecedentedly high levels. Reagan aimed to create a navy with a large

Kiev

Displacement	42,672 tonnes (42,000 tonnes)	**Armament**	4 x 3-inch (76mm) guns; 8 x
Length	274m (898ft 11in) (overall)		30mm (1.2in) cannon; 10 x 21-
Beam	41m (134ft 6in)		inch (530mm) torpedo tubes; 4 x
Draught	10m (32ft 10in)		SA-N3 and 4 x SA-N-4 SAMs,
Propulsion	4-shaft steam turbines		plus 8 x SS-N-12 missiles
Speed	32 knots	**Complement**	2500
		Aircraft	33

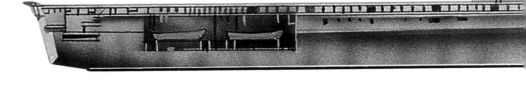

number of carriers. Plans to reactivate some of the Essex-class carriers were abandoned when it became clear that they could not operate up-to-date aircraft, while the remaining two Midways (*Midway* and *Coral Sea*) would be retired as new Nimitz-class ships came into service. *Coral Sea* would see action before she retired, thanks to the Libyan leader, Colonel Muammar Khaddafi.

AMERICA AND LIBYA

The first confrontation between America and Libya came in 1981. Colonel Khaddafi had seized power in a coup in 1967, replacing a pro-western government. He established links with the Soviet Union to purchase arms, and became a major cause of concern in the Mediterranean/Middle East region. Khaddafi unilaterally declared an

ABOVE: Three A-7E Corsairs fly above USS *Eisenhower*. The Corsair enjoyed a distinguished career, beginning in Vietnam. Further action occurred over Lebanon, Grenada and Libya, and finally in the Gulf War.

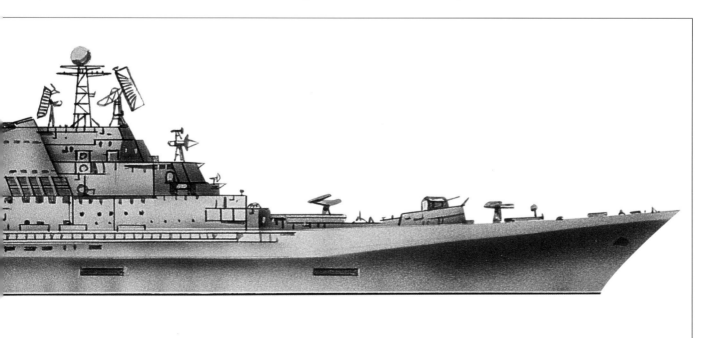

Grumman F-14 Tomcat

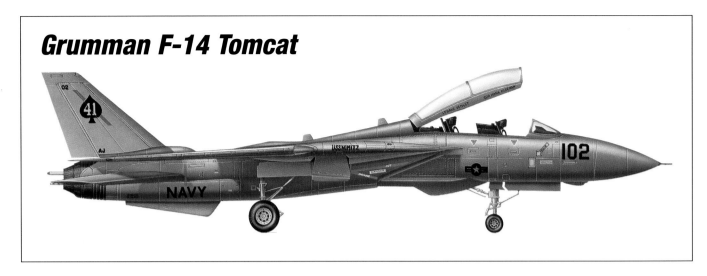

ABOVE: Widely regarded as the finest interceptor flying anywhere in the world, the Tomcat replaced the Phantom as the main fighter type on board American carriers, with its first cruise in 1975. Armed with the AIM-54 Phoenix missile, it is capable of engaging enemy targets at extremely long range.

extension of Libyan territorial waters, enclosing the Gulf of Sidra (also known as the Gulf of Sirte). The Americans refused to recognize this claim, regarding it as a breach of international law (as did most other nations). This was the original source of their dispute. Khaddafi's support for the Palestine Liberation Organization, coupled with Libyan intervention against Chad, meant that Khaddafi came to be regarded as a major threat. Reagan's more assertive foreign policy led him to order American ships accompanying the *Nimitz* to conduct 'freedom of navigation' exercises in the Gulf of Sidra to demonstrate the illegitimacy of Khaddafi's claim to those waters. On 19 August 1981, two F-14s from fighter squadron VF-41 were conducting a routine patrol when they were steered onto a radar contact by *Nimitz*. The contact turned out to be two Libyan air force Sukhoi-22 'Fitter-Js'. As the Tomcats approached the Fitters, a

flash of flame was seen under the wing of one of the Sukhois. Both Tomcat pilots (Cdr Hank Kleeman and Lt Larry 'Music' Muczynski) took this to be a missile launch. The missile failed to hit either Tomcat, and the F-14s manoeuvred for an opportunity to fire back. Muczynski achieved a good firing position within a matter of seconds, and fired a single Sidewinder at one of the Fitters. The missile tracked well and exploded as it went up the jet pipe of the Su-22. Kleeman waited for the second Fitter to cross the sun (so as to prevent the Sidewinder's infra-red homing seeker from being confused by that heat source), and once it had done so, he fired too. This was a direct hit. Within a matter of minutes, the F-14s had destroyed two hostile aircraft. Although the fleet remained on high alert in case Khaddafi tried to retaliate, the rest of the exercise passed without incident.

In 1983, the Americans formed part of a

USS *John F. Kennedy*

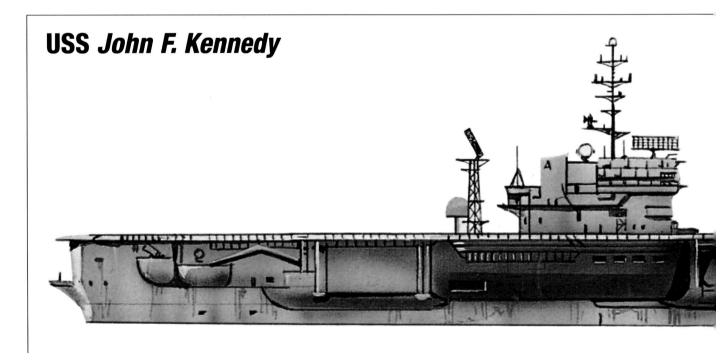

United Nations peacekeeping force sent to Lebanon, following the Israeli invasion of that country the year before. The locals opposed the presence of the Americans, and on 24 October, a massive truck bomb destroyed the US Marine compound in Beirut, killing 242 men.

Two American carriers, the *John F. Kennedy* and the *Independence,* were stationed off the coast, but were not employed in the aftermath of the bombing of the Marine barracks, since there was no clear retaliatory target for them to attack. On 3 December 1983, two F-14s from *JFK* were on a reconnaissance mission when Syrian forces fired at least 10 SAMs against the aircraft. Both escaped, but it was decided to launch a strike against the Syrians. A mix of A-6s and A-7s attacked Syrian positions and munitions sites. One of the Intruders was shot down while attacking a SAM site. The pilot was killed and the bombardier/navigator was taken prisoner (he was released later). As the air wing commander from *Independence* (Cdr Edward Andrews) was coordinating a rescue effort to recover the A-6 crew, his A-7 was also shot down. Andrews ejected and was quickly rescued from the sea by a US helicopter. Overall, the 1983 raids were a failure, and the US soon withdrew from Lebanon (as did British and French forces) when it was clear that there was no peace for the peacekeepers to uphold. Further operations against Libya in 1986 and 1989 were more successful.

OPERATION EL DORADO CANYON

Khaddafi's response to the 1981 Gulf of Sidra incident was wrapped up in his general attitude towards the West. By the mid-1980s, Khaddafi was openly supporting the PLO, and there were strong suspicions that he was supporting other groups that the Americans and their allies regarded as terrorists. In 1985, a London policewoman, Yvonne Fletcher, died when diplomats in the Libyan embassy opened fire on demonstrators and hit and killed her. President Reagan responded by making it clear that terrorist attacks would be met by strong action. Khaddafi in turn declared a 'line of death' across the Gulf of Sidra, threatening to engage any forces that entered the region. This prompted Reagan to send units of the Sixth Fleet into the Gulf on another freedom of navigation exercise. Led by *Saratoga, America* and *Coral Sea*, the fleet entered the Gulf as part of Operation Prairie Fire. On 24 March 1986, Libyan SAMs were fired against aircraft from the carriers, and the response was swift. A-7s attacked the SAM site with HARM anti-radar missiles. This was followed by an attempt by units of the Libyan navy to threaten US ships, which was thrown into disarray when Intruders sank a Combattante II-class patrol boat, followed some hours later by a Nanuchka-class corvette. Another Libyan patrol boat made the mistake of threatening the cruiser USS *Yorktown* – which obliterated the Libyan vessel with a salvo of Harpoon missiles. Hopes that this action would persuade Khaddafi to mend his ways were dashed when a bomb exploded in a disco in Berlin on 6 April. One American soldier was killed.

Intelligence intercepts convinced Reagan that the Libyans were behind the Berlin bomb, and he decided to react vigorously.

Displacement	79,502 tonnes (78,250 tons)	**Armament**	3 x octuple Sea Sparrow SAM
Length	323.8m (1062ft) (overall)		launchers plus 3 x 20mm (0.8in)
Beam	39.42m (129ft 4in)		Phalanx CIWS
Draught	10.67m (35ft)	**Complement**	2900 plus 2500 air wing
Propulsion	4-shaft geared steam turbines	**Aircraft**	82–90
Speed	33.6 knots		

RIGHT: The *Nimitz* was the second nuclear-powered aircraft carrier to enter service, and is the lead ship of a class currently planned to consist of 10 vessels. Appropriately, the *Nimitz* was the first of the class to see action, when two F-14s from one of her fighter squadrons shot down two Libyan Su-22s in 1981.

Operation El Dorado Canyon was launched on 15 April in response. The main strike force comprised USAF F-111s from RAF Lakenheath in England, but carrier aircraft were extremely busy. Targets around Benghazi were allocated to the Navy, and were attacked that night. Eight A-6Es from *Coral Sea* attacked the Benina airfield, accompanied by six F/A-18 Hornets and six A-7Es. At least eight Libyan aircraft were destroyed, and others were damaged. Six A-6s from *America* attacked the Al Jamahiriyah barracks, while other carrier aircraft provided support. F-14s and F/A-18s flew top cover in case the Libyan air force sought to interfere, while EA-6B Prowlers jammed SAM radars and communications.

The raids had a salutary effect on Khaddafi, whose enthusiasm for supporting terrorist groups was probably reduced. They also proved the versatility of carrier aircraft once again. The F-111s were forced to fly a circuitous route to the target after America's European allies (apart from Britain) refused to allow the aircraft to overfly their territory. This increased the length of the transit to and from the target and required massive tanker support. Over 60 tanker aircraft were deployed to bases in Britain, which prompted speculation that air strikes were about to take place. Although Khaddafi appears not to have gained any advantage from this warning, the carriers were proceeding about their business with rather less press coverage. The carrier aircraft were far closer, and could, in fact, have conducted the mission against all the Libyan targets had they been required to do so.

THE GULF

The Iran–Iraq war became a major cause of concern for the West when both sides (but particularly Iraq) started targeting oil tankers. In 1987, this led to the deployment of US forces to protect tankers, with convoys beginning in July. Within a short time, aircraft from *Enterprise*, along with Marine and Army helicopters, were engaging Iranian naval vessels. Intruders and Corsairs inflicted a number of nasty reverses on the Iranians, and the tanker war began to lose its attraction for both sides, neither of which was anxious to drag America into the war. The war ended with a ceasefire in July 1988, and both Iran and Iraq set about rebuilding. This was to provide the context for the next major involvement of American supercarriers in world affairs.

By 1990, the Cold War was virtually at an end, as the policies adopted by Mikhail Gorbachev brought the dissolution of Soviet control over Eastern Europe, and, ultimately, of the Soviet Union itself. Western governments immediately made plans to capitalize on the 'peace dividend' by reducing defence spending, but these plans had to be postponed when another war broke out in the Persian Gulf. Saddam Hussein's already slender reputation as a great strategist took a serious blow when he invaded Kuwait on 2 August 1990. Saddam believed that the Americans – and thus the rest of the world – would not intervene. He was sadly mistaken. President George Bush, supported by British Prime Minister Margaret Thatcher, feared that Saudi Arabia might be next, and sent forces to the region to protect the kingdom. As key parts of this force, the *Eisenhower* and *Independence* provided additional air support. If Saddam had intended to invade Saudi Arabia, he was deterred, and a massive build-up of an allied coalition to force him out of Kuwait began. Six carriers were sent to the region: *Saratoga*, *America*, *John F. Kennedy* and *Theodore Roosevelt* positioned themselves in the Red Sea, while *Ranger* and *Midway* entered the Gulf itself.

The campaign to liberate Kuwait began on the night of 16/17 January 1991 with massive air strikes against Iraq. As the air campaign developed, the carriers played a prominent part in operations. As well as attacking targets in Kuwait and Iraq itself, American carrier aircraft operating in conjunction with Westland Lynx helicopters from Royal Navy ships and Royal Air Force Jaguar attack aircraft decimated the Iraqi navy. Intruders and Corsairs made the first combat use of the AGM-84E SLAM (Stand-off Land Attack Missile) against a variety of targets, with considerable success (some of the footage from the guidance systems being broadcast on television news across the world). Two F/A-18s demonstrated their versatility when they shot down two Iraqi aircraft while loaded with four 907kg (2000lb) bombs. After destroying the Iraqi aircraft, the Hornets went on and bombed their targets.

Although the US Air Force played the lead role in the Gulf War, the contribution by the carriers and their aircraft was important.

BELOW: F-14 Tomcats sit nose-to-tail on the *John F. Kennedy*. The aircraft here are from VF-32 'Swordsmen': two aircraft from this squadron were responsible for the destruction of two Libyan MiG-23s in 1989.

Saddam Hussein's forces collapsed in confusion in the face of a ground offensive that began on 24 March 1991 and ended 100 hours later. Saddam claimed this was an overwhelming victory for Iraq – an eccentric interpretation of events. Saddam's refusal to comply with UN resolutions led to the establishment of 'no-fly zones', which at the time of writing are still being maintained. US carrier aircraft have played a full part, and in punitive strikes against targets like SAM sites and weapons facilities.

THE POST-GULF WORLD

Once the Gulf War was over, the American carrier fleet faced another major challenge to its budget. Within 10 years, the carrier fleet and the aircraft on board the ships had changed dramatically. The A-7, having served in the Gulf with two squadrons, was retired in 1991. Production of the F-14D, with new engines and better avionics, was cut back to the extent that only three squadrons were able to fully equip with this model, and one of these had to revert to the F-14B (which at least had the new engines). To increase the Tomcat's versatility, its air-to-ground capability was enhanced. F-14Bs and F-14Ds equipped with the LANTIRN targeting pod are regarded as among the most effective strike aircraft available to NATO. The A-12 stealth aircraft was cancelled after huge cost

over-runs. Plans to upgrade the A-6 were abandoned, and the aircraft were withdrawn from service in the late 1990s. These changes meant that the air wings aboard carriers took on a completely new complexion. Instead of carrying over 80 aircraft, American supercarriers in 2001 could be found carrying one squadron of around 14 Tomcats and three of F/A-18Cs. Reductions in the Navy F/A-18 force mean that US Marine Corps units have increasingly embarked upon the carriers as well. The S-3 Viking fleet has been relieved of its anti-submarine duties, and, much to the frustration of its crews, is now used largely in the air-to-air refuelling role, using a 'buddy' refuelling pack. At the time of writing (2002), there were rumours that the S-3 force would be the next to be cut.

The carrier fleet was also dramatically altered in the aftermath of the Gulf War. *Midway* was finally retired (*Coral Sea* having been deleted when CVN-72 entered service). Between 1993 and 1996, *Forrestal*, *Saratoga* and *Ranger* were withdrawn from service, along with *America*. *Independence* was retained for a while as the carrier based in Japan, but was replaced by *Kitty Hawk* in 1998 and retired. More Nimitz-class ships have entered service instead of the conventionally powered carriers – *Abraham Lincoln* (CVN-72) joined the fleet in 1989,

BELOW: The *Carl Vinson* was the third of the Nimitz-class ships to commission, joining the Navy in 1982. She was named for Congressman *Carl Vinson*, a prominent supporter of the US Navy, and the first man to witness the launch of a US Navy ship named after him. Aircraft from the *Vinson* participated in Operation Desert Fox in 1998, and have launched air strikes in support of the no-fly zones over Iraq.

but was not ready in time for the Gulf War. *George Washington* (CVN-73) entered service in 1992, while the *John C. Stennis* (CVN-74) was commissioned in 1995. CVN-75 (the USS *Harry Truman*) entered service in 1998. The USS *Ronald Reagan* joined the fleet in 2002, with one further carrier planned. Instead of the Reagan-era 15-carrier navy, there are now 12 active carriers, of which nine are nuclear-powered.

THE FUTURE OF THE SUPERCARRIER

Debate about what form carriers should take in the 21st century led to some discussion about using CVN-77 (which is currently without a name) as an evolutionary ship for the 'CVX', the future carrier of the US Navy. When the CVX enters service, it is likely to be equipped with a new, highly efficient electromagnetic launch system (EMALS), although this will almost inevitably still be known as a catapult. Vast increases in computing power and technology may reduce the size of the complement aboard the ship, with increasing automation. The air wing is a little easier to predict. The F-14 will be completely replaced in service by 2008 with the F/A-18E and F/A-18F Super Hornet. As the name suggests, this is a development of the F/A-18 Hornet. Critics claim that it is in fact a completely new aircraft that merely looks like a scaled-up F/A-

18, and that it is not an adequate replacement for the F-14D and F/A-18C in the air-to-air combat role. But tests and operational evaluations as the first of the new aircraft entered squadron service seem to suggest that it is a capable enough aircraft for most of the tasks it may be called upon to perform. In addition, the carriers will embark the Lockheed F-35 Joint Strike Fighter from 2008. A replacement for the overworked EA-6B Prowler is likely to come in the form of an electronic warfare version of the F/A-18F, but the E-2 Hawkeye seems set to soldier on well past its 50th birthday, albeit with radar and electronics that would have been thought of only in science fiction novels when it was first designed.

Although the American supercarrier fleet is in the midst of change, one thing remains clear: the supercarriers offer an impressive and effective means of projecting American power around the world when required. This is what they were designed to do, and they do it successfully. The supercarriers, despite their cost, have given the United States an unparalleled ability to project air power without the requirement for host nation support. The cost considerations have meant that the supercarriers have only been adopted by America. Other countries have adopted a more modest approach to operating aircraft at sea.

ABOVE: The Grumman E-2 Hawkeye entered US Navy service in 1964, to replace the E-1 Tracer in the airborne early warning role. Progressive upgrading has kept the aircraft fully up-to-date, and it is likely to remain a part of carrier air wings for some years to come. The French navy has also purchased the type for use aboard the *Charles de Gaulle*.

CHAPTER EIGHT

BRITISH AND FRENCH CARRIERS

In the late 1950s and early 1960s, it became clear that the Royal Navy's carriers were becoming too small. As aircraft grew in size to accommodate more avionics and carry greater weapon loads, they began to impose heavy demands upon carriers.

HEAVIER AIRCRAFT REQUIRED longer catapults to give them adequate flying speed, and all of the British carriers were disadvantaged. Only *Eagle* and *Ark Royal* were large enough to be considered for operation of the F-4 Phantoms the Royal Navy decided to buy in 1964 (although *Victorious* was also considered as a possible platform). *Albion* and *Bulwark* were converted to 'commando carriers' – that is to say they gave up fixed-wing aircraft and carried transport helicopters for their 'war load' of up to 900 Royal Marines. *Hermes* remained in service with an air group just over 20 strong, but when the Royal Navy adopted the Blackburn Buccaneer as its principal strike aircraft, *Hermes* could carry only seven or eight of them, along with a fighter complement of de Havilland Sea Vixens,

LEFT: A Dassault Rafale M takes off on a test flight, carrying an air defence warload of four MICA medium-range air-to-air missiles under the wings and fuselage, with two Matra 550 Magic infra-red homing weapons on the wing tips. The Rafale will replace the Super Etendard in French service, providing the French fleet with far greater capability.

Fairey Gannets for airborne early warning (AEW), and helicopters. The remaining carrier, *Centaur*, did not receive Buccaneers, and continued to operate a mix of Sea Vixens and Supermarine Scimitars.

Although *Ark Royal* and *Eagle* were candidates for carrying Phantoms, the Phantoms had to be modified to operate from their decks. A 102cm (40-inch) extension was added to the nose wheel leg to give a greater angle of incidence for take-off, and Rolls-Royce Spey engines were fitted (to give greater power at take-off) instead of the J79s found in American F-4s. Fitting Speys to the Phantom was a major task, and added great expense to the aircraft. The problem of small carriers was recognized even before the Phantoms were ordered, and the Royal Navy hoped to procure up to five 53,848-tonne (53,000-ton) carriers, known as the CVA-01 class. In July 1963, the Ministry of Defence announced that one carrier (the CVA-01 herself, which was to be called *Queen Elizabeth* in service) would be built. She would carry 36 Buccaneers and Phantoms, along with AEW aircraft and anti-submarine heli-

copters. The ship was controversial. After some years of prosperity, Britain was facing financial difficulties and defence spending, as always, was a likely target for cuts. At the same time as the Royal Navy required a new carrier, the Royal Air Force (RAF) was in urgent need of a new strike aircraft. Rejecting the adoption of the Navy's subsonic Buccaneer for this role, the RAF hoped to buy the TSR 2. This would have been a superb aircraft, but was cancelled in favour of the American F-111, since the latter was supposedly cheaper. Even so, buying F-111s and a fleet of CVA-01s was beyond Britain's means. In 1966, CVA-01 was cancelled, and the decision was taken that Britain would abandon aircraft carriers altogether in the early 1970s. Two years later, the F-111s were cancelled as the government declared that Britain would do little outside NATO, and that there was no conceivable circumstance – for example, an amphibious assault thousands of miles from Europe – where an aircraft carrier would be required.

The run-down of the carrier fleet was swift. *Centaur* was first to go, being relegat-

BELOW: *Ark Royal* on patrol. Although the Invincible class have been successful, they are really too small, carrying a maximum of about 20 aircraft. Britain's 1998 Strategic Defence Review confirmed that the three Invincibles will be replaced by two larger carriers capable of operating between 40 and 50 aircraft from around 2012.

British Aerospace Sea Harrier

ed to the role of depot ship in 1966. The following year, *Victorious* suffered a small fire while undergoing refit, and the government announced that she would be paid off and scrapped. *Hermes* was converted to commando carrier configuration, allowing *Albion* to be broken up in 1972. This was not all – the government announced that *Eagle* would not be converted for Phantoms after all, because it would cost too much (even though the Royal Navy carrier trials of the aircraft had been conducted from the ship). This was a questionable decision at best, but *Eagle* paid off in 1972, even though the new Conservative government took the decision to extend the life of Ark Royal. No 892 squadron, *Ark Royal*'s fighter unit, adorned the fins of it Phantoms with a large omega badge, to signify that they would be the last fixed-wing aircraft in the Royal Navy. They were not to know it, but they were wrong.

VERTICAL TAKE-OFF

The idea of making an aircraft that could take off and land vertically (as opposed to building a helicopter) was attractive to many designers, and to some senior military officers. It appeared to offer the prospect of not having to rely upon runways, desirable since runways were always likely to be among the first targets for enemy attack. Although building a vertical take-off and

landing (VTOL) aircraft sounded good, it was difficult to achieve. The solution came in the form of Hawker's P.1127 experimental aircraft, using a Rolls-Royce Pegasus engine that could deflect its thrust using vectoring jet nozzles. In the early 1960s, it was hoped that this technology would lead to the P.1154 supersonic VTOL combat aircraft, but this project was abandoned by the Royal Navy and the RAF after it became clear that they actually wanted two completely different aircraft, rather than slightly different versions of the P.1154. The Royal Navy bought the Phantom instead, and the RAF decided to adopt an operational version of the P.1127, to be known as the Harrier. The first Harrier entered RAF service with No 1 Squadron in 1969, six years after a P.1127 had operated successfully from the deck of *Ark Royal*.

The Royal Navy, meanwhile, settled down to life without carriers. To work out how the carrier-less fleet would work, a Future Fleet Working Party was set up. Rather embarrassingly, they concluded that the carrier-less fleet actually needed carriers. The rationale behind this startling conclusion was sound: AEW aircraft were still required to protect the fleet (although attacking aircraft could be engaged by missiles fired from ships, AEW aircraft gave greater warning of their approach than surface radar), and the fleet needed to be able to fend off enemy

ABOVE: A British Aerospace Sea Harrier FA.Mk 2 serving with front line squadrons on HMS *Invincible* and *Illustrious*. Sea Harriers were deployed extensively by British forces in operations over the former Yugoslavia.

reconnaissance aircraft (memories of the FW 200 Condor had not gone away). The Working Party were effectively told that they had come up with the wrong answer, and were wound up. But the logic of their conclusions endured.

FROM DECK CRUISER TO CARRIER

When CVA-01 was being designed, two classes of ship were put forward to act as escorts for the new carrier. The Type 82 Destroyer was to provide air defence, while a new helicopter cruiser would operate a number of Sea King helicopters for anti-submarine work. Only one Type 82 was built (HMS *Bristol*), and the design evolved into the smaller Type 42. The helicopter cruiser, on the other hand, grew. It soon became clear that many senior naval officers thought the helicopter cruiser might operate more than just helicopters. The dimensions of the ship increased as the design matured. The initial intention in 1967 was for a ship that could carry six Sea King helicopters in an external hangar, much in the same way that destroyers and other ships accommodated their single helicopters. It was then decided to increase the number of Sea Kings to nine in the hangar, with another three on deck. This meant that the hangar would have to be placed in the hull, along with two aircraft lifts and a flight deck that looked remarkably similar to that found on an aircraft carrier (albeit without catapults or arrester gear). This type of deck became known as a 'through deck' and the name of the type of

ship was changed to 'Through Deck Cruiser'. Cynics altered this to 'See Through Cruiser' on the grounds that the Navy clearly wanted the ship to operate VTOL aircraft.

Momentum for the new carriers (although the Navy was sensitive about using this term) grew. The Harrier proved successful in its operations with the RAF, particularly when using a short rather than vertical take-off to increase the war load it could carry. From being a VTOL type, the Harrier became a VSTOL (vertical and short take-off and landing) aeroplane. In 1973, Lieutenant Commander Doug Taylor produced a document (actually a Masters thesis for the University of Southampton), in which he advocated the use of a ramp to give extra upward momentum to the VSTOL aircraft's take-off run. The Navy issued a requirement for a VSTOL aircraft in 1972, and in 1973 placed an order for the first ship, HMS *Invincible*. In 1975, possibly the worst kept secret about the new 'cruisers' was revealed when the Royal Navy announced that it would purchase a naval version of the Harrier (the Sea Harrier), equipped with radar, to act as a short-range fighter aircraft. Taylor's 'ski-ramp' was added to the design in 1977. *Invincible* entered service in 1980, by which time two other carriers were planned. These were to have been named *Illustrious* and *Indomitable*, but public affection for the old *Ark Royal* (particularly after the BBC television series *Sailor* had won impressive audiences) meant that the third carrier, projected to enter service in the mid-1980s was rechristened *Ark Royal* to perpetuate the famous name.

FURTHER CUTS

In 1978 the old *Ark Royal* was decommissioned from Royal Navy service, leaving Britain without a conventional aircraft carrier. *Hermes* and *Bulwark* were still in service as commando and anti-submarine carriers, but a further round of defence cuts in 1979 (after the election of Margaret Thatcher's government) saw *Bulwark* paid off into reserve. This was merely the start. In 1981, as Britain faced another financial crisis, the Secretary of State for Defence, John Nott, conducted a more in-depth review. The results were startling. As Nott explained in a conference held at the British Joint Services Command and Staff College 20 years later, he had little choice. The British Army simply could not be cut back without reducing the size of the forces in Germany: at the height of the Cold War, this was unthinkable. The RAF was in the midst of a new equipment programme, and was important to NATO for two reasons. As well as the units needed in Germany to meet a Warsaw Pact invasion, Britain needed strong air defences to safeguard her role as 'an unsinkable aircraft carrier' capable of taking reinforcements from the United States for onward dispatch to the Central Front (in fact, it became clear to Nott that there were not enough air defence units). These factors made it politically

impossible to impose major cuts on the RAF, which left the Navy. Nott regretted the need to savage the Royal Navy, but it was the one service that could be targeted for major spending cuts. Nott concluded that as the Royal Navy would be used only for conducting anti-submarine operations in the Eastern Atlantic, the number of carriers could be reduced. *Hermes* would be withdrawn from service when HMS *Illustrious* entered service, projected to be at the end of 1982 or early 1983. The first of the new carriers, *Invincible*, would be sold to Australia (the Australians were looking to retire their sole carrier, HMAS *Melbourne*, which had begun life as HMS *Majestic* in 1948). The sale of *Invincible* would take place when the new *Ark Royal* (hereafter *Ark Royal* V to distinguish her from the fourth *Ark* that retired in 1978) entered service in around 1985. Nott also decided to dispose of the two amphibious landing ships *Fearless* and *Intrepid* and cut back further by retiring a number of the older ships, notably those in the reserve fleet. The cuts caused a major political furore. The Navy minister, Keith Speed, resigned, and a variety of retired admirals, political opponents and defence analysts lined up to berate Nott for his decisions. There was some support for Nott – some commentators claimed that Britain did not need aircraft carriers given her reduced status in the world. Others went further, claiming that the Sea Harrier (which had entered operational service in

BELOW: Away from home, a Sea Harrier FRS.1 from HMS *Illustrious*'s 800 Squadron conducts cross-deck operations from the USS *Eisenhower*. An A-6 Intruder and F-14 Tomcat are in the background. The Sea Harrier marks a completely different concept in carrier aircraft – the arrester wires the aircraft is rolling over are not required for STOVL aircraft, which follow the dictum 'it's better to stop then land, than land then try to stop!'.

Dassault Super Etendard

3-A-203 ARMADA 03 0753

1980) was of little real military value, and simply acted as some form of justification for the retention of carriers that were both unnecessary and lacking in real military capability. These commentators conceded that VSTOL allowed the Sea Harriers to put on some impressive air displays, but this was hardly the point. Further adding to the controversy was the decision to withdraw the ice patrol ship *Endurance* from the South Atlantic, operating around the Falkland Islands and South Georgia. Argentina had a long-standing claim over the Falklands, and it was argued that the withdrawal of *Endurance* might send entirely the wrong signals to the military junta in Buenos Aires.

INVASION

The issue of sovereignty over the Falklands had deep roots, and had been a major obsta-

cle to relations between Argentina and Britain. The Foreign and Commonwealth Office had made a number of attempts to settle the issue, but the implacable opposition of the Falkland Islanders to any plan that would transfer sovereignty to Argentina (or appeared to do so) thwarted all efforts. By 1982, Argentina was in serious difficulties. The ruling military junta had embarked upon a ruthless campaign of internal repression, which (accompanied by torture and 'disappearances') proved to be about the only policy that it was good at carrying out. It was certainly not blessed with a gift for economics, since the country was beset with a rampant inflation rate that appeared to change (always in an upward direction) every day, and sometimes more frequently than that. The British Government's apparent lack of interest in the Falklands prompted the head of the

Veinticinco de Mayo

Displacement	20,218 tonnes (19,900 tons) (full load)	Propulsion	2-shaft steam turbines
Length	211.28m (693ft 2in) (overall)	Speed	24 knots
Beam	24.38m (80ft)	Armament	12 x 40mm (1.6in) cannon
Draught	6.55m (21ft 6in)	Complement	1500
		Aircraft	21

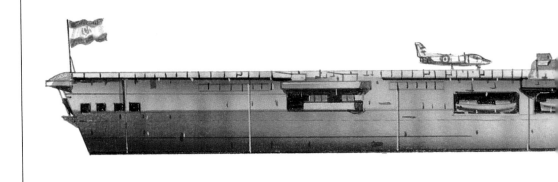

Argentine Navy, Admiral Jorge Anaya, to suggest invading them. The President, General Leopoldo Galtieri, was persuaded. After an illegal landing on South Georgia by a group of scrap merchants who raised the Argentine flag, Argentine forces invaded on 2 April 1982. Galtieri was confident that the invasion would go unchallenged. Despite the fascistic nature of its government Argentina was a bulwark against communism, and thus on good terms with the United States. Galtieri reasoned that the US would tell Britain that there was nothing that could be done, and Argentina would have achieved the goal of claiming the Falklands as hers. Even if the British wanted to react militarily, Galtieri mused, what could they do? Retaking the Falklands would require the Royal Navy to travel almost halfway around the world, to mount an amphibious operation miles from a friendly port, within range of Argentine aircraft and with an air defence force reliant upon an aircraft far less capable than Argentina's Mirage fighters. Galtieri and the junta concluded that Britain would be forced to accept the takeover. This was a serious misjudgement. Even as Argentina's junta were celebrating the success of the invasion, Britain began to assemble a task force to retake the islands. At the centre of the force were HMS *Hermes* (now converted to carry Sea Harriers) and HMS *Invincible*. They left Portsmouth on 5 April 1982, heading for a war that no one had expected, and in which carriers were to be essential.

VSTOL VINDICATED: THE FALKLANDS WAR

The carriers had embarked a very different air complement to that which had been intended when the VSTOL carriers were first mooted. Rather than being optimized for anti-submarine work, *Hermes* and *Invincible* carried Sea Harriers to give the fleet the air cover it required. *Hermes*, the larger of the two vessels, carried 12 Sea Harriers, made up of 800 Squadron and reinforcements drawn from the training unit, 899 Squadron. She also carried nine Sea Kings from 826 Squadron for anti-submarine work, and nine Sea King HC 4s from 846 Squadron, which would provide transport for the Marines. *Invincible* embarked eight Sea Harriers from 801 Squadron, and 11 Sea Kings provided by 820 Squadron. By 14 April, lead units of the Task Force were able to close on South Georgia to execute Operation Paraquet, the plan to retake the island. This went well, and by the evening of 26 April, South Georgia was back in British hands. The rest of the Task Force proceeded towards the Falklands, preparing to conduct the sort of operation that British politicians had specifically ruled out when they cancelled CVA-01 and ran the carrier fleet down in the 1970s. Once the carriers were within range of the islands, the British declared a Total Exclusion Zone (TEZ) around the Falklands in which they would engage any Argentinean forces.

Although the Argentine Navy was equipped with ships that were, in general,

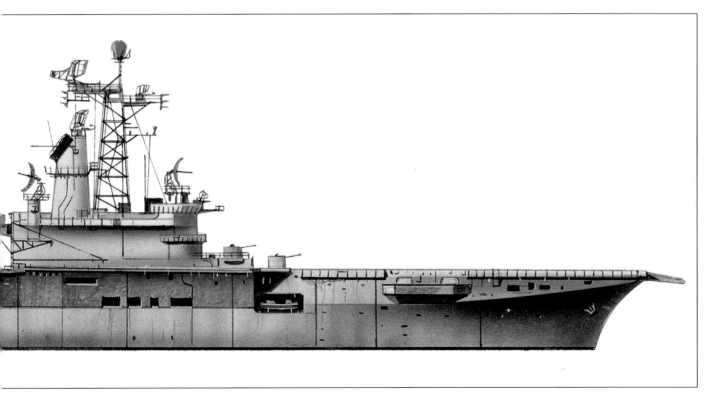

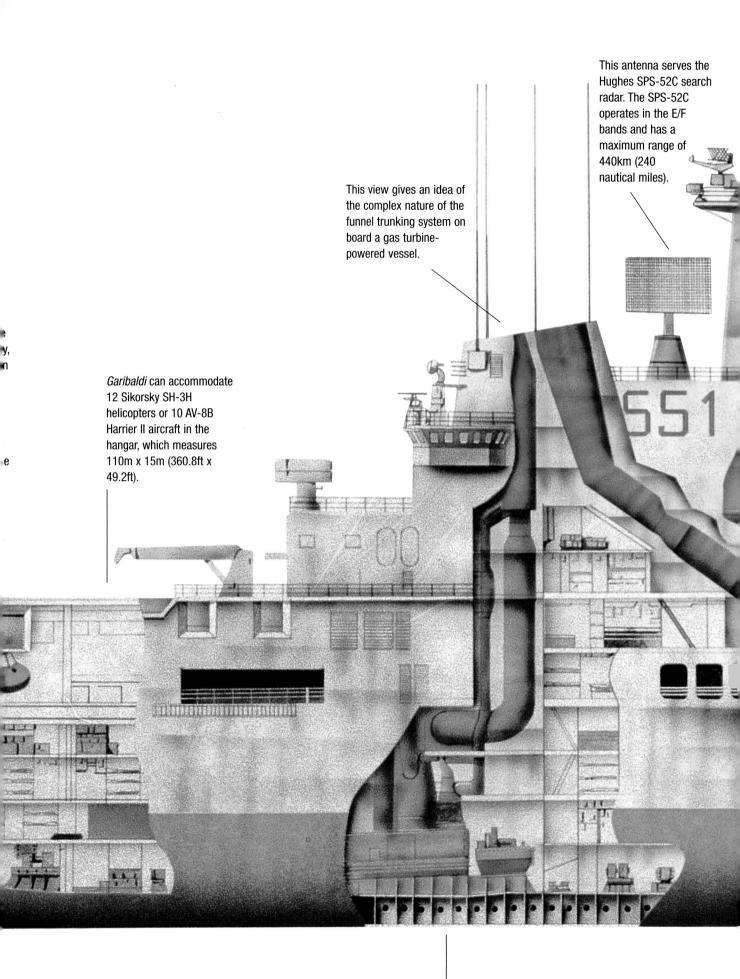

This antenna serves the Hughes SPS-52C search radar. The SPS-52C operates in the E/F bands and has a maximum range of 440km (240 nautical miles).

This view gives an idea of the complex nature of the funnel trunking system on board a gas turbine-powered vessel.

Garibaldi can accommodate 12 Sikorsky SH-3H helicopters or 10 AV-8B Harrier II aircraft in the hangar, which measures 110m x 15m (360.8ft x 49.2ft).

The *Garibaldi* employs four Fiat/GE LM 2500 gas turbines, delivering around 60MW (81,000shp), giving the ship a top speed of around 55.5km/h (30 knots).

Giuseppe Garibaldi

The *Garibaldi* represented a major change for the Italian navy, giving the nation an aircraft carrier for the first time. *Garibaldi* is typical of STOVL carriers, giving an affordable alternative to the giant nuclear-powered supercarriers of the US Navy.

As part of the ship's defensive armament, *Garibaldi* carries three turrets with twin 40mm (1.6in) cannon. These can be used against aircraft or surface targets. Each fires at 300 rounds per minute, while the 40mm (1.6in) shell has a maximum range of 12.5km (6.8 nautical miles).

Otomat TESEO launcher. Unlike other carriers, *Garibaldi* has potent anti-shipping capability through surface-to-surface missiles. The Otomat is a joint venture with France. The Mk 2 has a 210kg (463lb) warhead, and a range of 160km (86 nautical miles).

The primary anti-su⬛ helicopter of the Ital⬛ the SH-3H joined th⬛ 1968, procurement continuing until 198⬛ SH-3H can be used ⬛ anti-submarine and shipping roles (equi⬛ with the Marte miss⬛ latter).

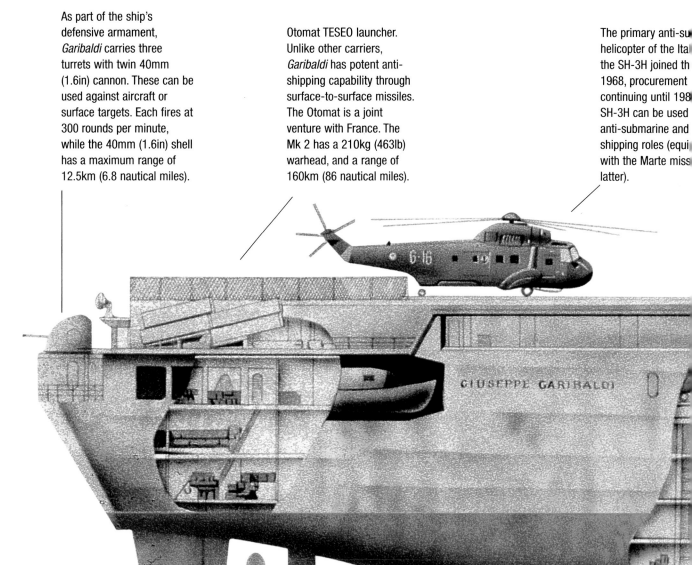

RIGHT: HMS *Ark Royal* is seen here during the late 1980s, with her full air wing on deck. Eight Sea Harrier FRS 1s from 801 Squadron, along with the Sea King AEW 2s of 849 Squadron, can be seen at the bow and in the centre of the flight deck, while Sea King HAS 5 anti-submarine helicopters are at the stern. At the bow, the launcher for Sea Dart surface-to-air missiles and a 20mm (0.8in) Phalanx Close-in-Weapon System (CIWS) are prominent. The Sea Dart launcher has since been removed, to allow the deck to be extended, giving more room for the operation of the RAF's Harrier GR 7.

far older than those in British service, they possessed a potentially formidable asset in the form of their own aircraft carrier, the *Vienticinco de Mayo*. This ship began life as HMS *Venerable*, before she was sold to the Royal Netherlands Navy as HMNS *Karel Doorman* in 1948. After withdrawal from Dutch service, the ship was sold to Argentina in 1968. Although limited in comparison with later carriers, the *Vienticinco de Mayo* could embark an air group of Skyhawks and the Dassault Super Etendard – the latter with the Exocet anti-shipping missile.

To meet this threat, the Royal Navy were forced to undertake a major upgrade of the Sea Harriers while they were heading for the Falklands. The United States agreed to replace NATO stocks of the advanced AIM-9L Sidewinder, allowing the Sea Harriers to be fitted for these weapons rather than the older AIM-9G models that they normally carried. This meant that the aircraft had to be fitted with software to allow the new Sidewinders to be fired. Similarly, a software package for loft-bombing had to be installed. The Sea Harriers had not been cleared to drop BL.755 Cluster Bombs or to fire 51mm (2-inch) rockets. Within a week, these upgrades had been incorporated, vastly enhancing the effectiveness of the small force.

The first 20 Sea Harriers upgraded to these standards were followed on 27 April 1982 by eight more aircraft drawn from other sources (including trials aircraft), and incorporated into the newly formed 809 Squadron, which flew to Ascension Island before embarking aboard the merchant ship *Atlantic Conveyor*. Although the Sea

Harrier force stood at 28, this was almost all that the Royal Navy had: only 30 Sea Harriers had been built by April 1982, and it seemed inevitable that they would take losses, leaving the fleet without adequate air cover. As a result, it was decided to deploy a number of the RAF's Harrier GR 3 force to the Task Force, drawn from Number 1 Squadron. While the pilots were given training for operating from aircraft carriers, the Harriers were modified to permit them to carry Sidewinders, so that they could augment the air defence force. Some changes to the avionics systems were made, most notably the incorporation of a transponder to allow the aircraft to be identified more clearly by the aircraft carriers' radars. The first contingent of RAF Harriers flew out to Ascension Island in early May 1982, by which time the Sea Harriers had already seen action.

FIRST CLASH

The first contact between Sea Harriers and Argentine forces came on 21 April, when an Argentine air force Boeing 707 was intercepted as it attempted to shadow the Task Force. The Sea Harriers escorted the interloper, and enjoyed a number of repeat experiences until a message was sent to Buenos Aires that the next 'shadower' would be shot down. There were no further incidents.

On 1 May 1982, a single RAF Vulcan bomber attacked the airfield at Port Stanley. Although the weapons-aiming systems on the Vulcan were old and designed for dropping nuclear weapons (where accuracy was not that important) a bomb was planted on the runway, hampering operations (even

though the damage was quickly repaired). This was followed by an attack by 12 Sea Harriers at 0748 hours local time. Nine aircraft attacked Port Stanley airport, while the other three headed for the airstrip at Goose Green. The first four aircraft, each carrying three 454kg (1000lb) bombs, attacked Stanley in a toss bombing attack against anti-aircraft positions, before they were followed by the rest of the aircraft, which dropped a dozen cluster bombs and three more 454kg bombs.

Early that afternoon, there were a series of inconclusive encounters between the Sea Harriers and Argentine aircraft, until the two Harriers flown by Flt Lt Paul Barton and Lt Steve Thomas were steered towards two Mirages by HMS *Glamorgan*, acting in the fighter control role. Thomas made radar contact with the two Mirages, and took the lead. The two formations approached each other at high speed. The two British pilots saw that the Mirages were flying very close together, and immediately suspected a trap – but to their surprise, there were no other enemy aircraft. The two Sea Harriers engaged, beginning with a speculative burst of cannon fire from Barton. This was ineffective, but within a matter of seconds he had achieved a lock-on with his Sidewinder. He squeezed the trigger, and after four seconds the missile struck the Mirage and blew it to pieces. Thomas then manoeuvred against the second Mirage, and launched a missile. He saw it chasing the enemy Mirage into cloud, but did not see whether or not it had destroyed its target: only after the war did he learn that the pilot had struggled back to Stanley, only to be shot down and

HMS *Hermes*

Displacement	29,160 tonnes (28,700 tons)	**Speed**	28 knots
Length	226.9m (744ft 4in)	**Armament**	2 x quadruple Seacat SAM
Beam	27.4m (90ft)		launchers
Draught	8.7m (28ft 6in)	**Complement**	1350
Propulsion	2-shaft geared steam turbines	**Aircraft**	28

SPECIFICATIONS		Propulsion	4 gas turbines driving two shafts
Giuseppe Garibaldi		Speed	30 knots
		Armament	6 x Otomat SSM launchers; 2 x octuple
Displacement	14,070 tonnes (13,850 tons) full load		Albatros SAM launchers; 3 x twin 40mm
Length	180m (591ft) overall		(1.6in) cannon; 6 x 325mm (12.7in)
Beam	33.4m (110ft)		torpedo tubes
Draught	6.7m (22ft)	Complement	825
		Aircraft	16–18

LEFT: A TAV-8B Harrier II of the Italian navy, aboard the *Giuseppe Garibaldi*. The Italian navy employs the radar-equipped AV-8B Plus as its main combat aircraft, with the TAV-8B (which does not have radar) being employed for type conversion and continuation training. Although the TAV-8B has underwing pylons, it is not intended for use in a combat role.

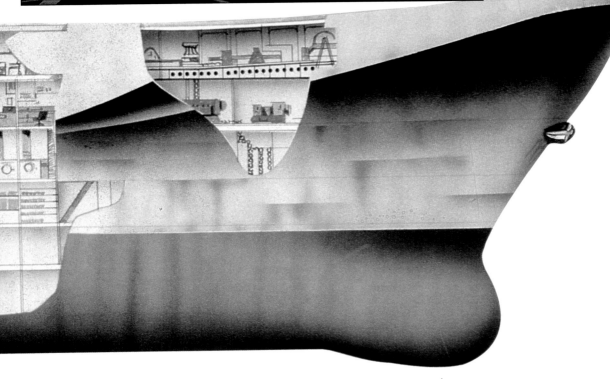

Garibaldi has a Raytheon DE 1160 Low Frequency sonar, although it is doubtful that a high-value asset such as a carrier would be used for offensive anti-submarine patrols.

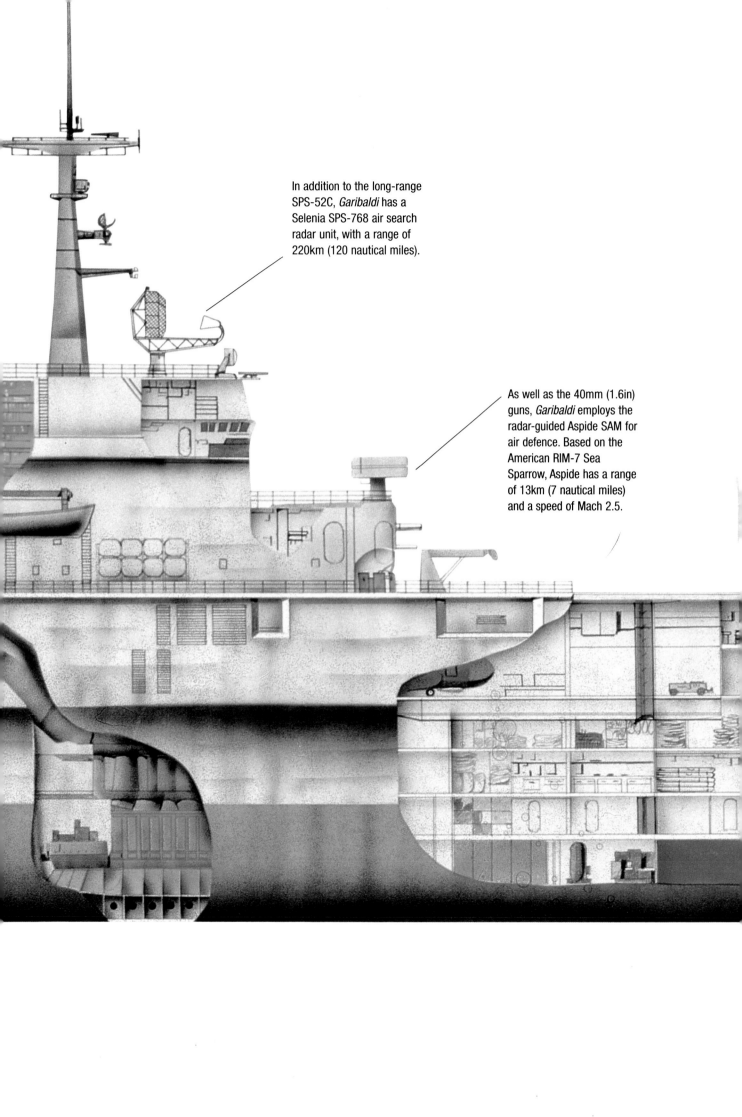

In addition to the long-range SPS-52C, *Garibaldi* has a Selenia SPS-768 air search radar unit, with a range of 220km (120 nautical miles).

As well as the 40mm (1.6in) guns, *Garibaldi* employs the radar-guided Aspide SAM for air defence. Based on the American RIM-7 Sea Sparrow, Aspide has a range of 13km (7 nautical miles) and a speed of Mach 2.5.

RIGHT: HMS *Hermes* is seen here in the commando carrier role, with four Sea King HC 4 and three Wessex HU 5 transport helicopters on deck. The two smaller helicopters visible on the rear landing spots are Westland Gazelles from the Royal Marines air squadron. Although *Hermes* is not carrying any Sea Harriers in this picture, the ski ramp to permit their operation is extremely prominent. *Hermes* retired from service in 1985, after HMS *Ark Royal* was commissioned, and was subsequently sold to India.

killed by nervous anti-aircraft gunners who mistook him for a British aircraft. By the end of 1 May, as well as the Mirage destroyed by Barton, Flt Lt Tony Penfold had shot down an Argentine IAI Dagger fighter-bomber and Lt Alan Curtiss had destroyed an enemy Canberra bomber.

After the Vulcan raid and the initial success of the Sea Harriers the Argentines withdrew their Mirages for homeland defence (fearing an attack against the mainland), leaving the less handy Skyhawks and Daggers to the mercy of the Sea Harriers.

On 4 May 1982, the Sea Harriers suffered their first loss when Lt Nick Taylor was killed after taking a direct hit from anti-aircraft guns as he bombed the airstrip at Goose Green. Two days later, two Sea Harriers and their pilots were lost after apparently colliding while on patrol in bad weather. There was then a lack of engagements until 21 May, when the British landed at San Carlos. Two Skyhawks were shot down by Lt Cdrs Mike Blissett and Neil Thomas, followed later that day by two Daggers destroyed by the commanding officer of 801 Squadron, Lt Cdr Nigel 'Sharkey' Ward, and Steve Thomas. This set the pattern for future encounters. On 8 June, Flt Lt Dave Morgan accounted for two Skyhawks, and his wingman, Lt David Smith, destroyed a third: these were the last air-to-air encounters of the war before the

Argentines surrendered on 14 June 1982.

Although the Royal Navy lost a number of ships to Argentine air attack, there was little doubt that the carriers and their Sea Harriers had played an essential part in retaking the Falklands. The 28 Sea Harriers flew over 1,100 Combat Air Patrol (CAP) and 90 offensive support sorties. They had fired 26 Sidewinders and an unrecorded amount of 30mm (1.2in) cannon ammunition, and had destroyed 21 aircraft with no loss in air combat. The overwhelming success enjoyed by the Sea Harriers meant that the RAF Harrier GR 3s were not required for air combat duties, and were instead used to provide support to ground units as they advanced towards Port Stanley.

LESSONS OF THE FALKLANDS

Although the Falklands campaign was a success, it was a close run affair. It was quite clear that the task force had been in dire need of airborne early warning aircraft, and a version of the Sea King helicopter was fitted with radar to fulfil this task. In addition, the Sea Harriers had relied heavily upon pilot skill, since their avionics suite was quite basic compared to other fighters. The small size of the Sea Harrier also meant that it was relatively lightly armed, carrying just two Sidewinders. This problem was addressed by the introduction of twin missile launchers that arrived in service shortly after the end of the war. The long-term solution, though, was the introduction of new radar and the ability to carry longer-ranged radar-guided weapons. This would take some time to achieve.

VSTOL CARRIERS AFTER THE FALKLANDS

The success of the Sea Harrier was not only encouraging for the Royal Navy. The Indian navy had decided to convert its carrier INS *Vikrant* (formerly HMS *Hercules*) to carry Sea Harriers in place of its outmoded Hawker Sea Hawks, and the new aircraft began operating in 1983. Unlike the Royal Navy's ships, the *Vikrant* had the ability to launch conventional aircraft, employing the Breguet Alizé in the anti-submarine role until 1987. Furthermore, the Spanish navy had enthusiastically operated the American version of the Harrier, the AV-8A, from its old carrier *Délado* (which had begun life as the American light carrier *Cabot* in World War II). The operation of the AV-8s (known as Matadors in Spanish service) prompted the decision to buy a new vessel, the *Príncipe de Asturias*. The Italian navy also introduced a carrier capable of operating VSTOL aircraft in the form of the *Giuseppe Garibaldi*. The Spanish chose to replace their Matadors with the AV-8B version of the Harrier, and the Italians ordered the radar-equipped AV-8B Plus (once a law from 1922 preventing the navy from operating aircraft had been revoked). These ships provided their owners with the ability to project air power, although there were those who questioned whether or not Italy and Spain really needed this capability.

There were no longer any questions about the Royal Navy's need to do so, and changes were made to the British carrier fleet throughout the 1980s and 1990s. *Hermes* was retired in 1986, and then sold to India:

HMS *Invincible*

Displacement	19,812 tonnes (19,500 tons) (full load)	**Propulsion**	Gas turbines driving 2 shafts
Length	206.6m (677ft)	**Speed**	28 knots
Beam	27.5m (90ft)	**Armament**	One Sea Dart SAM launcher
Draught	7.3m (24ft)	**Complement**	1320
		Aircraft	21

renamed *Viraat*, she was operated alongside *Vikrant* until the latter was retired in 1996. The decision to sell *Invincible* to Australia was revoked (and the Australian navy retired *Melbourne* in 1986 with no replacement). *Invincible* was joined by *Illustrious*, which arrived in service in June 1982 after heroic efforts by dockyard staff to prepare her well ahead of her scheduled commis-

sioning date, followed in 1985 by the fifth *Ark Royal* (*Ark Royal* V). The Sea Harrier upgrade programme led to the introduction of the Sea Harrier FA 2 in 1995. The FA 2 was given a state of the art Blue Vixen radar, widely held to be at least the equal of any equivalent radar in the world, and could carry up to four AIM-120 active radar guided missiles. With the end of the Cold War,

Clémenceau

Displacement	31,496 tonnes (31,000 tons)	**Speed**	33 knots
Length	265m (869ft 5in)	**Armament**	8 x 100mm (3.9in) guns
Beam	31.7m (104ft)	**Complement**	1338
Draught	8.6m (28ft 3in)	**Aircraft**	40
Propulsion	2-shaft geared steam turbines		

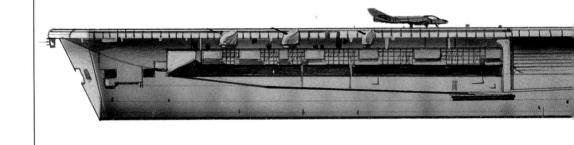

the carriers (two of which are kept operational at any one time) have been used much more frequently. The strength of the air group is enhanced by use of RAF Harrier GR 7s (the British version of the AV-8B) for the attack role. The GR 7's larger wing allows it to carry greater loads, and its use permits the Sea Harriers to be used mainly in the air-to-air role, although they can also be seen carrying bombs. Although the Royal Navy has made great use of its VSTOL carriers, not every navy is convinced that they offer better capabilities than conventional vessels.

FRANCE, BRAZIL AND ARGENTINA

The French navy commissioned two new carriers in the early 1960s to replace the earlier ships that were only capable of operating piston-engined aircraft. *Clémenceau*

and *Foch* were initially short of a suitable aircraft, until the Aéronavale (French fleet air arm) decided to purchase the Dassault Etendard. The Etendard was designed as a land-based fighter in response to a NATO competition, but it failed to win. The Aéronavale, however, decided that it exactly met their requirements. A version of the F-8 Crusader was chosen to fill the fighter role, while anti-submarine and maritime reconnaissance tasks were conducted by the Breguet Alizé and the Aérospatiale Super Frelon helicopter. *Foch* and *Clémenceau* saw little action in the early part of their lives. In the mid-1970s, an upgraded version of the Etendard, the Super Etendard (also sold to Argentina), was ordered, beginning operations after the carriers had been refitted in the later part of the decade. In 1983, Super Etendards from *Clémenceau* attacked

BELOW: The first two Dassault Rafale Ms were delivered to the Aéronavale in December 2000, and new aircraft are reported to be entering service at a rate of two per month. The Rafale will replace the now-retired Crusader and Super Etendard in French naval service.

Dassault Rafale

Syrian gun positions in retaliation for attacks on French peacekeeping forces in Lebanon. By the time of the Gulf War in 1990, both carriers were due for replacement by nuclear-powered vessels, which would operate the Dassault Rafale strike fighter, along with Grumman E-2 Hawkeye early warning aircraft. The cost of the new carriers meant that one was cancelled, and the *Charles de Gaulle* entered service almost 10 years later than planned. When *de Gaulle* joined the fleet, it was found that the flight deck was too small to operate the Hawkeyes safely, and the ship suffered a number of embarrassing engine and propeller problems. To add to the saga, the Rafale was not ready to join the ship. The Super Etendards had to continue, while the venerable Crusaders only were retired at the end of 2000. Nonetheless, once the problems are solved, *Charles de Gaulle* promises to offer a flexible operating platform in support of French military operations: as demonstrated in the Kosovo campaign of 1999, host nation support for land-based aircraft may be given grudgingly and subject to certain conditions (or it may not be given at all), while carriers suffer no such constraints.

Foch and *Clémenceau* were retired from service, with the former being sold to Brazil. This gave the Brazilian navy the chance to operate combat aircraft, and they bought second-hand A-4 Skyhawks for the role. This ended the odd situation where Brazil had a carrier (*Foch*, renamed *Sao Paulo*, replacing the *Minas Gerais*, yet another second-hand British light fleet carrier), but no combat aircraft, while Argentina had combat aircraft, but no carrier after the *Vienticinco de Mayo* was laid up (though in theory the carrier could be returned to service quickly if needed). It seems likely that the Argentine navy will be forced to operate its aircraft only from land bases for some time to come, unless it goes on exercise with the Brazilians.

THE FUTURE

Despite the increasing expense of operating carriers, several navies other than that of the United States remain willing to do so. Thailand deployed its first carrier in the late 1990s, equipping it with retired Spanish AV-8As, while India has purchased one of the aircraft carriers that the Soviet Union (and then Russia) never quite managed to place in service. The Russian carriers are STOBAR (short take-off and barrier assisted recovery) vessels, using a navalized version of the MiG-29 'Fulcrum'. This reflects a general preference for larger vessels carrying more aircraft and capable of generating a larger number of sorties.

RIGHT: A computer-generated image of the Lockheed Martin F-35 Joint Strike Fighter. The JSF is being built for the US Air Force, Marine Corps and US Navy, and the Royal Navy intends to buy the aircraft to replace Sea Harriers. As well as conventional-landing versions, a short take-off and vertical landing version is planned for the Marine Corps. Service entry for JSF is planned for 2008, while British aircraft will be employed from two new carriers that will enter service some time in the second decade of the 21st century.

The Royal Navy has ...d a similar conclusion: although the Invi.....s will remain in service until the secon.....de of the 21st century, they will be repl.....v much larger ships (as yet unnamed, bu.....vn as the CV(F) or Future aircraft carrie.....to take up to 50 combat aircraft. These c.....' will use the Lockheed F-35 Joint S. Fighter, but at the time of writing, the dec sion on whether these would be the short take-off/vertical landing (STOVL) or conventional take-off and landing variant has not been taken. The decision to adopt such ships demonstrates the view that aircraft carriers are increasingly useful, in an era of 'low-intensity' conflict where politics or lack of infrastructure may make operation from land bases difficult. Carriers also offer the ability to provide additional aircraft strength for a military operation without crowding airfields on land. Although the British and French carriers cannot offer the 70 or 80 aircraft of the American supercarriers, they still provide a useful additional number of combat aircraft.

It is important to recognize that carriers are not perfect solutions. They cost a huge amount of money, and since they are such attractive targets for an enemy, they have to be defended by other ships – these vessels cost a great deal of money too. Also, carrier-based aircraft are largely reliant upon land-based refuelling aircraft. Although carriers can embark aircraft capable of carrying refuelling pods to support operations, these are not as capable as large tanker aircraft. Despite these disadvantages, the strategic exibility offered by carriers is enormous, 1 much appreciated by the navies that op ate them.

It is interesting to wonder what Eugene Ely would have made of it all. When he made his pioneering flights in 1910, the notion of ships carrying up to 80 aircraft would have seemed absurd. The idea that some of them might carry bomb-loads 10 times heavier (or more) than the entire weight of Ely's aircraft would have been ridiculed. Anyone suggesting that some of these aircraft might be able to take off and land vertically would have been thought a fool or a lunatic. This, though, is what Ely's flights led to. Although the carrier and its aircraft are expensive, they remain an essential military tool for those nations that can afford them, and will do so for years to come.

ABOVE: The prototype of the F/A-18F Super Hornet lands aboard the USS *John C. Stennis* while on initial sea trials. The Super Hornet was developed from the earlier F/A-18, and is considerably larger. The F/A-18E and F/A-18F first joined the fleet with VFA-115 'Eagles', with the first carrier deployment of the type in June 2002.

INDEX

PICTURE CREDITS

Philip Jarrett: 42, 104.
TRH Pictures: 6-7, 8, 9, 11, 13, 16, 18, 22 (US Navy), 23, 25, 26-27, 29, 30-31, 33, 35, 36, 37, 41, 46, 47, 48, 49, 50-51, 52 (US Navy), 53 (USNA), 54,
    55 (USNA), 57 (US Navy), 58, 59, 61 (USNA), 62, 63, 64-65, 66, 71 (both), 74 (US Navy), 75, 77, 80, 81, 82 (both), 84, 86-87, 90, 94, 95 (both), 99,
    100, 101, 106, 107, 108-109, 110, 111, 112, 114, 116, 119, 120 (US Navy), 123, 126, 127, 130, 131, 132-133 (US Navy), 135 (US Navy), 143 (US
    Navy), 145, 147, 150, 151 (Mike Roberts), 152 (US Navy), 153 (US Navy), 154-155 (Dassault), 156 (Royal Navy), 158 (E. Nevill), 159 (US Navy),
    162 (Royal Navy), 166 (US Navy), 168 (Royal Navy), 170, 172, 173 (McDonnell Douglas).
Artworks: Aerospace Publishing Ltd